Java™ and SOAP

Related titles from O'Reilly

Also available

Java™ and SOAP

Robert Englander

O'REILLY®

Beijing · Cambridge · Farnham · Köln · Paris · Sebastopol · Taipei · Tokyo

Java™ and SOAP
by Robert Englander

Copyright © 2002 O'Reilly & Associates, Inc. All rights reserved.
Printed in the United States of America.

Published by O'Reilly & Associates, Inc., 1005 Gravenstein Highway North, Sebastopol, CA 95472.

O'Reilly & Associates books may be purchased for educational, business, or sales promotional use. Online editions are also available for most titles (*safari.oreilly.com*). For more information contact our corporate/institutional sales department: (800) 998-9938 or *corporate@oreilly.com*.

Editor:	Mike Loukides
Production Editor:	Emily Quill
Cover Designer:	Emma Colby
Interior Designer:	Melanie Wang

Printing History:

May 2002:	First Edition.

Library of Congress Cataloging-in-Publication Data

Englander, Robert.
    Java and SOAP/ Robert Englander.
        p. cm.
    ISBN 0-596-00175-4
    1. Internet programming. 2. Object oriented programming. 3. Simple object access protocol.
        4. Java (Computer programming language) I. Title.

QA76.76.H94 B54 2002
005.2'76--dc21   2002023322

Once again, for my daughter Jessica.

Table of Contents

Preface

The Simple Object Access Protocol, or SOAP, is the latest in a long line of technologies for distributed computing. It differs from other distributed computing technologies in that it is based on XML, and also that thus far it has not attempted to redefine the computing world. Instead, the SOAP specification describes important aspects of data content and structure as they relate to familiar programming models like remote procedure calls (RPCs) and message passing systems.

These specifications live squarely in the world of XML. SOAP is not bound to a specific programming language, computing platform, or software development environment. There are SOAP implementations that provide bindings for a variety of programming languages like C#, Perl, and Java™. Without these implementations SOAP remains in the abstract: a great concept without manifestation. It is the binding to software development languages that makes SOAP come alive, and that is what this book is about. Java is a natural for XML processing, making it perfect for building SOAP services and client applications. If building SOAP-aware software in Java is what you want to do, this book is just what you need to get started.

Intended Audience

This book is for everyone interested in how to access SOAP-based web services in Java, as well as how to build SOAP-based services in Java. It's written for programmers, students, and professionals who are already familiar with Java, so it doesn't spend any time covering the basic concepts or syntax of the language. If you aren't familiar with Java, you may want to keep a copy of a Java language book, like O'Reilly's *Learning Java* or *Java in a Nutshell,* close by.

A Moment in Time

The SOAP specification is still evolving. This book describes SOAP according to Version 1.1 of the spec. Although the concepts and techniques covered should continue to be relevant in future SOAP releases, there will certainly be important additions to SOAP as new versions of the spec are finalized. The Java implementations we'll be looking at will continue to evolve as well. Obviously, the descriptions and examples in this book will become dated or even obsolete over time—and that time will probably be sooner rather than later, given the speed at which web services are evolving. In fact, the handwriting is already on the wall: Apache SOAP Version 2, on which many of the examples are based, is destined to be replaced by Apache SOAP 3 (also known as Axis), which is currently available in an early release and is discussed briefly in Chapter 9. Axis, in turn, is committed to supporting the JAX RPC and JAXM API specifications, which are themselves still under development. An early access release of the reference implementation for these specifications is available from Sun Microsystems (and discussed in Chapter 11); this release is more recent than the most recent release of Axis. And it would be foolish to think that the JAX Pack specifications will mark the end of the evolutionary process. However, when the inevitable happens, you'll be armed with the knowledge and understanding necessary to keep pace with the changes.

How This Book Is Organized

The chapters in this book are organized so that each one builds upon the information presented in previous chapters, so it's best if you read the chapters in order.

Chapter 1, *Introduction*
>   This chapter provides an overview of SOAP, including related technologies, problem spaces, and comparisons to other solutions. It also introduces Apache SOAP and GLUE, the SOAP implementations that will be used throughout the book.

Chapter 2, *The SOAP Message*
>   This chapter describes the SOAP Envelope, a structured XML document that carries the payload of a SOAP transaction between client and server. It covers all aspects of a SOAP Envelope, including Headers, SOAP Body elements, and Faults. Some details of the SOAP HTTP binding are also included.

Chapter 3, *SOAP Data Encoding*
>   This chapter covers the data encoding of a SOAP transaction, including rules for encoding and serializing data elements. It starts out with a description of namespaces, and then delves into the serialization of both simple and complex data types.

Chapter 4, *RPC-Style Services*

This chapter goes deep into SOAP-based remote procedure call (RPC) style services. Extensive coverage of service methods and parameters is provided, along with the details of service deployment and activation mechanisms.

Chapter 5, *Working with Complex Data Types*

This chapter looks at the creation of services with complex method parameters and return values such as arrays and Java beans. It covers the mechanisms available for mapping these types to Java classes on both client and server systems.

Chapter 6, *Custom Serialization*

This chapter covers the use of nonstandard custom data types, picking up where Chapter 5 left off. It looks at some of the tools and APIs used to pass instances of custom data types as parameters and return values. It also details the techniques of writing Java classes for serializing and deserializing custom types.

Chapter 7, *Faults and Exceptions*

This chapter describes SOAP Faults, along with their relationship to Java exceptions. It looks at the default mechanisms provided, as well as techniques for generating and extending the contents of Faults.

Chapter 8, *Alternative Techniques*

This chapter starts out by describing the use of SOAP message-style services, an alternative to the RPC model. It also looks at passing literal XML inside of a SOAP Envelope, and finishes up with a look at SOAP Attachments.

Chapter 9, *SOAP Interoperability and WSDL*

This chapter looks at getting SOAP clients and servers, developed using different technologies, to work properly together. An introduction to the Web Services Description Language (WSDL) is provided. Examples are developed that cover clients and services built using Apache SOAP and GLUE, a sneak peek at Apache Axis, and Java clients accessing Microsoft .NET services.

Chapter 10, *SOAP Headers*

This chapter looks at the use of SOAP Headers, which provide a means to pass data between clients and services that lie outside the scope of the SOAP Body. It covers the development of an intermediary service that acts as a message router to another service. Some Java classes are developed for extending the Apache SOAP framework in order to work with SOAP Headers.

Chapter 11, *JAX-RPC and JAXM*

This chapter examines the emerging standard: the Java API for XML-based RPC (JAX-RPC). It's a look at an early release of Sun's reference implementation. This chapter covers the development of both a service and a client, and also looks at using the tools to develop code for accessing services described by WSDL. A final commentary on JAXM is also included.

Conventions Used in This Book

`Constant Width` is used for:

- Anything that might appear in a Java program, including keywords, operators, data types, constants, method names, variable names, class names, interface names, and Java package names.
- Command lines and options that should be typed verbatim on the screen.
- Namespaces.

Italic is used for:

- Pathnames, filenames, and Internet addresses, such as domain names and URLs. Italics is also used for executable files.

Making fine distinctions in a book like this is generally a losing battle. But I have tried to distinguish between namespaces (constant width) and URLs (italic), even though they look identical. Likewise, I've tried to distinguish between Java methods (constant width and ending in a pair of parentheses) and the methods exported by the SOAP service (constant width, no parentheses).

This icon signifies a note relating to the nearby text.

This icon signifies a warning relating to the nearby text.

How to Contact Us

I've certainly tried to be accurate in my descriptions and examples, but errors and omissions will inevitably exist. If you find mistakes, or you think I've left out important details, or you'd like to contact me for some other reason related to this work, you can contact me directly at:

rob@mindstrm.com

Alternately, address comments and questions concerning this book to the publisher:

O'Reilly & Associates, Inc.
1005 Gravenstein Highway North
Sebastopol, CA 95472
(800) 998-9938 (in the United States or Canada)
(707) 829-0515 (international/local)
(707) 829-0104 (fax)

There is a web page for this book, which lists errata, examples, or any additional information. You can access this page at:

http://www.oreilly.com/catalog/javasoap

To comment or ask technical questions about this book, send email to:

bookquestions@oreilly.com

For more information about books, conferences, Resource Centers, and the O'Reilly Network, see the O'Reilly web site at:

http://www.oreilly.com

Retrieving Examples Online

The code for the examples throughout this book is available online at:

http://www.mindstrm.com/javasoap

Acknowledgments

My good friend Rinaldo DiGiorgio continues, to this day, to keep me interested in Java and its related technologies. I don't think anyone has been a greater influence on my Java work than he has. Thanks, Rinaldo, for keeping me on the right path.

Many thanks go to David Askey and Anne Thomas Manes for reviewing the book and providing valuable feedback. They managed to find errors and offer advice that makes this a better book than it would have been without their help. Thanks to Lorraine Pecorelli for reading every chapter and making sure the words made sense. My deepest appreciation goes to Mike Loukides, the editor of this book. There were many obstacles to getting this project finished, and Mike's commitment and loyalty was key to turning the effort into a book. A thank you also is due to the O'Reilly design and production crew.

And finally, thanks to my family, Jessica and Carolyn, for their support. I'm not going to thank my friends this time—they were no help at all!

CHAPTER 1

Introduction

In the history of software development, new approaches frequently bring discarded ideas back into the mainstream of common practice. Each time an idea is revisited, prior successes and failures become invaluable aides in improving the concept and making its implementation better, or at least more usable. Now I'm not saying that we keep reinventing the wheel; rather, we keep going back and improving the wheel. And doing so can often be the catalyst for new ideas and new technologies that were not possible with the old wheel.

We've seen centralized computing with mainframes and their associated terminals come back disguised as application servers and thin clients. We've seen the concept of P-Code return in the form of interpreted languages like Java and Visual Basic. The universe of software development seems to expand and contract like, well, the cosmic Universe. If you wait around long enough, you may just be able to use the work you're doing today at some time in the future.

The point is, really, that a good idea is a good idea, regardless of whether it's a new idea. Timeliness is what matters most. So it goes for the world of distributed computing. The concept isn't new, but it gets revisited constantly. Pervasive infrastructure and technologies like the Internet, web browsers, and their associated protocols have allowed us to go back and advance the state of distributed computing. The evolution's latest craze is web services.

Web services are basically server functions that have published the interface mechanisms needed to access their capabilities. They're being implemented in a wide variety of technologies, but have a very important thing in common: they are providers of computational services that can be accessed using a standardized protocol. For instance, you might find a stock quote service that can return current stock market pricing and trading information based on a company's stock symbol. This is a very specific function, and that's the essence of web services. They do not provide the breadth of capability found in application servers—they provide small, focused capabilities that are likely to prove useful when combined with other services. You can imagine an online trading application that makes use of web services ranging from stock quotes to trade execution to banking transactions. The vision of web services is that it will ultimately be possible to create complex applications on the fly—or at least, with minimal development time—by combining bits and pieces of data and services that are distributed across the Web. Sun's slogan used to be "The network is the computer," and that vision is certainly coming to fruition.

RPC and Message-Oriented Distributed Systems

Distributed systems exist, for the most part, as loosely coupled entities that communicate with each other to accomplish some task. One of the most common models used in distributed software is the remote procedure call (RPC). One reason for the popularity of RPC systems is that they closely resemble the function/method call syntax and semantics that we as programmers are so familiar with. Technologies like Java RMI, Microsoft's COM, and CORBA all use this kind of model. Of course, you have to jump through many hoops before making the ever-familiar method call to a remote system, but even with all that it still feels remarkably like making a local method call. Often, once the method call returns we don't care how it happened.* Much of the work in providing that abstraction to programmers at the API level is what makes up the majority of the distributed systems implementations.

Another popular model for distributed computing is message passing. Unlike the RPC model, messaging does not emulate the syntax of programming language function calls. Instead, structured data messages are passed between parties. These messages can serve to decouple the nodes of the distributed system somewhat, and message-based systems often prove to be more flexible than RPC-based systems. However, that flexibility can sometimes be just enough rope for programmers to hang themselves.

It seems that a reasonable, and powerful, compromise might be to combine these two models. Can you imagine a system that provides for the familiarity and ease of use of RPC-style invocations, along with some of the flexibility of message-type systems? It seems to me that it would require the definition of a data format that could describe itself, while at the same time conforming to a standard set of rules governing that very description. Hmmm...

---

* I'm not suggesting that you turn a blind eye to the fact that you're making calls to remote systems. Imagine, for instance, the ramifications of iterating over a remote array of ten thousand objects by using an array accessor method that goes out to the remote system for every array element. Not exactly efficient!

Self-Describing Data

In programming parlance, the term *self-describing data* is itself self-describing. Put another way, if the question is, "What is self-describing data?" then the answer is, "Data that describes itself." Not a very useful definition. But that's the result of designing a flexible data format to be used by many, many people.

Let's look at a very simple example. Let's say we were designing a message-style distributed system for delivering stock quotes. We could design the response message format to be something like this:

- The first 10 characters contain the stock symbol, right-padded with spaces
- The next 10 characters represent the last price, right-padded with spaces
- The next 10 characters represent the volume, right-padded with spaces
- The next 20 characters represent the timestamp of the quote
- The next 10 characters represent the bid price
- The next 10 characters represent the ask price

You get the point. This is a fixed format message. It doesn't describe itself; rather it is described by the spec provided in the bullet list above. There's no flexibility here. And sometimes there's no need for any flexibility—it's not a one-size-fits-all scenario. But wouldn't you agree that there is some room for improvement? Let's consider the possibility that the values for last price, bid price, and ask price could be formatted in two different ways. The first format uses standard decimal notation, for example, 25.5. The other format uses fractions, so the same value would be encoded as 25 1/2. A self-describing format would have a provision for indicating which format is used for each of the price fields.

Now take this same concept and apply it to the overall structure of the message, as well as to its constituent parts. This gives you the flexibility to fully describe the contents of a message. For example, you could make some of the fields in the stock quote response optional. Maybe you've requested the quote after the market has closed, and maybe that renders the values for bid and ask prices useless. Then why return them at all? A self-describing format could specify its content, thereby having no need to return useless data.

In order for self-describing data to be truly useful, everyone has to use the same language for describing the data. I don't mean a programming language; I mean the language for expressing the description. What we need is a new way of describing and formatting these messages; a new grammar, so to speak. This new grammar would dictate the standard rules governing the format of these messages. In fact, this is where we really see the value of self-describing data: not so much to eliminate the problem of returning useless data, but to get everyone talking the same language. If I write a stock application that uses 11 characters to represent the stock symbol, it won't be able to talk to your stock server that uses 10 characters. But if we're exchanging self-describing data, the problem partially disappears: each piece of data says what it is in some standard way, so there's a much better chance that software coming from different people and organizations will be able to communicate.

XML

We've all been staring a form of self-describing data in the face every time we use a web browser. HTML is a good example of a standard data format that is quite flexible due to its provision for self-describing elements. For example, the color and font to be applied to a particular section of text are described right along with the text itself. This kind of self-describing data is commonly referred to as a *markup language*. The content is "marked-up" with instructions for its own presentation. This is very nice, and it obviously has gained an incredible level of industry acceptance. But HTML is not flexible enough to accommodate content that was not anticipated by its designers. That's not a knock on HTML; it's just the truth. HTML is not extensible.

The Extensible Markup Language (XML) is just what we're looking for. XML is a hierarchical, tag-based language much like HTML. The important difference for us is that it is fully extensible. It allows us to describe content that is specific to our own applications in a standard way, without the designers of the language having anticipated that content. For example, XML would allow me to create content to represent the stock quote response message from the previous section. It defines the rules that I must follow in order to accomplish that task, without dictating a specific format.

I'm not going to spend any time covering XML itself. If you're not familiar with XML, you may want to remedy that before you begin reading Chapter 2. Many books have been published on XML and related topics. A good starting point for general information is *XML in a Nutshell*, by Elliotte Rusty Harold and W. Scott Means (O'Reilly). For Java developers, *Java and XML* by Brett McLaughlin (O'Reilly) should be of particular interest.

API Specs Versus Wire-Level Specs

Java programmers are used to dealing with API-level specifications, where classes, interfaces, methods, and so on are clearly defined for the purpose of addressing a specific need. These specifications are designed to be independent of any specific implementation, focusing instead on the abstractions that must be implemented.

Consider the Java Message Service (JMS) specification. It fully describes the API that Java applications can use to access the features of message-oriented middleware (MOM) products. The motivation for a standard API is simple: if MOM vendors adopt the API, it becomes that much easier for programmers to work with the various product offerings. In theory, you could swap one JMS implementation for another without impacting the rest of your code. In practice, it means that product vendors might be somewhat handcuffed, unable to provide alternative APIs that leverage features and capabilities of their own products without sacrificing compliance. Nevertheless, API specifications have been around a long time, and they do achieve most of what they're intended to do.

However, the API specification approach, by itself, leaves a gaping hole in an extremely important area of software development: interoperability. You can't develop an application using Vendor A's JMS-compliant API to communicate with Vendor B's JMS-compliant server. The specification deals with only the API, not the format of the data being communicated between the parties. This seems to suggest that interoperability is not as important as commonality of programming syntax. Yes, it's a trade-off, but it's not always the right one.

A wire-level specification, on the other hand, deals exclusively in the content and format of the data being transmitted between parties: the data that's "on the wire." Instead of concentrating on APIs, it devotes itself to the representation used for distributed computing interactions. So you can pretty much guarantee that if you work with implementations from more than one vendor, the APIs will not be the same. However, you have a decent chance of getting distributed systems that were built using products from multiple vendors to work together. If you're doing any work in the area of web services, the wire-level specification approach is your ally; the API specification approach won't get you very far.

Overview of SOAP

One of the more recent forays into the world of distributed computing resulted in a wire-level specification called the Simple Object Access Protocol, or SOAP. The protocol is relatively lightweight, is based on XML, and is designed for the exchange of information in a distributed computing environment. There is no concept of a central server in SOAP; all nodes can be considered equals, or even peers.

The protocol is made up of a number of distinct parts. The first is the *envelope*, used to describe the content of a message and some clues on how to go about processing it. The second part consists of the rules for encoding instances of custom data types. This is one of the most critical parts of SOAP: its extensibility. The last part describes the application of the envelope and the data encoding rules for representing RPC calls and responses, including the use of HTTP as the underlying transport.

RPC-style distributed computing is the most common Java usage of SOAP today, but it is not the only one. Any transport can be used to carry SOAP messages, even though HTTP is the only one described in the specification. There has been significant discussion of using SMTP, BEEP, JXTA, and other protocols for carrying SOAP messages.

Using SOAP with Java

SOAP differs from RMI, CORBA, and COM in that it concentrates on the content, effectively decoupling itself from both implementation and underlying transport. An interesting concept for a Java book, wouldn't you say? After all, implementation and transport are likely to be built using Java. Yet SOAP in no way addresses Java or any other implementation strategy.

The reality is that SOAP is an enabler, incapable of existing on its own beyond the abstraction of the specification. To benefit from SOAP, or any other protocol, there have to be real implementations. Java is a great technology for implementing SOAP, and for building web services and applications that use SOAP as the "on the wire" data format.

SOAP Implementations

As I write this book, there are dozens of SOAP implementations, and new ones emerge all the time. Some are implemented in Java, some aren't. Some are free, some aren't. And inevitably some are good, and some aren't. It would be impractical to do a side-by-side comparison of every available implementation or even to give equal coverage to them all. On the other hand, it wouldn't be wise to focus on a single implementation, since that would present a bias that I don't intend. A reasonable compromise, and the one I've elected to use, is to select two interesting Java SOAP implementations and use them both extensively throughout the book. This gives you an opportunity to see different APIs and programming strategies. In Chapters 9 and 11, I'll break this rule and look briefly at a couple of other important SOAP technologies.

Apache SOAP

The Apache Software Foundation has an ongoing project known as Apache SOAP. This is a Java implementation of the SOAP specification that can be hosted by servers that support Java servlets. The examples in this book are based on Apache SOAP Version 2.2, which is available at *http://xml.apache.org/soap/index.html*. Four very important factors led me to choose this implementation: it supports a good deal of the specification, it has a reasonably large user base, the source code is available, and it's free.

Although Apache SOAP can be hosted by a variety of server technologies, I've chosen Apache Tomcat (Version 3.3 and Version 4), available at *http://jakarta.apache.org/tomcat/index.html*. The reasons are not particularly tied to SOAP, but it does work well in Tomcat. The use of Tomcat has no real impact on the examples in the book, so you can feel free to select some other server technology if you like.

Apache SOAP was developed at a time when there were no standards for a SOAP API. The SOAP specification doesn't address language bindings, so the implementors were forced to come up with their own APIs. More recently, the Java community has been working on standards for SOAP-based messaging and RPC APIs, known as JAXM and JAX-RPC, respectively. We'll take a look at these APIs in Chapter 11; they will be implemented by Axis, which is the next-generation Apache SOAP implementation. In an ideal world, JAXM and JAX-RPC would have been completed in time for me to give them the coverage they deserve, since they will almost certainly replace the APIs developed for Apache SOAP 2.2. In reality, though, the standard APIs are just solidifying now, and should be in final form just in time to make me write a second edition earlier than I'd like. The bulk of this book will focus on technology that you can use to write production code now. Once you have the concepts down, moving to a different API will not be a challenge.

GLUE

GLUE is an implementation of SOAP developed by a company called The Mind Electric (*www.themindelectric.com*). It's developed completely in Java, and can be hosted by a variety of servers that support servlets or can be run standalone using its own HTTP server. The GLUE examples in the book are based on GLUE Version 2, available at *http://www.themindelectric.com/products/glue/glue.html*. I chose GLUE for four reasons as well: it uses a very programmer-friendly approach, its APIs are quite different from those found in Apache SOAP, it relies on the Web Services Description Language (WSDL), and it's free for most uses.*

The GLUE APIs are also proprietary. I'd expect that a future version of GLUE would adopt standards like JAXM and JAX-RPC if the user community demanded it, but that, of course, remains to be seen.

Others

In Chapter 9 we'll work a little with some other technologies. Microsoft's .NET is a major player in the area of SOAP-based web services, so we'll look at what it takes to write Java applications that use SOAP to communicate with .NET services.

The Apache Software Foundation is currently working on a next-generation SOAP implementation called Axis. Although it's still a bit early to cover Axis in any detail, there's no doubt that it will some day replace or subsume Apache SOAP Version 2.X. We'll take a peek at writing a simple Axis application using the current release. (And, as I've already said, Chapter 11 will look at the JAXM and JAX-RPC proposed standards, which Axis will eventually implement.)

---

* Please refer to the GLUE license agreement.

The Approach

This book certainly does not cover every aspect of the SOAP technologies. My goal is to give you a good understanding of the major aspects of SOAP in the context of Java software development. You'll find that many of the examples are presented not only in Java source code, but also in the SOAP XML that is generated through the execution of the Java code. This will give you a sense of what the various APIs are actually accomplishing. Learning SOAP this way will allow you to go beyond the scope of this book with confidence, exploring the features and capabilities of the implementations I have covered as well those I have not.

No Security

One particular area is not covered in this book: security. How can you talk about a distributed computing technology without talking about security? The answer is actually quite simple: the SOAP specification does not deal with security. The current implementations rely on the security features of the hosting technology. Be it SSL, basic HTTP authentication, proxy authentication, or some other mechanism, all security is a function of the hosting technology and not part of SOAP itself. It's expected that either a future version of the SOAP spec or a separate SOAP Security spec will address that issue, but for now you'll have to rely on whatever your hosting technology supports.

The current spec does, however, mention the use of SOAP headers in security schemes, and you will find that some SOAP implementations follow that lead. Nonetheless, the mechanisms are likely to be specific to each implementation until a standard is adopted.

Getting Started

If you plan to work with the examples, you'll need to install all of the necessary software components, including the JDK, the SOAP implementations described earlier, and a number of other supporting technologies. All of these packages are reasonably well documented, so you should have no trouble getting them installed properly.

The chapters in this book are arranged so that each one builds on concepts of the preceding chapters. I suggest that you follow along in order, but of course that's entirely up to you. If you are already comfortable with XML or (even better) with some aspects of web services, you may find that you can jump around a bit.

CHAPTER 2

The SOAP Message

All SOAP messages are packaged in an XML document called an *envelope*, which is a structured container that holds one SOAP message. The metaphor is appropriate because you stuff everything you need to perform an operation into an envelope and send it to a recipient, who opens the envelope and reconstructs the original contents so that it can perform the operation you requested. The contents of the SOAP envelope conform to the SOAP specification,[*] allowing the sender and the recipient to exchange messages in a language-neutral way: for example, the sender can be written in Python and the recipient can be written in Java or C#. Neither side cares how the other side is implemented because they agree on how to interpret the envelope. In this chapter we'll get inside the SOAP envelope.

The HTTP Binding

The SOAP specification requires a SOAP implementation to support the transporting of SOAP XML payloads using HTTP, so it's no coincidence that the existing SOAP implementations all support HTTP. Of course, implementations are free to support any other transports as well, even though the spec doesn't describe them. There's nothing whatsoever about the SOAP payload that prohibits transporting messages over transports like SMTP, FTP, JMS, or even proprietary schemes; in fact, alternative transports are frequently discussed, and a few have been implemented. Nevertheless, since HTTP is the most prevalent SOAP transport to date, that's where we'll concentrate. Once you have a grasp of how SOAP binds to HTTP, you should be able to easily migrate your understanding to other transport mechanisms.

SOAP can certainly be used for request/response message exchanges like RPC, as well as inherently one-way exchanges like SMTP. The majority of Java-based SOAP implementations to date have implemented RPC-style messages, so that's where

---

[*] The spec can be found at *http://www.w3.org/TR/SOAP*. The SOAP 1.1 specification is not a W3C standard, but the SOAP 1.2 spec currently under development will be.

we'll spend most of our time; HTTP is a natural for an RPC-style exchange because it allows the request and response to occur as integral parts of a single transaction. However, one-way messaging shouldn't be overlooked, and nothing about HTTP prevents such an exchange. We'll look at one-way messaging in Chapter 8.

HTTP Request

The first SOAP message we'll look at is an RPC request. Although it's rather simple, it contains all of the elements required for a fully compliant SOAP message using an HTTP transport. The XML payload of the message is contained in an HTTP POST request. Take a quick look, but don't get too caught up in figuring out the details just yet. The following message asks the server to return the current temperature in degrees Celsius at the server's location:

```
POST /LocalWeather HTTP/1.0
Host: www.mindstrm.com
Content-Type: text/xml; charset="utf-8"
Content-Length: 328
SOAPAction: "WeatherStation"

<SOAP-ENV:Envelope
    xmlns:SOAP-ENV="http://schemas.xmlsoap.org/soap/envelope/"
    SOAP-ENV:encodingStyle="http://schemas.xmlsoap.org/soap/encoding/">
  <SOAP-ENV:Body>
    <m:GetCurrentTemperature xmlns:m="WeatherStation">
        <m:scale>Celsius</m:scale>
    </m:GetCurrentTemperature>
  </SOAP-ENV:Body>
</SOAP-ENV:Envelope>
```

The SOAP HTTP request uses the HTTP POST method. Although a SOAP payload could be transported using some other method such as an HTTP GET, the HTTP binding defined in the SOAP specification requires the use of the POST method. The POST also specifies the name of the service being accessed. In the example, we're sending the data to /LocalWeather at the host specified later in the HTTP header. This tells the server how to route the request within its own processing space. Finally, our example indicates that we're using HTTP Version 1.0, although SOAP doesn't require a particular version of HTTP.

The Host: header field specifies the address of the server to which we're sending this request, *www.mindstrm.com*. The next header field, Content-Type:, tells the server that we're sending data using the text/xml media type. All SOAP messages must be sent using text/xml. The content type in the example also specifies that the data is encoded using the UTF-8 character set. The SOAP standard doesn't require any particular encoding. Content-Length: tells the server the character count of the POSTed SOAP XML payload data to follow.

So far, all the headers have been standard HTTP headers that apply to any HTTP POST messages. The next one, however, is SOAP specific. The SOAPAction: header field is required for all SOAP request messages transported using HTTP.* It provides some information to the HTTP server in the form of a URI that indicates the intent of the message. This information is contained in an HTTP header field rather than in the message itself because it doesn't require the system to process the XML payload first. In turn, this means that the server can determine if it does not have the information or resources necessary to process the request without actually parsing the message. Although this field can contain data in any format or even be empty, the field itself must be present. The header SOAPAction: "WeatherStation" could indicate that our request requires an active connection to the weather station located on the roof of the building where the server resides. If the server knows that the weather station has fallen off the building and was subsequently crushed by a passing car, it can respond without bothering to process the SOAP payload. This may not be a common scenario, but the point is that the server can use the URI specified in the SOAPAction: field to gain some insight into the intent of the message, and act accordingly. It's also important to know that the URI need not take any particular form. It can be a URL, a name, a word, or even a number, as long as it has meaning to the server that receives the message.

If the SOAPAction: field contains an empty string (""), then the intent of the message is actually being provided by the HTTP request URI, which in the example is /LocalWeather. The server may interpret this URI to mean that it should access the weather station, or it might have some other meaning. If the field contains no data at all, then the message contains no information about the meaning or intent of the enclosed message. In that case, we'd expect the server to go ahead and process the XML payload.

HTTP Response

An RPC-style request message usually results in a corresponding HTTP response. Of course, if the server can't get past the information in the HTTP headers, it can reply with an HTTP error of some kind. But assuming that the headers are processed correctly, the system is expected to respond with a SOAP response. Here's the HTTP response to the RPC-style request from the previous example:

```
HTTP/1.0 200 OK
Content-Type: text/xml; charset="utf-8"
Content-Length: 359

<SOAP-ENV:Envelope
    xmlns:SOAP-ENV="http://schemas.xmlsoap.org/soap/envelope/"
    SOAP-ENV:encodingStyle="http://schemas.xmlsoap.org/soap/encoding/">
```

---

* This is a requirement in SOAP 1.1, but is expected to be optional in SOAP 1.2.

```
<SOAP-ENV:Body>
  <m:GetCurrentTemperatureResponse xmlns:m="WeatherStation">
      <m:temperature>26.6</m:temperature>
  </m:GetCurrentTemperatureResponse>
</SOAP-ENV:Body>
</SOAP-ENV:Envelope>
```

The response's HTTP header fields are, for the most part, similar to those of the request. The response code of 200 in the first line of the header indicates that the server was able to process the SOAP XML payload. The Content-Type: and Content-Length: fields have the same meanings as they did in the request message. No other HTTP header fields are needed; the correlation between the request and response is implied by the fact that the HTTP POST is inherently a request/response mechanism. You send the request and get the response as part of a single transaction.

Let's change the original request message so that the scale reads as follows:

```
<m:scale>Calcium</m:scale>
```

You know that one, right? No, there is no Calcium scale for temperature; we've constructed an erroneous request. So we go ahead and send the SOAP request to the server. Assuming the weather station hasn't really fallen off the building, the server processes the request. As we expected, our SOAP processing code does not understand the Calcium temperature scale, and generates the following error response:

```
HTTP/1.0 500 Internal Server Error
Content-Type: text/xml; charset="utf-8"
Content-Length: 525

<SOAP-ENV:Envelope
        xmlns:SOAP-ENV="http://schemas.xmlsoap.org/soap/envelope/"
    <SOAP-ENV:Body>
      <SOAP-ENV:Fault>
         <faultcode>SOAP-ENV:Client</faultcode>
         <faultstring>Client Error</faultstring>
         <detail>
            <m:weatherfaultdetails xmlns:m="WeatherStation">
               <message>No such temperature scale: Calcium</message>
               <errorcode>1234</errorcode>
            </m:weatherfaultdetails>
         </detail>
      </SOAP-ENV:Fault>
    </SOAP-ENV:Body>
</SOAP-ENV:Envelope>
```

The HTTP error code of 500 with the explanation "Internal Server Error" shows that an error occurred. Just as before, the header includes the Content-Type: and Content-Length: HTTP header fields. The SOAP spec says that if the message is received and understood, the response should be sent using a 2xx status code. When the server does not understand the message, or if the message is improperly formatted, is missing information, or cannot be processed for any other reason, the server must use

HTTP code 500 ("Internal Server Error"). That HTTP header is followed by a SOAP envelope, which includes its own fault code, fault string, and a detailed description of the error.

I'm not convinced that this is the best way to handle SOAP faults, or that using a transport protocol error is really a good way to package a SOAP error. Transport errors and SOAP errors really don't have anything to do with each other. After all, the response includes a proper SOAP message that describes the error in detail. However, in fairness to the developers of the SOAP spec, this error-handling procedure is in line with the way HTTP delivers errors in retrieving, say, HTML documents. I could still argue both sides, but that's the requirement and it certainly doesn't interfere with the SOAP processing.

Summarizing the HTTP Binding

That's just about all we need to cover about the SOAP HTTP binding. The beauty of it, really, is that HTTP is a well-established mechanism that works extremely well for transporting XML, and therefore it's a good way to transport SOAP messages.

Some of the details of the XML in the previous examples might be obvious to you, even though we haven't covered them yet. If you understand the XML, great. Otherwise, fear not. The purpose of the discussion so far has been to show you what the HTTP binding for SOAP looks like. In the next section we'll take a detailed look at the SOAP envelope, which is the XML payload that contains the SOAP requests and responses.

The SOAP Envelope

The SOAP envelope represents the entirety of the XML for a SOAP request or response.* The Envelope is the highest-level XML element in the message, and it must be present for the message to be considered valid. So in essence, the Envelope represents the XML document that contains the SOAP message. The Envelope can contain an optional Header element that, if present, has to be the first subelement of the Envelope. The Envelope must contain a Body element.† If the Envelope contains a Header element, then the Body element has to come right after the Header; otherwise the Body has to be the first subelement of the Envelope.

A SOAP envelope packaged and transported using HTTP is similar to a paper envelope sent using the postal service. The SOAP envelope is the paper envelope; the

---

* An exception to this occurs where an attachment is included. We'll look at that possibility in Chapter 8.

† There have been some discussions about providing for a Body-less Envelope in SOAP 1.2.

SOAP header (if present) and the SOAP body are the contents of the paper envelope; and the HTTP headers are the physical address information on the outside of the paper envelope.

With a little imagination we can complete the analogy. The return address on a paper envelope has no direct counterpart in the SOAP process; however, in both cases an undeliverable message is returned to sender. The only thing missing is the stamp. I guess this is where the analogy may break down a little. Still, although you probably don't pay specifically for sending an HTTP request to a server, you're probably paying for Internet service. So there's your postage stamp!

Namespaces

Understanding XML namespaces is important to understanding SOAP. I'm not going to cover all the details of XML namespaces, as that would take a long time and wouldn't reflect directly on the subject matter of this book. Nonetheless, I'll give you a quick description of XML namespaces as they relate to SOAP. Basically, namespaces are an XML mechanism for eliminating ambiguity between XML elements and attributes. In other words, they help us to understand the context, or meaning, of the element. Let's look at part of an earlier example:

```
<m:GetCurrentTemperature xmlns:m="WeatherStation">
      <m:scale>Celsius</m:scale>
</m:GetCurrentTemperature>
```

XML allows us to create something similar to programming language variables to represent namespaces. In the example above we've created a namespace identifier named m by using the namespace declaration xmlns:m="WeatherStation". Generally, the syntax of a namespace declaration in a SOAP message typically is:

```
xmlns:id="some URI"
```

The xmlns keyword tells the XML processor that we're defining a namespace. If the definition includes a qualifier name, then we're also creating a namespace qualifier that can be used to distinguish this namespace from other namespaces. If we don't specify a qualifier name, then we're defining a default namespace. The id is the identifier name we're declaring, in this case, the letter m. The last part is a URI that provides the context for the namespace. Although the URI is frequently a URL, it's important to realize that it's just an identifier; the recipient of a document won't try to download the content of the URI (which may not even exist). We can use the letter m to qualify elements that are within the same scope as the declaration itself.

Qualifying an XML element means associating it with a specific namespace. In this example, we qualify the GetCurrentTemperature XML element with the namespace WeatherStation by declaring the element as m:GetCurrentTemperature. This means that GetCurrentTemperature is associated with the WeatherStation namespace, represented by the identifier m.

Note that the namespace identifier m can be used to qualify the element in which it is declared. But there's nothing special about using m in this element. We aren't required to qualify the GetCurrentTemperature element with the namespace identifier m just because that element contains the namespace declaration as an attribute, but rather because we need to indicate where GetCurrentTemperature is defined. Putting the declaration in this element creates the scope for which the identifier m can be used. Clearly, it's valid to use the identifier at the same level as its declaration; that's what we did in the example. So the scope of the namespace is bounded by the element that contains the declaration. This means that the namespace ID can be used on the element that contains the declaration, any attributes of that element, and any subelements and associated attributes of the containing element. The namespace identifier is not within the scope of the XML elements that are higher up in the containment hierarchy. If you go back and look at the original example, this means that the namespace identifier m could not be used for attributes of the Body element because m would be out of scope. The scoping rules are similar to those used in block-oriented programming languages like Java, where the namespaces are pushed onto a stack as you enter bracketed blocks of code, and the stack is popped as you exit the block. Here's a Java code snippet that shows the same kind of scoping for variables var1 and var2:

```
int var1 = 10;
{
    int var2 = 2 * var1; // this is OK because var1 is in scope
}
var1 = var2; // this is invalid because var2 is out of scope
```

 XML supports something called a *default namespace*, which can result in namespace qualification being inherited without being explicitly expressed. A default namespace is declared by assigning a value to the attribute named xmlns without using an associated namespace identifier. Consider this example:

```
<GetCurrentTemperature xmlns="WeatherStation">
    <scale>Celsius</scale>
</GetCurrentTemperature>
```

In this case, both the GetCurrentTemperature element and the scale element are associated with the WeatherStation namespace.

Namespace qualification is often necessary to determine the intended meaning of the element or attribute. Consider the following example:

```
<truckmonitor>
    <scale>37F6A</scale>
    <weight>12000</weight>
    <scale>Celcius</scale>
    <temperature>25</temperature>
</truckmonitor>
```

This XML contains some data that may have been collected at a truck monitoring station. The first occurrence of the scale element specifies the scale used to weigh the truck. Later on, we have the same element name, scale, to describe the temperature scale used to measure the outside temperature at the monitoring location. So how are we to know the meaning of the two scale elements? You might feel that the overall structure is intuitive just by looking at it, but this may not always be the case.

Certainly one way to avoid this problem would be to use more descriptive names, or XML structures that better represent the meaning of the elements. But you may not always be in control of those things; you may be creating a composite document from XML fragments that come from many different sources. The use of appropriate namespace qualifications can lend a hand in resolving name conflicts and ambiguity. The following document is the same as the previous one, with the two scale elements properly qualified:

```
<truckmonitor xmlns:ns1="TruckScale" xmlns:ns2="Thermometer">
    <ns1:scale>37F6A</ns1:scale>
    <weight>12000</weight>
    <ns2:scale>Celcius</ns2:scale>
    <temperature>25</temperature>
</truckmonitor>
```

The first occurrence of scale is now associated with the TruckScale namespace, while the second occurrence of scale is associated with the Thermometer namespace. Did you notice that both of the namespace declarations are attributes of the same element? That's perfectly valid, since namespace declarations are nothing more than attributes, and an XML element can have more than one attribute.

SOAP defines two namespaces to be used by SOAP messages. The SOAP Envelope is qualified by the namespace http://schemas.xmlsoap.org/soap/envelope. We used this namespace in earlier examples by declaring the SOAP-ENV namespace identifier and using it to qualify the Envelope element. The namespace identifier http://schemas.xmlsoap.org/soap/encoding is used to declare the encodingStyle attribute, which we'll discuss more later. Note that the encodingStyle attribute is namespace-qualified using the SOAP-ENV identifier. Here's a quick look at it again:

```
<SOAP-ENV:Envelope
        xmlns:SOAP-ENV="http://schemas.xmlsoap.org/soap/envelope/"
        SOAP-ENV:encodingStyle="http://schemas.xmlsoap.org/soap/encoding/">
    . . .
    . . .
</SOAP-ENV:Envelope>
```

The Envelope Element

The Envelope is the topmost element of the XML document that represents the SOAP message. The Envelope is the only XML element at the top level; the rest of the SOAP message resides within the Envelope, encoded as subelements. A SOAP message must have an Envelope element. The Envelope can have namespace declarations, as shown in the earlier examples, and needs to be qualified as shown earlier, using the http://schemas.xmlsoap.org/soap/envelope namespace. That's why the element name is shown as SOAP-ENV:Envelope. It is also common for the Envelope element to declare the encodingStyle attribute, with the attribute namespace-qualified using the declared namespace identifier SOAP-ENV as well.

All subelements and attributes of the Envelope must themselves be namespace-qualified. These elements and attributes are also qualified by SOAP-ENV, just as the Envelope is qualified. For the remainder of this chapter and the rest of the book, we'll use the SOAP-ENV namespace identifier to mean the http://schemas.xmlsoap.org/soap/envelope namespace. This should make for easier reading. Keep in mind that it's the namespace itself that matters, not the name used for the qualifier.

The Header Element

The SOAP header is optional. If it is present, it must be named Header and be the first subelement of the Envelope element. The Header element is also namespace-qualified using the SOAP-ENV identifier.

Most commonly, the Header entries are used to encode elements used for transaction processing, authentication, or other information related to the processing or routing of the message. This is useful because, as we'll see, the Body element is used for encoding the information that represents an RPC (or other) payload. The Header is an extension mechanism that allows any kind of information that lies outside the semantics of the message in the Body, but is nevertheless useful or even necessary for processing the message properly.

Header elements should limit the use of attributes to those elements that are immediate children of the Header element itself. The spec says that this *should* be done, meaning that although one can use them on elements deeper in the element hierarchy underneath the Header element, the recipient is required to ignore the attributes on such elements.

Here's an example of a SOAP header that contains an immediate child element named username. We don't apply any attributes to the username element, but we do namespace-qualify it. The username element identifies the user who is making the request.

```
<SOAP-ENV:Header>
    <ns1:username xmlns:ns1="JavaSoapBook">
      Jessica
    </ns1:username>
</SOAP-ENV:Header>
```

The actor Attribute

A SOAP message often passes through one or more intermediaries before being processed. For example, a SOAP proxy service may stand between a client application and the target SOAP service. We'll see an interesting example of this in Chapter 10, where we'll develop a SOAP application service that proxies another service on behalf of the client application, which actually specifies the ultimate service address. Therefore, the header may contain information intended solely for the intermediary as well as information intended for the ultimate destination. The actor attribute identifies (either implicitly or explicitly) the intended recipient of a Header element.

It's important to understand the requirements that SOAP puts on an intermediary. Essentially, it requires that any SOAP Header elements intended for use by an intermediary are not passed on to the next SOAP processor in the path. Header elements represent contracts between the sender and receiver. However, if the information contained in a Header element intended for an intermediary is also needed by a downstream server, the intermediary can insert the appropriate Header in the message to be sent downstream. In fact, the intermediary is free to add any Header elements it deems necessary.

If an actor attribute doesn't appear on a Header element, it's assumed that the element is intended for the ultimate recipient. In essence, this is equivalent to including the actor attribute with its value being the URI of the ultimate destination.

Let's extend the previous example by adding an actor attribute. Say that the message is being sent to an intermediate application server located at *http://www.mindstrm.com/AppServer*. We want that application server to log the name of the user that made the request, and then pass the request on to the final destination server. To do so, we set the actor for the username element to *http://www.mindstrm.com/AppServer*:

```
<SOAP-ENV:Header>
    <ns1:username
          xmlns:ns1="JavaSoapBook"
          SOAP-ENV:actor="http://www.mindstrm.com/AppServer">
          Jessica
    </ns1:username>
</SOAP-ENV:Header>
```

The proxy application server sees that the username element is intended for itself and not for the final destination, and uses the data appropriately. It removes the username element from the header before passing the message on to its ultimate destination. As you can see, the actor attribute is namespace-qualified by the SOAP-ENV identifier. That's because the actor attribute is defined by SOAP and specified by the associated http://schemas.xmlsoap.org/soap/envelope namespace.

The mustUnderstand Attribute

SOAP includes the concept of optional and mandatory header elements. This doesn't mean that the inclusion of the elements is mandatory—that is an application issue. Instead, "mandatory" means that the recipient is required to understand and make proper use of the information supplied by a Header element. This requirement allows us to accommodate situations in which a recipient of a SOAP message can't perform its job unless it knows what to do with the data provided by a specific Header element. In this case the element can include the mustUnderstand attribute with an assigned value of 1.

This may be necessary if the sending application is upgraded with a new version, for example. That new version may use some new information that has to be processed by the server in order for the result to be useful. Of course you'd expect that there would be a corresponding upgrade to the server, but maybe that hasn't happened yet. Because of the version mismatch, the older version of the server does not understand the new SOAP header element that it received from the upgraded client application. Let's say, for example, that the username header element must be understood by the recipient; if it is not, the message should be rejected. We can include this requirement in the SOAP message by assigning the mustUnderstand attribute the value of 1. (The value 0 is essentially equivalent to not supplying the attribute.) Let's modify our previous example to indicate that the recipient must understand the username element:

```
<SOAP-ENV:Header>
    <ns1:username
        xmlns:ns1="JavaSoapBook"
        SOAP-ENV:actor="http://www.mindstrm.com/AppServer"
        SOAP-ENV:mustUnderstand="1">
        Jessica
    </ns1:username>
</SOAP-ENV:Header>
```

If the recipient of this message does not understand the username element, it is required to respond with a SOAP fault. The response might look something like this:

```
HTTP/1.0 500 Internal Server Error
Content-Type: text/xml; charset="utf-8"
Content-Length: 373

<SOAP-ENV:Envelope
        xmlns:SOAP-ENV="http://schemas.xmlsoap.org/soap/envelope/"
    <SOAP-ENV:Body>
        <SOAP-ENV:Fault>
            <faultcode>SOAP-ENV:MustUnderstand</faultcode>
            <faultstring>SOAP Must Understand Error</faultstring>
            <faultactor>http://www.mindstrm.com/AppServer</faultactor>
        </SOAP-ENV:Fault>
    </SOAP-ENV:Body>
</SOAP-ENV:Envelope>
```

The fault response includes a faultcode, a faultstring, and a faultactor; the faultactor indicates where the fault took place. We'll look more closely at faults later in this chapter.

The encodingStyle Attribute

The encodingStyle attribute specifies the data encoding rules used to serialize and deserialize data elements. It is important to understand that SOAP does not specify any default rules for data serialization. SOAP does, however, specify a simple data typing scheme commonly supported by SOAP implementations. This is the subject of the next chapter, so we won't get into the details of the encoding rules here. However, it's important to understand how to specify the encoding style to be used for serializing and deserializing the element data in the SOAP message.

The encodingStyle attribute is namespace-qualified using the SOAP-ENV namespace identifier. In the following example we specify the encodingStyle attribute as part of the Envelope element; we'll see examples in later chapters that make this declaration in the Body element instead. Either way works, as long as you recognize that the encodingStyle attribute applies to the element in which it was declared as well as all of its subelements (i.e., it's in-scope).

```
<SOAP-ENV:Envelope
    xmlns:SOAP-ENV="http://schemas.xmlsoap.org/soap/envelope/"
    SOAP-ENV:encodingStyle="http://schemas.xmlsoap.org/soap/encoding/">
    . . .
    . . .
</SOAP-ENV:Envelope>
```

You can supply more than one URI in the declaration. In that case, the first URI must be the most specific, and the last must be the least specific. Here's an example:

```
SOAP-ENV:encodingStyle="http://www.mindstrm.com/tightEncoding
http://www.mindstrm.com/looseEncoding"
```

In this case, the system looks for the encoding rules first using *http://www.mindstrm.com/tightEncoding*.[*] If the rule can't be found using that URI, the system then tries *http://www.mindstrm.com/looseEncoding*. It's possible to turn off the currently scoped encoding style by specifying an empty string for the URI (""). This declaration applies to the current element and all of its subelements.

---

[*] It's tempting to think of the system trying to download tightEncoding, particularly since the URI happens to be a URL. But that isn't the case; the system just looks in its own tables to see whether it understands tightEncoding, and acts accordingly.

Envelope Versioning

The SOAP spec doesn't define a numbering system for declaring which version of the SOAP envelope you're using. In SOAP 1.1, all envelopes must be associated with the `http://schemas.xmlsoap.org/soap/envelope` namespace,* which we've used in all of the previous examples. That's it. No other versioning information is used for SOAP envelopes at this time. If a SOAP message is associated with any other namespace, or if no namespace is declared, then the recipient has to respond with a SOAP version mismatch. Here is an example of a SOAP fault response for this situation:

```
HTTP/1.0 500 Internal Server Error
Content-Type: text/xml; charset="utf-8"
Content-Length: 311

<SOAP-ENV:Envelope
        xmlns:SOAP-ENV="http://schemas.xmlsoap.org/soap/envelope/"
    <SOAP-ENV:Body>
       <SOAP-ENV:Fault>
          <faultcode>SOAP-ENV:VersionMismatch</faultcode>
          <faultstring>SOAP Envelope Version Mismatch</faultstring>
       </SOAP-ENV:Fault>
    </SOAP-ENV:Body>
</SOAP-ENV:Envelope>
```

The Body Element

The SOAP `Body` element is mandatory in SOAP 1.1. If there is no SOAP header, the `Body` must be the first subelement of the `Envelope`; otherwise it must directly follow the SOAP `Header` element. The `Body` element is also namespace-qualified using the `SOAP-ENV` identifier.

The `Body` element contains the SOAP request or response. This is where you might find an RPC-style message that contains the method name and its parameters, or a one-way message and its relevant parts, or a fault and its details. SOAP `Body` elements are not completely defined by the SOAP specification; we'll cover that subject in great detail later. In fact, SOAP defines only one kind of `Body`: the SOAP `Fault`.

Let's take another look at one of the earlier examples of an envelope with a SOAP `Body` element. In this case the request is an RPC. We've namespace-qualified the `Body` element using the same `SOAP-ENV` namespace identifier that we used for the other SOAP-defined elements and attributes.

```
<SOAP-ENV:Envelope
        xmlns:SOAP-ENV="http://schemas.xmlsoap.org/soap/envelope/"
        SOAP-ENV:encodingStyle="http://schemas.xmlsoap.org/soap/encoding/">
    <SOAP-ENV:Body>
        <m:GetCurrentTemperature xmlns:m="WeatherStation">
```

---

* For SOAP 1.2, the namespace is `http://www.w3.org/2001/12/soap-envelope`.

```
        <m:scale>Celsius</m:scale>
      </m:GetCurrentTemperature>
    </SOAP-ENV:Body>
  </SOAP-ENV:Envelope>
```

SOAP Faults

The `Fault` is the only `Body` element entry defined by SOAP. It's used to carry error information back to the originator of a SOAP message. The `Fault` element must appear as an immediate subelement of the `Body` element, and it can't appear more than once.

SOAP defines four subelements of the `Fault` element. Not all of these are required, and some are appropriate only under certain conditions. These elements are described in the following sections. You'll probably recognize that we've seen all of these in previous examples, so you may want to flip back and look at them again after you've read these descriptions.

The faultcode Element

The `faultcode` element provides an indication of the fault that is recognizable by a software process, providing an opportunity for the system receiving the fault to act appropriately. The code is not necessarily useful to humans—that is the purpose of the `faultstring` element described in the next section. The `faultcode` element is mandatory, and must appear as a subelement of the `Fault` element. SOAP defines a number of fault codes for use in the `faultcode` element. These codes are associated with the `http://schemas.xmlsoap.org/soap/envelope` namespace. Here are brief descriptions of the SOAP-defined fault codes:

VersionMismatch
> Indicates that an invalid namespace was associated with the SOAP `Envelope`.

MustUnderstand
> Means that there was a SOAP `Header` element that contained the `mustUnderstand` attribute with a value of 1, and either the attribute was not understood or the semantics associated with the attribute couldn't be followed.

Client
> Indicates that there was some error in the formatting of the SOAP message or that the message did not contain the appropriate or necessary information. The client should assume that the message is not suitable to be sent again without making the appropriate changes. We saw an example of this when we requested the local temperature using an invalid temperature scale.

Server
> Indicates that the message could not be processed due to reasons not related to the formatting or contents of the received message. This can be interpreted to

mean that the message could be re-sent without modification possibly processed at some later time. For example, the back-end database server needed to complete the requested action may be currently offline, but may be back online later.

These fault codes are extensible; this means that they can be extended using a dot notation, where the name following each dot serves to provide more specific detail. For example:

```
Server.WeatherStationFailure
```

While this can still be considered a `Server` error, it provides more information by indicating that there was some problem with the weather station equipment needed to fulfill the request. We could extend this fault code even further, as follows:

```
Server.WeatherStationFailure.SmashedToPieces
```

This fault code lets us know that the weather station equipment is beyond repair, possibly because it fell off the building and was subsequently crushed. Remember, however, that these codes are meant to be processed by software. Extended fault codes should be defined in anticipation of possible situations or conditions, allowing the recipient of the fault to act accordingly. (I'm not sure that smashed equipment would qualify as an anticipated condition.)

The faultstring Element

This element is also mandatory, and must appear as a subelement of the `Fault` element. Its purpose is to provide a human-readable description of the fault; it's not designed to be processed by the recipient the way the `faultcode` element is. It is expected that the sender will populate this element with a reasonable description that would make sense to the reader within the context of the original request.

The faultactor Element

This element is required only under certain conditions, and when present must be a subelement of the `Fault` element. It is the corollary to the actor header attribute described earlier. It provides an indication of the system that was responsible for the fault. Earlier, we talked about SOAP intermediaries and used a proxy application server as an example. There, the proxy generated the fault because it didn't understand what to do with the `username` element. Because the application proxy was not the intended ultimate recipient of the original message, it was required to include the `faultactor` element, identifying itself as the source of the fault. The value of this element is the URI of the fault generator.

If the source of the fault is the ultimate destination of the message, the `Fault` element is not required to include a `faultactor` element. However, this element may be included even under these circumstances.

The detail Element

The detail element provides information related to faults that occur due to errors associated with the Body element of the request message. If the contents (or lack of contents) of the Body preclude the proper processing of the message, then the detail element must appear as a subelement of the Fault. On the other hand, if the fault is not related to the Body element of the message, the detail element must not be included; SOAP specifies that the absence of a detail element indicates that the fault is unrelated to the processing of the Body element.

In particular, the detail element cannot be used to further describe faults related to SOAP Header elements. In the earlier example, the proxy application server was not able to further describe the fault using a detail element because the problem was unrelated to the contents of the Body.

Another Fault Example

Here's another complete example of a SOAP fault:

```
HTTP/1.0 500 Internal Server Error
Content-Type: text/xml; charset="utf-8"
Content-Length: 595

<SOAP-ENV:Envelope
        xmlns:SOAP-ENV="http://schemas.xmlsoap.org/soap/envelope/"
   <SOAP-ENV:Body>
     <SOAP-ENV:Fault>
        <faultcode>SOAP-ENV:Client</faultcode>
        <faultstring>Client Error</faultstring>
        <faultactor>http://www.mindstrm.com/LocalWeather</faultactor>
        <detail>
           <m:weatherfaultdetails xmlns:m="WeatherStation">
              <message>No such temperature scale: Calcium</message>
              <errorcode>1234</errorcode>
           </m:weatherfaultdetails>
        </detail>
     </SOAP-ENV:Fault>
   </SOAP-ENV:Body>
</SOAP-ENV:Envelope>
```

This is really the same response we used earlier in the chapter. The only difference is that this time we included the faultactor element to identify the source of the fault. So this example includes an instance of every SOAP fault code, as well as a detail element describing the fault a little further.

At this point, we're finished looking at the SOAP message itself. Our next step is to look at the encodings that are used in messages.

CHAPTER 3

SOAP Data Encoding

When sending data over a network, the data must comply with the underlying transmission protocol, and be formatted in such a way that both the sending and receiving parties understand its meaning. This is what we refer to as *data encoding*. Data encoding encompasses the organization of the data structure, the type of data transferred, and of course the data's value. Just like in Java, it is the data that gets serialized, not the behavior. Data encoding and serialization rules help the parties involved in a SOAP transaction to understand the meaning and content of the message. The model for SOAP encoding is based on XML data encoding, but the encoding constrains or alters those rules to fit the intended purpose of SOAP. I think you'll find that the data requirements of most systems can be easily represented using the encoding rules presented here.

Schemas and Namespaces

Namespaces provide the mechanism used to determine how element and attribute names are interpreted. Because XML allows arbitrary element names, it needs a mechanism for specifying which dictionary should be used to look up the meaning of any given name. The encoding style defined in section 5 of the SOAP specification is the most commonly used encoding style in SOAP. This encoding style, which is defined in the schema referenced by the `http://schemas.xmlsoap.org/encoding` namespace, is often referred to as "SOAP Section 5." In SOAP messages, this namespace is by convention referenced using a namespace qualifier such as `SOAP-ENC` or `soapenc`. In our examples we will use the `SOAP-ENC` namespace qualifier to refer to this namespace.

It's important to understand that, in SOAP, schemas are used as references to definitions of data elements. They aren't used to validate SOAP message data in standard SOAP processing, although there's nothing stopping you from doing that on your own. References to schemas are often used as namespaces in order to qualify a serialized data element. It's up to the developer or the underlying framework to understand the structure or meaning of the data and to code to it accordingly.

SOAP Section 5 incorporates all of the built-in data types of XML Schema Part 2: Datatypes.* This schema defines most of the basic data types you'll use, either directly or as part of your own types. The general practice is to declare a namespace identifier named xsd and associate it with the namespace http://www.w3.org/2001/XMLSchema. As we saw in the previous chapter, this declaration is usually done as an attribute of the SOAP Envelope or SOAP Body.

Another common namespace identifier used for data encoding is xsi, which is associated with the namespace http://www.w3.org/2001/XMLSchema/instance. The easiest way to explain this identifier is with an example. Imagine that we want to declare that the data type of a particular XML element is a float as defined by the XML Schema of 2001. We do this by using the type attribute from xsi, which is an instance data type. The xsi:type attribute specifies the data type of the encoded data value. Here's an example of its use:

```
<xyz xsi:type="xsd:float">3.14159</xyz>
```

 Note that the schema from 2001 is not the only one out there. Schemas from 1999 and 2000 are also commonly used, and others will emerge. SOAP implementations should be able to handle any of the possibilities because the message will contain a reference to the appropriate schema.

The following namespace identifiers are commonly found in SOAP literature and implementations. Let's take a look at their declarations so that you'll recognize them:

```
xmlns:SOAP-ENC="http://schemas.xmlsoap.org/encoding/"
xmlns:xsi="http://www.w3.org/2001/XMLSchema/instance/"
xmlns:xsd="http://www.w3.org/2001/XMLSchema/"
```

Terminology

In order to fully understand SOAP encoding, it's important to look at some of the terminology. These terms are described in the SOAP spec, but we're going to expand on that a little and look at some examples using both Java and XML.

The term *value* is used to describe the actual data encoded in an XML element. The data is a string of characters. The interpretation of that string can be just about anything you'd normally think of in Java programming: a number, a name, a date, or something more elaborate. The values found in a SOAP message are always associated with a given type. We'll talk about types shortly; for now suffice it to say that the data type of a given value is never undefined in SOAP. There should always be some way to determine the correct type for any value in the message.

---

* This spec can be found at *http://www.w3.org/TR/xmlschema-2/*.

SOAP makes a distinction between simple values and compound values. A *simple* value does not contain any named parts; it just contains a single piece of data. The data values associated with programming language types like strings, integers, and floats would all be considered simple values. Here are a few examples in Java with their corresponding examples in SOAP:

```
int a = 10;                     <a xsi:type="xsd:int">10</a>
float x = 3.14159;              <x xsi:type="xsd:float">3.14159</x>
java.lang.String s = "SOAP";    <s xsi:type="xsd:string">SOAP</s>
```

Each of the variables above contains simple values of the associated type. The data is not split into multiple parts, and no other names or mechanisms are needed to get at the data.

A *compound* value contains multiple pieces of data that have some relation to each other. The individual pieces of data may be accessed by indicating an ordinal position in a sequence of values, as with a traditional array. They could be accessed using values that are keys to an associative array, like a hash table. And they could be accessed using the names of the constituent parts, as with a struct in C. Whatever the mechanism, there is always a way to distinguish a specific data value within a compound value, and that mechanism is referred to as an *accessor*. It's also possible for a constituent part of a compound value to be a compound value itself. Here are some examples of compound values in both Java and SOAP:

```
int[3] iArray = {10, 20, 30};

<iArray xsi:type=SOAP-ENC:Array SOAP-ENC:arrayType="xsd:int[3]">
    <val>10</val>
    <val>20</val>
    <val>30</val>
</iArray>

class Sample
{
    public int iVal = 10;
    public java.lang.String sVal = "Ten";
}
Sample samp = new Sample();

<Sample>
    <iVal xsi:type="xsd:int">10</iVal>
    <sVal xsi:type="xsd:string">Ten</sVal>
</Sample>
```

In this example, ordinal accessors are used to get at the values in the Java array variable iArray. To get at the parts of the Java variable samp, we use the named accessors iVal and sVal. We'll look more closely at some compound types, including arrays and structs, in the section "Compound Types."

In SOAP, as in most programming languages, values are associated with an appropriate data type. We've already touched on this in discussing simple and compound data values; each of these values had an associated type. Just like in Java, we declare instances of types and then assign values to them.

Serialization Rules

The XML elements in a SOAP message are either *independent* or *embedded*. Because of the hierarchical nature of XML, most elements are embedded as subelements of other elements. Independent elements, then, are not subelements of any other elements; they appear at the top level of a serialization.

All of the values in a SOAP message are encoded as the content of an element. Data values cannot appear by themselves outside the confines of an element. That does not mean, however, that every XML element contains a value. For instance, compound data types like structs or arrays contain subelements that contain the actual data values. The elements that define these compound data values do not contain the data directly. Compound types will be covered a little later.

References

SOAP Section 5 also permits elements to reference the values contained in other elements. In this case, no value is provided with the element; instead, an attribute identifies the element in which the actual data value is to be found. The data value must be contained in an independent element, appearing at the top level of a serialization.

The element containing the data value must contain an attribute named `id` of type ID. The value of the `id` attribute is the name that other elements use to reference the value. Here is such an element:

```
<lastName id="name-1">Englander</lastName>
```

The `lastName` element is a perfectly valid accessor in its own right. In addition, it has an identifier that allows other elements to reference the data value.

Elements that access a value in another element have no data values themselves. They are empty elements containing an `href` attribute that references the value. The `href` attribute is of type `uri-reference` defined in the XML Schema specification; the value of this attribute references the `id` attribute of the element that contains the data value. Here's an example of an accessor element that references the value of the `lastName` element used previously:

```
<surName href="#name-1"/>
```

This ability to reference the values of other elements is important for a couple of reasons. First, it has the potential to reduce the size of a SOAP message. Imagine that you're sending a message that contains the names of members of the Englander family. The XML could look something like this:

```
<member>
    <firstName>Rob</firstName>
    <lastName>Englander</lastName>
</member>
<member>
    <firstName>Jessica</firstName>
    <lastName>Englander</lastName>
</member>
<member>
    <firstName>Arnold</firstName>
    <lastName>Englander</lastName>
</member>
    . . .
    . . .
    . . .
```

As you can see, there's a great deal of duplicated data. References allow us to minimize the repetition because many accessors can refer to the same element. When that occurs, the value is called a *multi-reference* value. Let's take another crack at it using multiple references:

```
<surName id="Last-Name">Englander</surName>
<member>
    <firstName>Rob</firstName>
    <lastName href="#Last-Name"/>
</member>
<member>
    <firstName>Jessica</firstName>
    <lastName href="#Last-Name"/>
</member>
<member>
    <firstName>Arnold</firstName>
    <lastName href="#Last-Name"/>
</member>
    . . .
    . . .
    . . .
```

In this case, every member of the family has a lastName element that references the value found in the surName element. Of course, in this contrived example we haven't really saved much space (if any). However, if the data value were considerably larger, this technique would save considerable space. The savings become more apparent when the value being referenced is a compound element.

Saving space is not the only reason for using multi-reference variables. The technique is also useful when serializing a graph, or collection, of objects where many of those objects have references to the same object. In this case it is important to maintain those relationships when reconstructing the objects during deserialization. Let's look at an example of this in Java. The following code shows a class called `Employee` that contains properties for the employee's first and last names, his or her title, and the employee's manager (also an employee). Following that is some code that defines a manager named `Rob` and three employees named `Ben`, `Andrew`, and `Lorraine`, who all work for `Rob`.

```
Class Employee {
    protected java.lang.String _firstName;
    protected java.lang.String _lastName;
    protected java.lang.String _title = "Worker Bee";
    protected Employee _manager;
    public Employee(java.lang.String first, java.lang.String last,
                    Employee mgr) {
        _firstName = first;
        _lastName = last;
        _manager = mgr;
    }
    public void setTitle(java.lang.String title) {
        _title = title;
    }
    public java.lang.String getTitle() {
        return _title;
    }
    public java.lang.String getFirstName() {
        return _firstName;
    }
    public java.lang.String getLastName() {
        return _lastName;
    }
    public Employee getManager() {
        return _manager;
    }
}
Employee _rob = new Employee("Rob", "Englander", null);
_rob.setTitle("Slave Driver");
Employee _ben = new Employee("Ben", "Jones", _rob);
Employee _andrew = new Employee("Andrew", "Smith", _rob);
Employee _lorraine = new Employee("Lorraine", "White", _rob);
```

Figure 3-1 shows the relationships between the three Worker Bees (Ben, Andrew, and Lorraine), and the Slave Driver manager (Rob). Clearly we wouldn't want to replicate the object referenced by the variable _rob. That wouldn't properly represent the relationship between these objects. We want each of the Worker Bee employee objects to reference the same object as their manager. If it's not clear to you why the distinction is important, imagine that rob gets promoted to Senior Slave Driver. We wouldn't want to call getManager( ) on each of the employee objects and then call setTitle( ). We would want to make the change once to the _rob object.

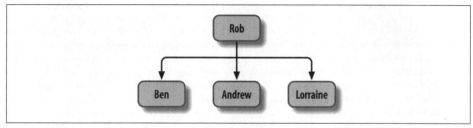

Figure 3-1. An employee hierarchy

In SOAP, multi-reference variables preserve these kinds of object relationships so that object graphs are represented properly on both sides of a SOAP transaction. The XML for the relationships established in this example could look something like this:

```
<rob id="Rob">
    <firstName>Rob</firstName>
    <lastName>Englander</lastName>
    <title>Slave Driver</title>
</rob>
<ben>
    <firstName>Ben</firstName>
    <lastName>Jones</lastName>
    <title>Worker Bee</title>
    <manager href="#Rob"/>
</ben>
<andrew>
    <firstName>Andrew</firstName>
    <lastName>Smith</lastName>
    <title>Worker Bee</title>
    <manager href="#Rob"/>
</andrew>
<lorraine>
    <firstName>Lorraine</firstName>
    <lastName>White</lastName>
    <title>Worker Bee</title>
    <manager href="#Rob"/>
</lorraine>
```

Indicating Type

Every element that contains a value must also indicate the type of the data. There are a few different ways to indicate the data type. The first mechanism is to include an xsi: type attribute as part of the element. This means that the attribute is named type, as defined by the namespace indicated by xsi. The value assigned to xsi:type must be a valid type identifier such as xsd:float, xsd:string, etc. In the second mechanism, the value can be an element of an array that already constrains the type of its constituent parts to a particular data type. In this case, no explicit type declaration for the individual values is necessary; we'll see this later when we talk about arrays. Finally, the element name itself can be related to some type that can be determined by looking at the associated XML schema. The following extract from an XML schema defines a compound data type:

```
<element name="Automobile" type="Automobile"/>
<complexType name="Automobile">
    <element name="make" type="xsd:string"/>
    <element name="model" type="xsd:string"/>
    <element name="year" type="xsd:int"/>
</complexType>
```

The data type Automobile contains elements named make and model of type string, as well as a year of type int. Now let's look at an instance of type Automobile based on this schema:

```
<niceCar xsi:type="Automobile" >
    <model>Corvette</model>
<make>Chevrolet</make>
    <year>1999</year>
</niceCar>
```

This XML defines an instance of type Automobile: a 1999 Chevrolet Corvette. Because the schema for the Automobile type already specifies the data types for the constituent parts, we don't need to declare the types in the example.

Simple Types

SOAP makes use of the simple types as defined in the XML Schema Part 2: Datatypes, in the section called "Built-in datatypes." That section of the specification talks about integers, floats, strings, etc., as well as a variety of data types derived from the base types. For instance, a positiveInteger is a simple type that is based on the int type, but is constrained to allow only positive values.

 Just because a data type is declared as a built-in type, don't assume that it will automatically be supported by every SOAP implementation. The smartest thing you can do is check the documentation for the system you're using. You are probably safe with types like xsd:int, xsd:string, and xsd:float. And I think you'll find that quite a few more are implemented pretty much everywhere as well, but just check first.

If you take a look at the XML Schema specification, you'll find a large number of simple types. Table 3-1 shows a few of the simple types and associated example values.

Table 3-1. Simple types defined by XML Schema

Type	Example
int	–41
float	3.14159
string	"Java and SOAP"
positiveInteger	100

Here are the examples from Table 3-1 as they might appear in an XML document:

```
<iVal xsi:type="xsd:int">-41</iVal>
<fVal xsi:type="xsd:float">3.14159</fVal>
<sVal xsi:type="xsd:string">Java and SOAP</sVal>
<pVal xsi:type="xsd:positiveInteger">100</pVal>
```

The data types are explicitly declared using the xsi:type attribute so that you can see clearly what the types are. Remember, however, that this is not the only way to associate an element with a type.

Strings

You may encounter two different type declarations for string elements. The first is xsd:string, which we used in an earlier example. The second is SOAP-ENC:string, which is a type based on xsd:string that allows the use of the id and href attributes used for multi-reference values. These string types are not exactly the same as string types in programming languages, such as Java's java.lang.String. Some restrictions are placed on the SOAP string types that prohibit the use of special characters, such as those used in forming proper XML markup. Clearly, characters like < and > would interfere with the overall structure of the XML document if they were to appear within a string value. Take a look at this example:

```
<value xsi:type="SOAP-ENC:string">embedded < is no good</value>
```

The inclusion of the < character in the string value is a problem because that character has special meaning in XML. That's not to say that it's impossible to encode a string such as this one; you just have to use replacement characters or some type other than SOAP-ENC:string. Escape sequences for the brackets, such as < and >, are one solution. Another way to resolve this issue is to use MIME base64 encoding, because the base64 alphabet doesn't include any prohibited characters. We'll take a look at base64 encoding shortly.

Enumerations

Enumerated values are, essentially, a group of names that represent other values. In the C programming language, the enum keyword allows you to use descriptive names in place of integer values. For instance, instead of using the values 1, 2, and 3 to represent the colors red, yellow, and green, you might define an enumerated type that uses the color names in place of the values. At runtime, the system replaces the names with the associated values. This is more or less a programming convenience that can lead to more readable and understandable source code.

One problem with enumerated types is that the values used to represent them internally are not standardized. There is no standard integer value that represents the name Green, for instance. So there is an inherent problem with transmitting enumerated values from one system to the other. The actual values used internally are more than likely unique to the application. In the C language, the values often default to an integer sequence starting with 0. In this case, the order in which the names are defined in the enumeration type determines the values; the first entry is defined as 0, the second as 1, and so on. However, the syntax allows the programmer to override that behavior and define each entry independently. So the actual values are a programming detail not likely to be the same from one program to the next. Some programming languages, like Java, don't even support enumerations.[*] But that doesn't diminish the usefulness of enumerated types.

SOAP encodes enumerated types by encoding the name of the value. In the case of the traffic signal, the SOAP encoding ignores the internal implementation value in favor of the name of the color. Here is an XML snippet that shows the encoding of the state of an imaginary traffic signal:

```
<trafficSignal>
    <signalState xsi:type="xsd:string">Green</signalState>
</trafficSignal>
```

The sending application does not encode the internal representation of the value of Green; instead it uses the name Green itself. It's up to the recipient to resolve the value Green into its own appropriate internal value. It's also possible to define an enumeration type in a schema. Here's what the traffic signal schema definition might look like:

```
<element name="TrafficSignalState" type="TrafficSignalState"/>
<simpleType name="TrafficSignalState" base="xsd:string">
    <enumeration value="Red"/>
    <enumeration value="Yellow"/>
    <enumeration value="Green"/>
</simpleType>
```

Using this schema definition, we could encode the trafficSignal value as:

```
<trafficSignal>
    <TrafficSignalState>Green</TrafficSignalState>
</trafficSignal>
```

Binary Encoding

SOAP recommends that binary data, referred to in the SOAP specification as *byte arrays*, be encoded using the MIME base64 encoding algorithm. Since there is no data that cannot be represented in binary, this means that a SOAP document can encode any data type using the base64 character set. This has the added benefit of substituting characters that may have special meaning to certain protocols.

Although it's not appropriate to cover all the details of base64 encoding here, it might be useful to walk through a simple example. Base64 encoding uses an alphabet

---

[*] Java, of course, has an Enumeration interface, which is a mechanism for accessing the elements of a collection. That feature isn't related to a C-style enumerated type.

composed of 6-bit values. Each of these values has a defined substitution character. Table 3-2 shows the base64 alphabet.

Table 3-2. Base64 character set

6-bit value	Base64 character
0-25	A - Z
26-51	a - z
52-61	0 - 9
62	+
63	/
PAD	=

To encode your binary data you must break it down into 6-bit pieces. If the total number of bytes in your data is not divisible by 6, fill it out to the right with zeros. Base64 encoding was designed for email, which constrains each line of data to 76 characters. In the SOAP world we are not bound by that limit, so you don't have to break the data on that boundary; you can insert new lines anywhere convenient.

Let's say we want to encode the string "<data>". Those braces are a problem in string encoding, but it'll work out fine in base64. First, let's look at the hexadecimal representation of each byte of data:

Character	<	d	a	t	a	>
Hex value	0x3C	0x64	0x61	0x74	0x61	0x3E

Next we'll convert to binary and break it up into 6-bit pieces. This gives us exactly 8 pieces, so we don't need to pad the data. Here are the 6-bit binary pieces along with their decimal equivalents and associated base64 characters:

6-bit value	001111	000110	010001	100001	011101	000110	000100	111110
Decimal value	15	6	17	33	29	6	4	62
Base64 value	0	F	P	h	d	F	D	+

Now we can encode the data using base64 encoding and represent it in XML as:

```
<value xsi:type="SOAP-ENC:base64">OFPhdFD+</value>
```

To do the decoding, first convert each character of the string into its equivalent 6-bit value. Next regroup the bits into 8-bit values, using each one to form one byte of the decoded data. You should get back to the original string: "<data>".

Base64 encoding can be useful for transmitting any kind of binary data. However, if you're thinking about using this encoding style to transmit a 10 MB bitmap file, you may want to think again. Base64 increases the size of the data by about 1/3, which can be significant in some environments. That's not to say it won't work, of course, and it may be just fine for your application.

 One common technique for handling large data objects is to send a URL that references the data instead of sending the data itself. The recipient can then use that URL to retrieve the data out-of-band. This is a good technique when you want to keep your SOAP message small, especially if the data may not be used by the recipient.

Another technique, which we'll talk about in Chapter 8, is to send the data as a MIME attachment. This doesn't reduce the overall size of the message, but it does keep the data out of the SOAP payload, improving the performance of the SOAP processing.

Polymorphic Accessors

The term *polymorphism* is used frequently in object-oriented software design and development. It means that a thing (usually an object) can take on the appearance of other things. Although this book is not about object-oriented programming, let's talk about what we usually think of as polymorphism in Java and then look at what it means in SOAP.

Consider our earlier Java class called Employee. We used the Employee class for managers as well as regular employees. Of course in the real world there are characteristics and behaviors of managers that are not present in regular employees (no, I don't mean personality traits, although we're all aware of those differences!). For instance, a manager class may include a collection of employees under his or her care (or control, depending on your perspective). We could create a Manager class that derives from the Employee class, and then add the manager-specific stuff to that new class. This works because managers are also employees. In other words, managers are a type of employee, so an instance of a Manager object can also take the shape of an Employee object. If the Manager instance is passed to some function as an Employee reference, the receiving method will not know or care that the object is actually a Manager instance. It sees it as an Employee instance. This is an example of polymorphism.

Another example of polymorphism is the variant type in Microsoft COM (Component Object Model) programming. The variant represents a data value and an associated data type indicator. The data type indicator tells the user which accessor to use when retrieving the data.

In SOAP, the mechanisms of polymorphism are not nearly as elaborate as they are in Java; SOAP polymorphism more closely resembles the COM variant. If you've looked at the SOAP specification, you may have noticed that the entire section on polymorphism is just a few lines long. Polymorphism in SOAP means only that an accessor includes a type declaration. That's it. The following XML fragment shows an accessor named quantity. In the first case, assume that quantity is defined to be of type xsd:int according to some schema. Therefore, no type declaration is used. The value cannot take on different types. In the second case, the quantity accessor includes a type declaration, allowing the accessor to take on a data type of xsd:float. The second form is a polymorphic accessor.

```
<quantity>37</quantity>
<quantity xsi:type="xsd:float">37</quantity>
```

We'll see some important uses of polymorphic accessors when we look at heterogeneous arrays and generic compound types.

Compound Types

The SOAP specification talks mostly about two kinds of compound data types: structs and arrays. Here's how the spec defines these types:

Struct
A compound value in which accessor name is the only distinction among member values, and no two accessors have the same name.

Array
A compound value in which ordinal position is the only distinction among member values.

We touched on these definitions earlier when we talked about the terminology of SOAP encoding. These data structures are common to many programming languages, and there's nothing different about the way SOAP defines them.

Structs

Many programming languages support structs, though not all in the same way. For instance, in the C programming language you can define a compound structure using the struct keyword. This keyword essentially allows you to define a data type or instance that comprises named parts, where each part can be an instance of any other valid data type. In C++ you can use the struct keyword in the same way you can in C. However, you'd most often use a special (and more functional) structure called a class. In Java there is no explicit concept called a struct, but just like in C++ we can use a class to provide the same thing as a struct.

Here is a Java class that contains fields representing some characteristics of a guitar:

```
class Guitar {
    public java.lang.String _manufacturer;
    public java.lang.String _model;
    public int _year;
}
```

This may not be the best way to represent a guitar in a real-world Java application, but it is perfectly valid and closely resembles the struct available in C and C++. An XML schema fragment corresponding to this class could look like the following.

```
<element name="Guitar" type="Guitar"/>
<complexType name="Guitar">
    <element name="manufacturer" type="xsd:string"/>
    <element name="model" type="xsd:string"/>
    <element name="year" type="xsd:int"/>
</complexType>
```

Here's an example of a serialized Guitar instance using this schema:

```
<Guitar>
    <manufacturer>Epiphone</manufacturer>
    <model>Sheraton II</model>
    <year>1997</year>
</Guitar>
```

Arrays

Instances of SOAP arrays are declared using the data type SOAP-ENC:Array. The elements of an array can be any valid SOAP type, even arrays themselves. Arrays must have a SOAP-ENC:arrayType attribute that specifies the data type of the elements as well as the dimensions of the array.

Let's start off by looking at an array declaration for a one-dimensional array of five floating-point values. The actual values are omitted for now (we'll get to that subject next).

```
<someNumbers xsi:type="SOAP-ENC:Array" SOAP-ENC:arrayType="xsd:float[5]">
    . . .
    . . .
</someNumbers>
```

An array is serialized as a series of element values, where the order of the elements represents their ordinal positions. The actual element name for each value in the array is not significant because array members are accessed by position; XML requires that some name be used for each array element, but SOAP doesn't care what the name is. Often you'll find that every element of a serialized array uses the same name, but that's not a requirement. The SOAP specification suggests using the element's data type as the element name. That, too, is only a suggestion. I like to use names that reflect the contents of the array if at all possible. Here is an array with the data values filled in:

```
<someNumbers xsi:type="SOAP-ENC:Array" SOAP-ENC:arrayType="xsd:float[5]">
    <number>1.234</number>
    <number>2.345</number>
    <number>3.456</number>
    <number>4.567</number>
    <number>5.678</number>
</someNumbers>
```

Since the elements are serialized in the order they appear in the array, you can determine their ordinal position by inspection. Like Java and many other languages,

SOAP starts array indexing at 0. So the value 4.567 is at ordinal position 3 (the 4th element of the array).

In the case of multi-dimensional arrays, elements are listed in row-major order. This means that the ordinal position farthest to the right changes the fastest. Figure 3-2 is a two-dimensional array containing the integer values 1 through 6. The dimensions of the array are 3 by 2, and the figure shows the major dimension down and the minor dimension across.

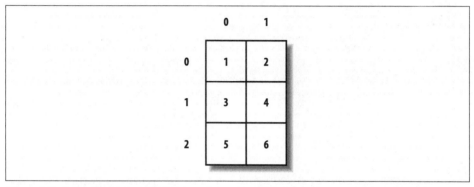

Figure 3-2. A two-dimensional array

The SOAP-ENC:arrayType allows you to specify the size of each dimension of a multi-dimensional array by separating each dimension size with a comma. Here's what the encoding of the array in Figure 3-2 might look like:

```
<values xsi:type="SOAP-ENC:Array" SOAP-ENC:arrayType="xsd:int[3,2]">
    <value>1</value>
    <value>2</value>
    <value>3</value>
    <value>4</value>
    <value>5</value>
    <value>6</value>
</values>
```

So far, the arrays we've looked at are homogeneous: every element of the array is of the same data type. But it's also possible to encode heterogeneous arrays, where each value is of a different type. This is one place where polymorphic accessors are important. To create a heterogeneous array, the SOAP-ENC:arrayType is assigned the value xsd:ur-type. This type means that the data types of the enclosed array values are not being constrained by the SOAP-ENC:arrayType attribute, but instead each data value is encoded to include its data type. Here is an array that contains values of different types:

```
<mixedNuts xsi:type="SOAP-ENC:Array" SOAP-ENC:arrayType="xsd:ur-type[3]">
    <nut xsi:type="xsd:float">3.14159</nut>
    <nut xsi:type="xsd:string">SOAP</nut>
    <nut xsi:type="xsd:int">8141992</nut>
</mixedNuts>
```

SOAP also permits the size of an array dimension to be omitted. This means that the number of values in a particular dimension of the array can be determined by looking at the members that are encoded in the array. So the first line of the `mixedNuts` example could also be written as follows:

```
<mixedNuts xsi:type="SOAP-ENC:Array" SOAP-ENC:arrayType="xsd:ur-type[]">
```

By inspecting this XML, we are able to determine that this one-dimensional array is of size 3.

Partial arrays

In some cases an array won't be fully populated. In other words, there may be one or more elements in an array that have no value. In the following Java code, the array `contestants` is a one-dimensional string array of size 10, but only the elements at positions 6, 7, and 8 contain data values:

```
java.lang.String contestants[] = new java.lang.String[10];
contestants[6] = "Rob";
contestants[7] = "Arnold";
contestants[8] = "Scott";
```

If we were to use the standard encoding for this array, we'd need to encode every element, even though most of those values are null. Null values shouldn't be confused with empty values. In the case of our string array, there is a difference between an element that contains an empty string and an element that is null. We certainly want to encode empty strings because that properly reflects the data that exists. In the example above, the values in the `contestants` array at all positions other than 6, 7, and 8 are null; they do not contain instances of `java.lang.String`. We could encode those null elements by supplying an `xsi:null` attribute for each one, with a value of 1. These elements won't contain any data:

```
<contestants xsi:type="SOAP-ENC:Array" SOAP-ENC:arrayType="xsd:string[10]" >
    <name xsi:null="1"/>
    <name xsi:null="1"/>
    <name xsi:null="1"/>
    <name xsi:null="1"/>
    <name xsi:null="1"/>
    <name xsi:null="1"/>
    <name>Rob</name>
    <name>Arnold</name>
    <name>Scott</name>
    <name xsi:null="1"/>
</contestants>
```

This is perfectly fine, but it's not very efficient. SOAP allows you to encode this kind of array by omitting everything but the block of elements that contain values. To do so, include the `SOAP-ENC:offset` attribute in the array declaration. The value of this attribute represents the ordinal (zero-based) position of the first element actually included in the array. So we could encode the `contestants` array as follows:

```
<contestants xsi:type="SOAP-ENC:Array" SOAP-ENC:arrayType="xsd:string[10]"
             SOAP-ENC:offset="[6]">
    <name>Rob</name>
    <name>Arnold</name>
    <name>Scott</name>
</contestants>
```

This is certainly more efficient than transmitting all the null array values. Note that the SOAP-ENC:arrayType attribute still specifies that the array has a size of 10. This is important, as we want the receiver of this array to use the proper array size.

Sparse arrays

The use of the SOAP-ENC:offset attribute works perfectly if the data values present in the partially transmitted array are contiguous, as they were in the contestants example. But certainly this isn't the only possible scenario of partially populated arrays. What if the data values are in noncontiguous positions, as in the following code?

```
java.lang.String contestants[] = new java.lang.String[10];
contestants[1] = "Rob";
contestants[5] = "Arnold";
contestants[8] = "Scott";
```

This is what's known as a sparse array. SOAP provides for sparse arrays by allowing each transmitted element of the array to specify its own ordinal position by including a SOAP-ENC:position attribute. So we can now encode the array as:

```
<contestants xsi:type="SOAP-ENC:Array" SOAP-ENC:arrayType="xsd:string[10]">
    <name SOAP-ENC:position="[1]">Rob</name>
    <name SOAP-ENC:position="[5]">Arnold</name>
    <name SOAP-ENC:position="[8]">Scott</name>
</contestants>
```

The encoding of partially transmitted and sparse arrays has the potential of being far more efficient than encoding all of the null values in a partially populated array. You should be aware, however, that many of the current SOAP implementations don't support these constructs. I'm sure that over time, and hopefully by the time you read this, SOAP implementations will support partial and sparse arrays.

Generic Compound Types

There are times when the exact format of a serialized compound data value is not known in advance. This might be because there is no schema definition for the data type, or it might occur as the result of a general database query. For example, let's say you are using SOAP to query a database by sending an SQL query like the one shown here:

```
select * from guitars;
```

In case you're not familiar with SQL syntax, this statement asks for all the records from the table named guitars, and returns all the fields from each record in that table. However, we may not know in advance the names of the fields, or even how many fields there are. Table 3-3 represents a simple database table called guitars, containing two records. The table contains three fields: manufacturer, model, and year.

Table 3-3. The guitars table

Manufacturer	Model	Year
Gibson	Les Paul	1958
Fender	American Stratocaster	2001

Even though we don't know in advance the fields to expect back from our SQL query, a valid SOAP response could contain the following serialized data:

```
<guitars>
    <guitar>
        <manufacturer xsi:type="xsd:string>Gibson</manufacturer>
        <model xsi:type="xsd:string">Les Paul</model>
        <year xsi:type="xsd:int">1958</year>
    </guitar>
    <guitar>
        <manufacturer xsi:type="xsd:string>Fender</manufacturer>
        <model xsi:type="xsd:string">American Stratocaster</model>
        <year xsi:type="xsd:int">2001</year>
    </guitar>
</guitars>
```

This XML contains generic compound data. It's up to the receiver of this data to figure out how to deal with it. Both struct and array constructs can be used within generic types. The format of each guitar element resembles that of a SOAP struct, and the guitars element looks very much like an array, even though it isn't declared using xsi:type="SOAP-ENC:Array". The elements of each guitar use polymorphic data accessors, since their data types may not be known in advance.

Default Values

The SOAP specification talks briefly about the handling of default values. It states that the omission of an element from the transmitted data can imply that a default value is to be used. The C++ language provides a good programming analogy to this topic, since it allows you to define default values for method parameters, thus allowing the caller to omit values for those parameters. Here's what just such a method definition in C++ looks like:

```
int getValue (int param1, int param2 = 1);
```

In this case, the default value for param2 is 1. So if the caller doesn't provide a value for that parameter when calling getValue( ), the system uses the value 1. Although there is no support for this kind of syntax in Java, it is certainly possible to define SOAP transactions that support default values.

Let's say that an order entry system expects a compound element named order, where each item in the order contains a quantity, an item number, and a description. We might want to say that the default value for the quantity is 1, so that the sender is not required to include a quantity for an item if they are ordering only one. In this case we might serialize an order as:

```
<order>
    <item>
        <quantity>2</quantity>
        <itemNum>1020304</itemNum>
        <description>Really cool device</description>
    </item>
    <item>
        <itemNum>1020305</itemNum>
        <description>Some other device</description>
    </item>
</order>
```

We did not include a quantity element for the second item. Instead, we expect the recipient to use the default value. The important point is that SOAP does not define default values, nor does it mandate them. It's up to the sender and recipient to do the right thing.

The SOAP Root Attribute

Linked lists, trees, and directed graphs are common data structures. However, we've yet to see a serialization mechanism that identifies where the starting point, or root, of such a structure might be. The SOAP root attribute is used for just this purpose. Assigning the value of 1 to the SOAP-ENC:root attribute of an element identifies it as the root of a structure such as a linked list.

Here is some Java code for the nodes of a singly linked list of integers, followed by an instance of a list containing three nodes. The nodes contain the values 50, 60, and 70, and they are placed into the list in ascending order with the node containing the value 50 being the head (or root) of the list.

```
class Node {
    int _value;
    Node _next;
    public Node(int value, Node next) {
        _value = value;
        _next = next;
    }
}
Node n3 = new Node(70, null);
Node n2 = new Node(60, n3);
Node n1 = new Node(50, n2);
```

The variable n1 is the root of the list. Here's what the serialization for this list might look like:

```
<list>
    <node>
        <value id="node-3" xsi:type="xsd:int">70</value>
        <next xsi:null="1"/>
    </node>
    <node>
        <value id="node-2" xsi:type="xsd:int">60</value>
        <next href="#node-3"/>
    </node>
    <node>
        <value SOAP-ENC:root="1" id="node-1" xsi:type="xsd:int">50</value>
        <next href="#node-2"/>
    </node>
</list>
```

We used value references to link one node to the next, and the SOAP-ENC:root attribute to indicate the head of the list.

CHAPTER 4

RPC-Style Services

Although SOAP is not limited to a particular style of distributed computing, it lends itself to a remote procedure call (RPC) model. This is only what you would expect; according to the SOAP specification, one of SOAP's design goals is to encapsulate and exchange RPC calls. This approach maps very nicely to Java programming because method calls on Java objects can be easily translated to RPC calls. We'll start this chapter by looking at the structure of SOAP RPC request and response messages. From there we'll implement some RPC services in Java and deploy those services in both Apache SOAP and in GLUE. And, of course, we'll write some Java code to make use of those services.

SOAP RPC Elements

Creating a SOAP RPC request uses the SOAP structure and encoding described in Chapters 2 and 3. No new XML or data encoding styles are needed for RPC. Let's take a look at what's required to represent an RPC method call in SOAP:

- The target object
- Method name
- Method parameters
- SOAP header data

Target Object URI

The target object URI is, essentially, the resource address of the service that we want to use. You see resource addresses all the time when you browse the Web—you navigate to a web page by specifying the page's resource address. For instance, to look at the page describing the author of O'Reilly's JavaBeans book, you'd use the URL *http://www.oreilly.com/catalog/javabeans/author.html*. The protocol, server address, and resource are all together. Let's break it down so you can see the parts. The server address is *www.oreilly.com*, the HTML page resource is */catalog/javabeans/author. html*, and the protocol is *http*.

This is exactly what we do to specify the target object in a SOAP RPC request message, with one difference: instead of an HTML page resource, the target object name is used. The target object name is carried by the transport (for example, by an HTTP header), not the SOAP message itself. This is the only part of a SOAP RPC message that is carried outside the message except for the SOAPAction attribute. In an Apache SOAP server, the target object for an RPC message is usually /soap/rpcrouter. This URI represents the resource that routes SOAP RPC messages in Apache SOAP. For a GLUE server, the target resource is usually /glue, followed by the name of the service itself. We'll look at the HTTP headers for both of these servers a little later.

Method Name

The method name is, as you might have guessed, the name of the method to be invoked. Back in Chapter 2 we talked about a service that provided the current temperature at a weather station. That service exposed a method called getCurrentTemperature. If you like to think in Java terms, you can think of the method name as a public method on an instance of a service object.

In the SOAP XML, the method being invoked is packaged as a SOAP struct* that contains an accessor for each parameter. The method name struct is an immediate child of the SOAP Body element. Let's look again at the getCurrentTemperature example:

```
<SOAP-ENV:Envelope
    xmlns:SOAP-ENV=
        "http://schemas.xmlsoap.org/soap/envelope/"
    SOAP-ENV:encodingStyle=
        "http://schemas.xmlsoap.org/soap/encoding/">
    <SOAP-ENV:Body>
        <m:GetCurrentTemperature xmlns:m="WeatherStation">
                <m:scale>Celsius</m:scale>
        </m:GetCurrentTemperature>
    </SOAP-ENV:Body>
</SOAP-ENV:Envelope>
```

Notice that the name of the method being invoked is namespace-qualified using the name of the service object. The namespace is supposed to be a URI that provides the target service with a mechanism to interpret the meaning of the method. The URI would normally point to a resource that describes the method, but in this example this will work just fine. But what service object are we talking about? It's not the target object. It's another object that is known to the target object by a particular name.

---

* The term struct is used here to mean the XML element hierarchy used to represent a service method and its parameters. For all you C programmers out there, don't confuse this with a C struct, which obviously has a different meaning.

In this case, the service object's name is WeatherStation. The mechanism used to map the names of service objects to their physical implementations is not specified by the SOAP specification. Each SOAP implementation has its own way of doing that, which we'll see in the section on "Deploying the Service."

The method signature may also be included as part of the method struct, but it isn't required to be there. In fact, the SOAP specification doesn't describe the format of the method signature, and signatures won't be used in this book (and aren't used by the servers I discuss). I mention method signatures only so you won't be confused if you run into an implementation that uses them.*

Method Parameters

The parameters to the method are modeled as accessors and are immediate child elements of the method struct. This is true for all in and in/out parameters; any out parameters will not appear in the method invocation struct. SOAP allows for the processing of methods with missing parameters, as we saw in Chapter 3. It's up to the application to decide whether or not to process a call with missing parameters. If leaving out parameters is not acceptable, the application should respond with a SOAP fault. Each accessor is named after the parameter name for the enclosing method, and its type is the same as the corresponding service method type.

The previous SOAP envelope has one parameter to the getCurrentTemperature method. The parameter is called scale, and is used to specify the temperature scale that should be used to return the result. This parameter is namespace-qualified using the service name, which is not unlike using a schema name to qualify the accessor. This means that the scale element is presented according to its definition in the WeatherStation namespace. We could have chosen to include an xsi:type attribute on scale, but omitting the attribute is valid as well. As long as the type matches the type that's specified in the schema referred to by the namespace, you don't have to specify the type in the SOAP message. You can even send a different type, as long as you specify what the type is.

Let's look at some Java code and see how it maps to a SOAP RPC method call. The DowJones30 class represents the current levels of the Dow Jones industrial average. DowJones30 contains a method called getCurrentLevel( ) that returns the Dow Jones industrial average for the current trading session. It also has a method called getPrice( ) that returns the current trading price for a member stock of the Dow Jones Industrial Average. getPrice( ) takes a string parameter called stock that represents the stock symbol, and a currency string parameter that specifies the currency that should be used when returning the price. The price is returned as a float.

---

* I doubt that you'll ever encounter a method signature as part of the SOAP message. There doesn't seem to be any industry acceptance of the concept, and it isn't implemented by any SOAP engines I've encountered.

```
public class DowJones30 {
    private float _level;
    public float getCurrentLevel() {
        return _level;
    }
    public float getPrice(String stock, String currency) {
        float result;
        // determine the price for stock and return it
        // in the specified currency
        return result;
    }
}
```

Now let's say we've already deployed a service named `DowJones` that is implemented by the `DowJones30` class. To invoke the `getCurrentLevel()` method of the `DowJones` service, we use a SOAP envelope that looks like this:

```
<SOAP-ENV:Envelope
    xmlns:SOAP-ENV=
        "http://schemas.xmlsoap.org/soap/envelope/"
    SOAP-ENV:encodingStyle=
        "http://schemas.xmlsoap.org/soap/encoding/">
    <SOAP-ENV:Body>
        <m:getCurrentLevel xmlns:m="DowJones">
        </m:getCurrentLevel>
    </SOAP-ENV:Body>
</SOAP-ENV:Envelope>
```

There are no parameters, since the `getCurrentLevel()` method does not take any parameters. Now let's call the `getPrice()` method, using the stock symbol IBM and a currency of USD (U.S. dollars) as parameters. Here's what the envelope would look like:

```
<SOAP-ENV:Envelope
    xmlns:SOAP-ENV=
        "http://schemas.xmlsoap.org/soap/envelope/"
    SOAP-ENV:encodingStyle=
        "http://schemas.xmlsoap.org/soap/encoding/">
    <SOAP-ENV:Body>
        <m:getPrice xmlns:m="DowJones">
            <m:stock>IBM</m:stock>
            <m:currency>USD</m:currency>
        </m:getPrice>
    </SOAP-ENV:Body>
</SOAP-ENV:Envelope>
```

Method Response

A method response also takes the form of a SOAP struct. The method struct contains an accessor for the return value, followed by accessors for each out and in/out parameter value in the same order they appear in the method signature,[*] if one exists.

---

[*] As mentioned earlier, the method signature referenced in the SOAP specification does not appear to have been implemented. It is mentioned here for your information only.

The names of the accessors for the out and in/out values correspond to their names in the method signature, but the names of the return values don't matter. My preference is to give the return value a name that reflects the method name itself. I tend to name service methods using a verb-noun style, which then allows me to name the return value accessor with the noun. For instance, if my service name is computeSize, then I name the return value accessor size.

It's become common practice to name the return value struct by appending the word Response to the name of the method that was invoked. So for a method called computeSize, the struct containing the result would be named computeSizeResponse. Although this is a common convention, it is not required, and you'll find that some SOAP implementations don't follow it.

Here's the SOAP envelope that might be returned by invoking the getCurrentLevel method:

```
<SOAP-ENV:Envelope
    xmlns:SOAP-ENV=
        "http://schemas.xmlsoap.org/soap/envelope/"
    SOAP-ENV:encodingStyle=
        "http://schemas.xmlsoap.org/soap/encoding/">
    <SOAP-ENV:Body>
        <m:getCurrentLevelResponse xmlns:m="DowJones">
            <m:currentLevel>10513.15</m:currentLevel>
        </m:getCurrentLevelResponse>
    </SOAP-ENV:Body>
</SOAP-ENV:Envelope>
```

Fault Response

If a SOAP RPC method call fails, a SOAP fault should be returned. Let's take a look at an example of a SOAP fault. Say we call the getPrice method of the DowJones service but specify an invalid currency parameter. The service might return a fault that looks like this:

```
<SOAP-ENV:Envelope
    xmlns:SOAP-ENV=
        "http://schemas.xmlsoap.org/soap/envelope/"
    SOAP-ENV:encodingStyle=
        "http://schemas.xmlsoap.org/soap/encoding/">
    <SOAP-ENV:Body>
        <SOAP-ENV:Fault>
            <faultcode>SOAP-ENV:Client</faultcode>
            <faultstring>Client Error</faultstring>
            <detail>
                <m:dowJonesfaultdetails xmlns:m="DowJones">
                    <message>Invalid Currency</message>
                    <errorcode>1234</errorcode>
                </m:dowJonesfaultdetails>
            </detail>
        </SOAP-ENV:Fault>
```

```
    </SOAP-ENV:Body>
  </SOAP-ENV:Envelope>
```

A SOAP RPC method call either fails or succeeds, but never both. So you'll never find a method response and a fault response together.

Optional Header Data

Processing an RPC sometimes requires information that is not part of the method signature. For instance, it may be necessary to pass a username to a service. A username is usually not appropriate as a parameter to the method call, but nonetheless is needed by the receiving application. Information like this can be encoded in the SOAP header, as described in "The Header Element" in Chapter 2. There can also be transport-specific data; for example, you may want to pass cookie information as part of your HTTP header in order to specify the HTTP session to use for this method invocation. In either case, this additional data is encoded outside the bounds of the SOAP body.*

Service Activation

The lifetime of an object is an important part of any distributed system, and is sometimes referred to as *service scope* or *service activation*. Whatever terminology is used, it encompasses the various possible object lifetime models available in the system. In SOAP systems based on HTTP, there are generally three service activation models:

Request-level service activation
> For each request made on a given service object, a new instance of the object is created that persists only until the request is complete. This kind of service activation is useful for service objects that don't maintain state.

Application-level service activation
> A single instance of the service object handles every method invocation for the entire lifetime of the service application. This kind of activation can be used for services that maintain state or that place a large burden on resources during object creation.

Session-level service activation
> A single instance of the service object is used for all method invocations for the lifetime of the session. Sessions are not necessarily a standard, as you may know. It's possible to implement sessions specific to your own applications by doing things like generating and passing tokens, or you can take advantage of existing approaches like the use of cookies. This is certainly one of those cases where you need to pass additional header information.

---

* Actually, sending transport-specific data such as a cookie is probably not such a good idea, because it binds you to a particular transport. Some other transport-independent session data would be more appropriate.

The SOAP specification doesn't define any requirements or behaviors for service object lifetime; there are no real requirements for SOAP implementations to support the three models described here. However, these activation models are found outside of SOAP as well, and you can expect to find them in many if not all of the SOAP implementations available. Each implementation may have its own unique way of setting the activation model for a service, but the behavior should be the same. You'll probably find that the service activation model for a service is specified as part of the service deployment. We'll cover this topic in practice when we talk about service deployment later in this chapter.

A Simple Service

Let's design a simple service called CallCounterService. This service keeps track of the number of method calls it receives. It's not exactly useful by itself, but it gives us a chance to get a service up and running to see how services are deployed and how the service activation models work. We'll place the classes for this example in the package javasoap.book.ch4. Make sure to create the appropriate directory for this package on your system and make it available on the classpath used by your server and client systems.

Here's the source code for the MethodCounter class, which implements the CallCounterService. Note that the Java class name does not have to be the same as the service name.

```
package javasoap.book.ch4;
public class MethodCounter {
    int _counter;
    public MethodCounter( ) {
        _counter = 0;
    }
    public int getCount( ) {
        return _counter;
    }
    public boolean doSomething( ) {
        _counter += 1;
        return true;
    }
}
```

As you can see, there is nothing special about the Java code. MethodCounter contains a variable called _counter that keeps track of the number of method calls made during the lifetime of the object. The class contains a method called doSomething( ) that increments the _counter variable and returns a Boolean value indicating whether the call was successful. There's also a method called getCount( ) that returns the number of times doSomething( ) has been called. We named the method getCount( ) according to the JavaBeans naming conventions for a read-only integer property named Count. We obey the JavaBeans conventions for a few reasons. First, it makes sense to follow standard conventions whenever we can. More important, we'll see later that some SOAP implementations can make use of JavaBeans properties without requiring the programmer to do extra work.

Note that our service class uses a no-argument constructor. This is important. Java SOAP implementations load service classes dynamically, usually by calling `Class.newInstance( )`. This method requires the class to have a constructor with no arguments. Of course, if we didn't explicitly include a constructor, a default no-argument constructor would have been created automatically. We include the constructor explicitly to highlight the fact that it's needed, regardless of how it is included.

Before we go any further, let's take a look at the SOAP envelope we would use to encapsulate the invocation of the doSomething( ) method:

```
<SOAP-ENV:Envelope
    xmlns:SOAP-ENV=
        "http://schemas.xmlsoap.org/soap/envelope/"
    SOAP-ENV:encodingStyle=
        "http://schemas.xmlsoap.org/soap/encoding/">
    <SOAP-ENV:Body>
        <m:doSomething xmlns:m="CallCounterService">
        </m:doSomething>
    </SOAP-ENV:Body>
</SOAP-ENV:Envelope>
```

The first child element of the SOAP Body is the method being invoked; the element is namespace-qualified using the service name (not the name of the class that implements the service). There are no parameters for the doSomething element, since there are no parameters to the doSomething( ) method of our service class.

Deploying the Service

Service deployment is not part of the SOAP specification, so each implementation has its own deployment procedure. We'll look at service deployment using two SOAP implementations: Apache SOAP and GLUE.

Deploying with Apache SOAP

In Apache SOAP, you must create a *deployment descriptor*, which is an XML file that contains information about the service and the Java class that implements the service. Let's take a look at a deployment descriptor for CallCounterService, implemented by the Java class javasoap.book.ch4.MethodCounter:

```
<isd:service
    xmlns:isd="http://xml.apache.org/xml-soap/deployment"
    id="urn:CallCounterService">

    <isd:provider type="java"
            scope="Application"
```

```
        methods="doSomething getCount">
    <isd:java class="javasoap.book.ch4.MethodCounter"
        static="false"/>
</isd:provider>
<isd:faultListener>
org.apache.soap.server.DOMFaultListener
</isd:faultListener>
<isd:mappings>
</isd:mappings>
</isd:service>
```

The outermost XML element is called service, which is namespace-qualified using the identifier isd, representing the http://xml.apache.org/xml-soap/deployment namespace. The service element also has an id attribute that is assigned the unique name of the service being deployed. I've prefixed the service name, CallCounterService, with urn. You don't need to do this, but it's a common practice that I'll follow, at least in this example. Just be aware that it's not a requirement.

The first child element is called provider, which describes the implementation of the service. As with all the child elements of service, this element is also namespace-qualified with the isd identifier from the parent element. Three attributes are used on the provider element. The first attribute is type, which tells Apache SOAP what implementation type this service is using; we assign it the value java. (Apache SOAP allows for service implementations other than Java, but we won't be covering them.) The scope attribute specifies the service activation model of the deployed service. Possible values for this attribute are Application, Session, and Request. These correspond to the activation models described earlier. We're using Application level service activation now; we will experiment with other values later. The third attribute of the provider element is called methods. This attribute lists the method names that are exposed by the service. These method names have to match the corresponding methods in the Java class that implements the service because Apache SOAP uses dynamic class loading and Java reflection in order to make method calls. The method names are separated by spaces. For this example we're exposing the doSomething and getCount methods.

The provider contains a child element that further describes the details of the service implementation. We assigned the type attribute a value of java, which corresponds to the child element name java. The java element has two attributes and no data. The class attribute is assigned the full name of the Java class that implements the service, in this case MethodCounter. An attribute called static indicates whether the exposed methods of the service implementation class are static.

The next element of the deployment descriptor is a child element of service called faultListener. The data value of this element is the full name of the Java class used to create a fault listener object. This object is responsible for building SOAP faults to be returned when a fault condition exists. We're using the org.apache.soap.server.

DOMFaultListener class, which is provided by Apache SOAP. In Chapter 7 we'll look more closely at SOAP faults and write our own fault listener.

The last element is called mappings. In Chapter 6 we'll use this section to define Java classes that manage the serialization and deserialization of custom Java types. For now we don't need any mappings, so there are no entries in the mappings section.

Next, we need to use the deployment descriptor to deploy our service. I've named the deployment descriptor file *CallCounterService.dd*; it doesn't matter what name you use, as long as it makes sense and is recognizable to you. At this point, you should start your server, if it isn't running already. Apache SOAP includes a Java application that you can use from a command line to deploy a service. This application is called the service manager client (org.apache.soap.server.ServiceManagerClient); it can deploy, undeploy, and list services. Here's what the command to deploy the service looks like:

```
java org.apache.soap.server.ServiceManagerClient
    http://georgetown:8080/soap/servlet/rpcrouter deploy CallCounterService.dd
```

The first parameter is the URL of the Apache SOAP RPC router; I'm running an Apache Tomcat server with Apache SOAP that accepts connections on port 8080. The server is a machine on the local network called georgetown. The second parameter, deploy, tells the service manager client that we are deploying a service. The last parameter, CallCounterService.dd, is the name of the file that contains the deployment descriptor. If all goes well, you won't see any output from the service manager client; you'll just return to the command prompt. If you get any exceptions or other error messages, look carefully at the output. Some likely problems are an incorrect classpath, or running the command from a directory other than the one that contains the deployment descriptor file.

After you've successfully deployed the service, you can verify it by calling the service manager client again. This time we'll ask the service manager to list all of the deployed services:

```
java org.apache.soap.server.ServiceManagerClient
    http://georgetown:8080/soap/servlet/rpcrouter list
```

The first parameter is the same as before: the URL of the Apache SOAP RPC router. list tells the service manager to list the currently deployed services. You should see the following response:

```
Deployed Services:
    urn:CallCounterService
```

Apache SOAP persists the information for the deployed services, so if you shut down the server that is hosting Apache SOAP and restart it at a later time, the services will still be available. It doesn't, however, persist the state of the objects that implement those services; they will start as if for the first time, with a new lifetime.

The Apache SOAP Admin tool

You might find it easier to use the web-based interface for Apache SOAP administration. The URL for this interface starts with the address and port of the server hosting Apache SOAP, followed by the SOAP Admin resource. I'm running Apache SOAP on georgetown on port 8080, so the URL is *http://georgetown:8080/soap/admin/index.html*. Figure 4-1 shows the main Apache SOAP administration page.

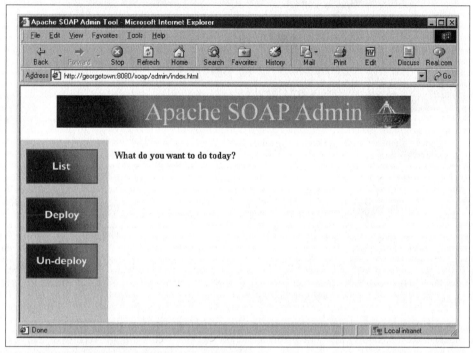

Figure 4-1. The Apache SOAP administration page

The List button takes you to a page that lists all of the deployed services. You'll see the urn:CallCounterService listed, as shown in Figure 4-2. The urn:CallCounterService link takes you to a page that shows the details of our service deployment, as shown in Figure 4-3. You can see all the deployment details that we specified in the deployment descriptor.

You can also deploy and undeploy services via this interface. If you click on Undeploy, you'll find a list of deployed services. To undeploy a service, just click on its link. If you like, go ahead and undeploy the urn:CallCounterService. You can also use the service manager client from the command line to undeploy a service:

```
java org.apache.soap.server.ServiceManagerClient
    http://georgetown:8080/soap/servlet/rpcrouter undeploy urn:CallCounterService
```

Figure 4-2. Currently deployed services

Now that the service is no longer deployed, click the Deploy button on the web interface. Figure 4-4 shows the form for service deployment. The information for deploying the service is already filled in.

To deploy the service, scroll down to the bottom of the form, where you'll find a button labeled Deploy. Click that button and the service will be deployed. You can use the web interface to look at the deployed service to make sure it looks the same as before. Apache SOAP makes no attempt to validate any of the information, so make sure you get it right.

There's an obvious security issue here. Would you want to allow anyone with the right URL to deploy or undeploy services? Not likely. Use the security features of the hosting technology in a production environment.

Deploying with GLUE

We can use the same Java class to implement CallCounterService in GLUE, because like Apache SOAP, GLUE does not require any special or extra code for services. However, the process of deploying GLUE services is quite different from that of Apache SOAP, and quite a bit simpler. GLUE provides a couple of ways to deploy services. We'll deploy the service by writing a standalone application that starts an

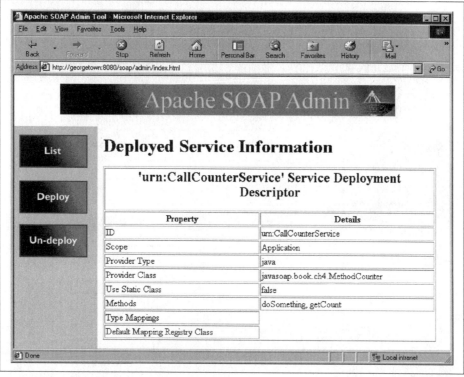

Figure 4-3. Service details

instance of GLUE's integrated HTTP server within our own code, and then use the GLUE classes and related methods to publish the service. Here's the application:

```
package javasoap.book.ch4;
import electric.util.Context;
import electric.registry.Registry;
import electric.server.http.HTTP;
public class CallCounterApp {
    public static void main( String[] args )
        throws Exception {

        HTTP.startup("http://georgetown:8004/glue");
        Context context = new Context();
        context.addProperty("activation", "application");
        Registry.publish( "urn:CallCounterService",
            javasoap.book.ch4.MethodCounter.class, context );
    }
}
```

The CallCounterApp class contains the required static main( ) method so it can be called from the command line. The HTTP.startup( ) method starts an instance of an HTTP server on my local machine georgetown on port 8004, and the resource used to

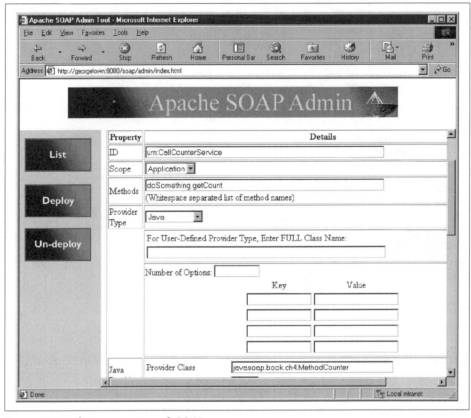

Figure 4-4. Deploying a service with SOAP

accept and route SOAP messages is */glue*. Putting that together gives us the full URL of *http://georgetown:8004/glue*, which is passed as a parameter to HTTP.startup( ).

After starting the server, we need to register our service with it. We start by specifying the activation model we want to use. To do so, we create an instance of the class electric.util.Context. This class is part of the GLUE APIs, and is used to assemble a collection of property names and associated values. To record the activation model, we call the addProperty( ) method of the context object, giving it the property name activation and the associated value application. Finally, we're ready to publish the service, using the publish( ) method of GLUE's electric.registry.Registry class. The first parameter passed is urn:CallCounterClass, which once again is the name of the service being published. The second parameter is the Java class that implements the service, MethodCounter. The context object is passed as the last parameter, indicating that we want to publish (deploy) the service using the application-level service activation model.

To start the application, we enter the following from a command-line prompt:

```
java javasoap.book.ch4.CallCounterApp
```

When we start the application, we'll see some output telling us the GLUE version number as well as the full URL of the GLUE resource that is listening for SOAP messages. This is the same URL that was passed to the `HTTP.startup( )` method. At this point the `urn:CallCounterService` service is deployed and ready to accept SOAP RPC method invocations.

How does GLUE know what methods are being exposed as part of the service? In the Apache SOAP deployment descriptor we specifically defined the methods that were exposed; we haven't done anything like that for GLUE. Instead, GLUE uses a number of techniques to determine the methods automatically. Therefore, the simplest way to deploy a service is to let GLUE figure out which methods to expose on its own. In later chapters we'll look at how to gain control over the methods that are exposed. For this example, GLUE exposes all the public methods of the `MethodCounter` class except for the constructor. You shouldn't be surprised that GLUE requires a no-argument constructor, just like Apache SOAP.

The GLUE console

GLUE includes a web-based interface that allows you to see the available services on a given server, edit them, and even deploy new services. The GLUE console is a special web application that can be started using the *console.bat* (or *console.sh*) script that is included in the */bin* directory of the GLUE installation. If you're using a command-line prompt in a Microsoft Windows environment, I suggest you navigate to that directory to execute the `console` command, because `console` is a Windows command as well. If you navigate to GLUE's */bin* directory first, you'll start the correct program.

By default, the GLUE console listens for HTTP connections to the local machine on port 8100 (i.e., *http://localhost:8100*). To run the console application on another port, specify that port number as an argument to the `console` command. The following command starts the console on port 8150:

```
console 8150
```

All the examples in this book use the default port of 8100. So go ahead and start the console application, then launch your web browser and go to *http://localhost:8100*. You will see the main GLUE console window shown in Figure 4-5.

For now, we're going to use only the first field of the GLUE console interface, labeled HOME. Remember that we have already started an instance of a GLUE server using the URL *http://georgetown:8004/glue*. Enter this URL in the HOME field of the console form, click on the HOME button, and you'll be taken to the page shown in Figure 4-6. This page includes the URL of the server's endpoint, the resource that manages the SOAP messages. It also shows all of the services currently available on that server. The first one, `system/admin`, is a special service used by GLUE. The second service is `urn:CallCounterService`, which we deployed earlier. The `urn:`

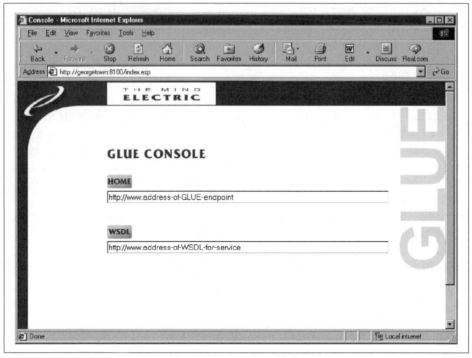

Figure 4-5. The GLUE console

CallCounterService link takes you to a page that describes the web service, shown in Figure 4-7.

Let's take a look at the information provided for a web service. The Description field provides a description of the service; its value is a default value that GLUE has generated for us. In later examples we'll provide a more useful description. The Endpoint field contains the full URL of the service. The WSDL field shows a URL that can be used to request a description of the service in the Web Service Description Language; we'll look at this in Chapter 9. The Class field shows the full class name of the Java class that implements the service, and the Mode field shows that the service activation model used by this service is application. Finally, the Methods field contains the methods that can be invoked on this service. These were automatically determined by GLUE.

The EDIT button takes you to a form that allows you to edit the description, Java class, and mode (service activation model) of the service. It also allows you to modify the URN (universal resource name). The URN is the actual name of the service, which in this case is urn:CallCounterService. Clicking the JAVA button gives you a listing of client-side Java classes that can be used to access the service. We'll get to this in the section "Calling the Service with GLUE."

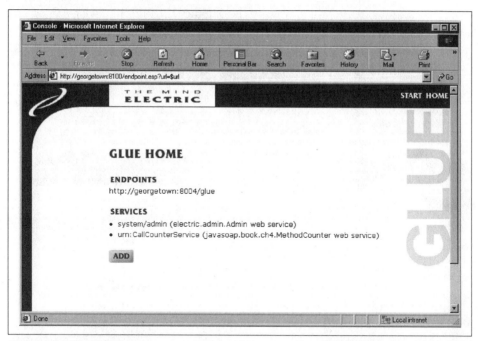

Figure 4-6. The GLUE home

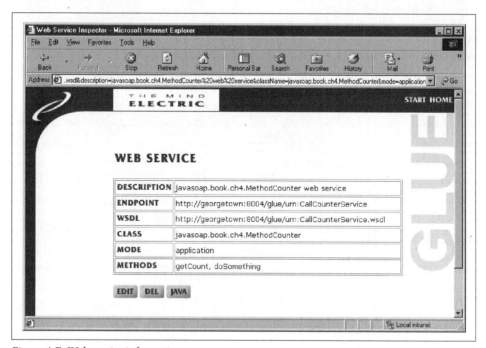

Figure 4-7. Web service information

You can undeploy (delete) the service by clicking the DEL button. If we go ahead and delete the service, the GLUE console responds with the page shown in Figure 4-8.

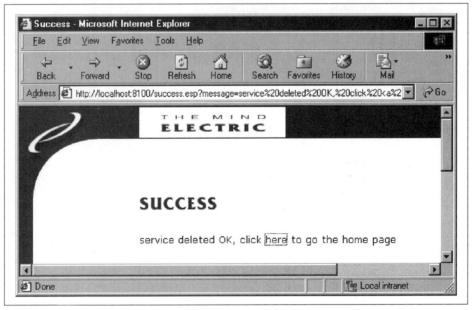

Figure 4-8. Successful deletion

At this point, click the "here" link to go back to the page that describes the available web services on the server. This will look similar to Figure 4-6 except that urn: CallCounterService will no longer be listed. Now click the ADD button, which takes you to a form for providing the information needed to deploy a service (Figure 4-9). I've entered the information for the urn:CallCounterService, this time providing a better description. I used the same URN, class, and mode used when we deployed the service from within the Java application.

Press the SAVE button to deploy the service. If you provide an invalid class name, the GLUE console will indicate a failure. Otherwise you'll be taken to the web service page (Figure 4-7).

Writing Service Clients

In the next few sections, we'll write some Java code that invokes methods on the services we've exposed in both Apache SOAP and GLUE. For now, we won't mix and match technologies—we'll use Apache SOAP APIs to call an Apache SOAP server, and GLUE APIs to call a GLUE server.

So what about interoperability? One of the most important aspects of SOAP as a wire protocol is that your choice of implementation should not prohibit you from

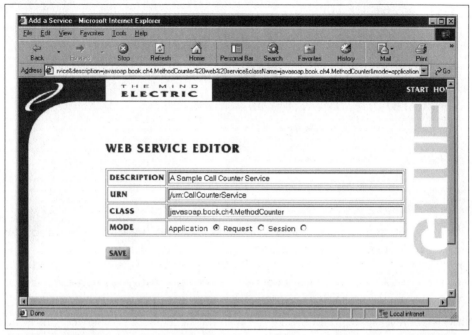

Figure 4-9. Adding a service through the console

communicating successfully with other SOAP implementations. However, there are still some problems with SOAP interoperability. Some technologies are better at it right now than others, and in some cases you have to jump through a few hoops to make different SOAP technologies communicate properly with each other. So let's put off this subject until Chapter 9, where we'll cover these issues in detail.

Calling the Service with Apache SOAP

Now that we have a service up and running, let's write some Java code that acts as a client of the service. Here's a simple Java application that invokes the getCount method of the urn:CallCounterService on our Apache SOAP server:

```
package javasoap.book.ch4;
import java.net.*;
import org.apache.soap.*;
import org.apache.soap.rpc.*;
public class GetCountApp {
    public static void main(String[] args)
        throws Exception {

      URL url =
        new URL(
          "http://georgetown:8080/soap/servlet/rpcrouter");
```

```
Call call = new Call();
call.setTargetObjectURI("urn:CallCounterService");
call.setMethodName("getCount");
try {
    Response resp = call.invoke(url, "");
    Parameter ret = resp.getReturnValue();
    Object value = ret.getValue();
    System.out.println("Result is " + value);
}
catch (SOAPException e) {
    System.err.println("Caught SOAPException (" +
                    e.getFaultCode() + "): " +
                    e.getMessage());
}
    }
}
```

This program starts by creating an instance of java.net.URL using the URL of the Apache SOAP RPC router of our Apache SOAP server. It then creates an instance of org.apache.soap.rpc.Call, a Java class that encapsulates a SOAP RPC method call. The setTargetObjectURI() method of the call object is used to specify the name of the service, and setMethodName() specifies the name of the method being invoked.

At this point we're ready to invoke the method on the specified service. Since the method invocation can throw a SOAPException, we put it within a try/catch block. If anything goes wrong we'll print out the fault code and message from the exception.

To make the method call, we use the invoke() method of the call object, with the URL that we set up earlier as the first parameter. The second parameter is a SOAP action URI, which is included as an HTTP header entry. We're not using a SOAP action, so an empty string is passed for this parameter. The invoke() method returns an instance of org.apache.soap.rpc.Response; upon successful return, this object contains the response from the server. For now let's assume that the call succeeds. After invoking the method, we call the getReturnValue() method of the response object. This method returns an instance of org.apache.soap.rpc.Parameter, which contains the return value, or response, of the service method call. Now we call the getValue() method of the parameter, which returns an instance of Object; the actual type of the object you get back depends on the return type of the method. This is an important point. Apache SOAP RPC method calls return instances of Java objects, not instances of Java primitives. In a case like this, where the service method being called returns an int value, the primitive return value is created as an instance of its corresponding Java object type—in this case, Integer. We could cast the return value to Integer, but instead we'll leave it as an Object instance and print the result using System.out.println(). This method implicitly calls toString(), which returns the Integer's value as a String.

Let's go ahead and run this application:

```
java javasoap.book.ch4.GetCountApp
```

If everything is set up correctly, you'll see the following output:

```
Result is 0
```

The result is 0 because we haven't yet made any calls to the doSomething( ) method that increments the value of the counter in the service object. This is great! We've successfully deployed and invoked a SOAP service in Java. Let's take a look at the SOAP payload that was used to invoke the service:

```
POST /soap/servlet/rpcrouter HTTP/1.0
Host: Georgetown
Content-Type: text/xml; charset=utf-8
Content-Length: 344
SOAPAction: ""

<?xml version='1.0' encoding='UTF-8'?>
<SOAP-ENV:Envelope
 xmlns:SOAP-ENV="http://schemas.xmlsoap.org/soap/envelope/"
 xmlns:xsi="http://www.w3.org/2001/XMLSchema-instance"
 xmlns:xsd="http://www.w3.org/2001/XMLSchema">

<SOAP-ENV:Body>
  <ns1:getCount xmlns:ns1="urn:CallCounterService">
</ns1:getCount>

</SOAP-ENV:Body>
</SOAP-ENV:Envelope>
```

All of the data in this SOAP document should be familiar to you. The information specific to this example is contained in the SOAP body, where you can see that the getCount element (which represents the method being invoked) is namespace-qualified by urn:CallCounterService, the name of the service on which the method is being invoked. While we're at it, let's look at the response sent back by the server:

```
HTTP/1.0 200 OK
Content-Type: text/xml; charset=utf-8
Content-Length: 468
Set-Cookie2: JSESSIONID=yqf5f6su31;Version=1;Discard;Path="/soap"
Set-Cookie: JSESSIONID=yqf5f6su31;Path=/soap
Servlet-Engine: Tomcat Web Server/3.2.3

<?xml version='1.0' encoding='UTF-8'?>
<SOAP-ENV:Envelope
 xmlns:SOAP-ENV="http://schemas.xmlsoap.org/soap/envelope/"
 xmlns:xsi="http://www.w3.org/2001/XMLSchema-instance"
 xmlns:xsd="http://www.w3.org/2001/XMLSchema">

<SOAP-ENV:Body>
 <ns1:getCountResponse
  xmlns:ns1="urn:CallCounterService"
  SOAP-ENV:encodingStyle=
    "http://schemas.xmlsoap.org/soap/encoding/">
   <return xsi:type="xsd:int">0</return>
 </ns1:getCountResponse>
```

```
    </SOAP-ENV:Body>
    </SOAP-ENV:Envelope>
```

The HTTP headers are shown so that you can see the entire response. Notice that the server is returning HTTP cookie values. Although we aren't using them now, those cookies will be useful when we use Session service activation for services.

Now look at the SOAP body. Since the name of the method that was invoked is getCount, the first child element of the body is getCountResponse, namespace-qualified by the service name. The SOAP-ENV:encodingStyle attribute is set to http://schemas.xmlsoap.org/soap/encoding. Within the getCountResponse element we find a single child element named return, which contains the return value of the getCount method. return is explicitly typed as xsd:int, and contains the data value 0.

Let's make a few calls to doSomething in order to bump up the counter:

```java
package javasoap.book.ch4;
import java.net.*;
import org.apache.soap.*;
import org.apache.soap.rpc.*;
public class GetCountApp2 {
    public static void main(String[] args)
        throws Exception {

        URL url =
          new URL(
            "http://georgetown:8080/soap/servlet/rpcrouter");

        Call call = new Call();
        call.setTargetObjectURI("urn:CallCounterService");
        try {
            call.setMethodName("doSomething");
            Response resp = call.invoke(url, "");
            resp = call.invoke(url, "");
            resp = call.invoke(url, "");
            call.setMethodName("getCount");
            resp = call.invoke(url, "");
            Parameter ret = resp.getReturnValue();
            Object value = ret.getValue();
            System.out.println("Result is " + value);
        }
        catch (SOAPException e) {
            System.err.println("Caught SOAPException (" +
                        e.getFaultCode() + "): " +
                        e.getMessage());
        }
    }
}
```

In this example, we first set the name of the method to doSomething using setMethodName( ), and then we execute call.invoke( ) three times. Then the method name is set to getCount and the service is invoked again. Like last time, the result of the getCount method is displayed. You should see the following output after running this application from a command-line prompt:

```
Result is 3
```

We've deployed urn:CallCounterService using application scope, meaning that a single instance of the service class is used for every service request. So each time the doSomething method is called, the _counter variable inside the MethodCounter instance is incremented. If you run the application again, the result will be 6. One more time and it'll be 9. Here you see application scope services in action, trivial as the example itself happens to be. If you want to get the counter back to 0, shut down the server you're using to host Apache SOAP and restart it.

 You'd think that an alternative to shutting down the server would be to undeploy and then redeploy the service. It doesn't work, though, at least not with a Tomcat server. Apparently the implementing service class is cached and reused if the service is redeployed. If you're using some other server to host Apache SOAP, you should check this out for yourself.

Calling the Service with GLUE

Now let's create an application that uses the GLUE APIs to communicate with the GLUE server we started earlier. GLUE takes a different approach to Java client programming. It allows you to access services via local Java interfaces. These interfaces contain methods that correspond to the exposed, or published, methods of the service. In this example, we want to write a Java interface that has the getCount( ) and doSomething( ) methods just as they appear in MethodCounter. Here's such an interface, named ICallCounterService.*

```
package javasoap.book.ch4;
public interface ICallCounterService {
  int getCount( );
  boolean doSomething( );
}
```

Next let's create an application that accesses the GLUE-hosted service urn: CallCounterService.

```
package javasoap.book.ch4;
import electric.registry.Registry;
import electric.registry.RegistryException;
public class GetCountApp3 {
  public static void main(String[] args) throws Exception
  {
    try {
```

---

* Starting interface names with an I is a common, but by no means universal, convention.

```
        ICallCounterService ctr =
          (ICallCounterService)Registry.bind(
            "http://georgetown:8004/glue/urn:CallCounterService.wsdl",
            ICallCounterService.class);
      System.out.println("Result is " + ctr.getCount( ));
    }
    catch (RegistryException e)
    {
      System.out.println(e);
    }
  }
}
```

GLUE allows us to bind the service interface to the service. Once this is accomplished, we simply use the interface as if it were a local object (which it is!). So the only step is to call the static bind( ) method of the electric.registry.Registry class. The first parameter is a URL to the WSDL file that describes the service. GLUE is based on WSDL, and automatically generates the WSDL description for the service. (WSDL is covered briefly in Chapter 9.) To create the proper URL, start with the address of the server and resource (*http://georgetown:8004/glue*) and add the name of the service, followed by *.wsdl*. The second parameter is the Java class that represents the interface, ICallCounterService.class. The return value of the Registry.bind( ) method is cast to an instance of the Java interface for the service, ICallCounterService.

After the call to Registry.bind( ) returns, we can use the ctr variable to call the getCount( ) and doSomething( ) methods as if it were nothing more than a local Java object. In this example we simply print out the result by calling ctr.getCount( ). Here's how to run the example:

```
java javasoap.book.ch4.GetCountApp3
```

The result of calling getCount( ) is 0 because there have not yet been any calls to doSomething( ):

```
Result is 0
```

The GLUE console can generate some Java code that makes it easier to access the service. To generate this code, go back to the GLUE console using your browser, then go to the urn:CallCounterService and click on the JAVA button. GLUE uses a different name for the interface (IMethodCounter) than I did, but the contents of the interface are otherwise the same. The helper class is called MethodCounterHelper. It encapsulates the Registry.bind( ) calls and the cast required to pass the correct interface. The helper class provides two static bind( ) methods. The first one takes no parameters and generates the URL of the service endpoint automatically. The other bind( ) allows you to specify another URL if you like. Here's the previous client application modified to use the Java interface and helper class generated by the console. Make sure that you use the appropriate package name for the interface and helper class. The GLUE console does not do that part, so it's up to you.*

```
package javasoap.book.ch4;
import electric.registry.RegistryException;
public class GetCountApp4 {
   public static void main(String[] args) throws Exception
   {
      try {
        IMethodCounter ctr = MethodCounterHelper.bind( );
        System.out.println("Result is " + ctr.getCount( ));
      }
      catch (RegistryException e)
      {
         System.out.println(e);
      }
   }
}
```

Using the helper class MethodCounterHelper cleans up the code a bit. For a small program like this, it's not a significant difference, but there would be a bigger payoff in a larger application. Compile the new client, together with the Java interface and helper class as part of the javasoap.book.ch4 package. Running this example from a command-line prompt gives us the same result as before.

The GLUE console also provides a way to invoke the methods of a service without writing any code. Go back to the urn:CallCounterService web service page in your browser. The methods that are listed in the METHODS field are hyperlinks; clicking on one of these links brings you to a form for invoking the selected service method. If you select the getCount method, you'll see the form shown in Figure 4-10. There are fields for the input parameters and return value, labeled INPUTS and OUTPUTS. If there were any parameters for the getCount method, there would be a place to enter a value. In this case there are none. Clicking on the SEND button invokes the service method. When the call returns, the result is displayed below the SEND button; if you do this now, you'll see a 0. This web interface provides a useful tool for checking the functionality of web services without having to write Java code.

Let's modify the GLUE example to make multiple calls to doSomething before calling getCount. Here's a new version of our client that uses the GLUE APIs to make multiple calls, using the interface and helper class generated by the GLUE console:

```
package javasoap.book.ch4;
import electric.registry.RegistryException;
public class DoSomethingApp {
   public static void main(String[] args) throws Exception
   {
```

---

* GLUE provides a utility called wsdl2java that generates Java code from a WSDL file, and has an option to generate the code for a specified package. We'll look at this utility in Chapter 9.

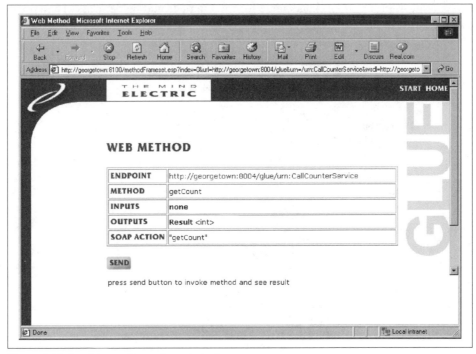

Figure 4-10. Invoking getCount through the browser

```
    try {
      IMethodCounter ctr = MethodCounterHelper.bind( );
      ctr.doSomething( );
      ctr.doSomething( );
      ctr.doSomething( );
      System.out.println("Result is " + ctr.getCount( ));
    }
    catch (RegistryException e)
    {
        System.out.println(e);
    }
  }
}
```

When you run this client for the first time, you get the following output:

```
Result is 3
```

If you run it again, the result will be 6, and so on, because the service is using application scope (activation mode). To reset the counter to 0, stop and then restart the CallCounterApp application, or use the GLUE console to delete the service and then add it back. With the GLUE console, the latter approach works just fine.

Deploying with Request-Level Scope

Up until now, all the examples we've created have been deployed using application-level scope (service activation). In this mode, a single instance of the implementing service class handles all of the method invocations. Let's change the deployment to request-level scope. With request-level scope, a new instance of the service object is created for each method invocation, and that object is destroyed when the invocation is complete.

First we'll change the example running under Apache SOAP by modifying its deployment descriptor. The only change required is to set the scope attribute of the provider element to Request; the rest of the deployment descriptor remains exactly the same:

```
<isd:service
    xmlns:isd="http://xml.apache.org/xml-soap/deployment"
    id="urn:CallCounterService">

    <isd:provider type="java"
          scope="Request"
          methods="doSomething getCount">
      <isd:java class="javasoap.book.ch4.MethodCounter"
          static="false"/>
    </isd:provider>
    <isd:faultListener>
    org.apache.soap.server.DOMFaultListener
    </isd:faultListener>
    <isd:mappings>
    </isd:mappings>
</isd:service>
```

Remember to undeploy and then redeploy the urn:CallCounterService using any of the techniques discussed earlier. You don't have to shut down the server the way we did before; now that we're using request-level scope, there shouldn't be any instance of MethodCounter in memory anyway. So you can use the command-line version of the service manager client to undeploy and redeploy the service, or you can use the Apache SOAP Admin browser application to do the same. If you decide to shut down the server and restart it, you'll still have to undeploy and redeploy the service because Apache SOAP maintains deployed services persistently.

Now that you've redeployed urn:CallCounterService using request-level scope, you can use the Apache version of the client application to access the service. Even though the application calls doSomething( ) multiple times before calling getCount( ), the result will always be 0. This is a direct consequence of request-level scope: whenever either of these methods is invoked, a new instance of the MethodCounter class is created, and that instance is destroyed when the invocation is complete. No state is maintained across invocations. Therefore, there's no way for the count to be anything but 0.

Let's do the same for the service running under GLUE. The easiest way to accomplish this is to use the GLUE console. Browse to the web services page for the urn: CallCounterService service, and then click the EDIT button. This takes you to the web service editor page shown in Figure 4-11.

Figure 4-11. The web service editor

To change the activation mode, click the corresponding radio button in the MODE field and select Request. Now click the SAVE button, and the service is redeployed using request-level scope.

 I've been using different terms for the service activation model. Sometimes I call it scope, sometimes activation mode, and other times service activation model. They all mean the same thing, but different implementations use different terms and I want you to get used to all of them. The words may be different, but they all still refer to the lifetime of the object that implements the service.

You can check that the service is now using request-level scope by running the DoSomethingApp application again. You will always get a result of 0. Again, the calls to doSomething and the call to getCount are all made against separate instances of the MethodCounter class.

Deploying with Session-Level Scope

Apache SOAP provides for session management by passing cookies via the HTTP headers. Earlier in this chapter, we saw an HTTP response from the server that included HTTP header entries called Set-Cookie and Set-Cookie2. The client application uses these cookies if it needs to make subsequent method invocations against the same session as the original request. The Apache SOAP API uses a simple technique for handling this. org.apache.soap.transport.http.SOAPHTTPConnection includes a method called setMaintainSession( ) that takes a single boolean parameter. This parameter, when set to true, tells the connection object to maintain the current session. The connection object implements this by keeping track of the cookies and sending them back to the server when the next method invocation takes place.

Go ahead and edit the deployment descriptor, setting the scope attribute to Session. Now run the client program again. You'll get the following output:

```
Result is 3
```

This output proves that the same instance of the service object was used for all of the method invocations. If you run it again you'll get the same result because a new instance of the session object is created on the first call to doSomething( ), and each subsequent method call uses the same service object. Because we're using the same instance of org.apache.soap.rpc.Call for every service call, we're also using the same instance of org.apache.soap.transport.http.SOAPHTTPConnection. You've probably guessed that the default behavior of org.apache.soap.transport.http. SOAPHTTPConnection is to maintain the session.

A common use for session-level scope is a shopping cart, where you want to keep track of the session between service method invocations. However, there may be times when you do not want to use the same session for all of your method calls, even though the service is deployed using session scope. In the next example, the SOAPHTTPConnection object is retrieved from the Call object after the first method invocation. Then a call to the connection's setMaintainSession( ) method is made with a parameter of false. This stops the connection from using the same session on subsequent service method calls.

```java
package javasoap.book.ch4;
import java.net.*;
import org.apache.soap.*;
import org.apache.soap.rpc.*;
import org.apache.soap.transport.http.*;
public class SessionApp {
    public static void main(String[] args)
        throws Exception {

        URL url =
          new URL(
            "http://georgetown:8080/soap/servlet/rpcrouter");
```

```
Call call = new Call( );
call.setTargetObjectURI("urn:CallCounterService");
try {
    call.setMethodName("doSomething");
    Response resp = call.invoke(url, "");
    SOAPHTTPConnection st =
      (SOAPHTTPConnection)call.getSOAPTransport( );
    st.setMaintainSession(false);
    resp = call.invoke(url, "");
    st.setMaintainSession(true);
    resp = call.invoke(url, "");
    call.setMethodName("getCount");
    resp = call.invoke(url, "");
    Parameter ret = resp.getReturnValue( );
    Object value = ret.getValue( );
    System.out.println("Result is " + value);
}
catch (SOAPException e) {
    System.err.println("Caught SOAPException (" +
                    e.getFaultCode( ) + "): " +
                    e.getMessage( ));
}
    }
}
```

Before the third call to doSomething( ), we call setMaintainSession( ) again with a parameter of true. Therefore, after the third call to doSomething( ), the SOAPHTTPConnection object will keep track of the session cookies. Then, when we call getCount( ), those cookies will be sent back to the server, ensuring that the same session object is used again. You should get the following output when you run the SessionApp application:

```
Result is 1
```

If you want to maintain a single session across multiple calls, make sure that you establish the session before the first call that should be part of that session. However, programming this way is a little sloppy, at least for my taste. I would prefer to create a new instance of the SOAPHTTPConnection and use it when I begin making calls using a single session. Of course, these considerations apply only to services deployed using session scope. If you'd like to give this a try, change the code within the try block to look like this:

```
call.setMethodName("doSomething");
Response resp = call.invoke(url, "");
resp = call.invoke(url, "");
SOAPHTTPConnection st = new SOAPHTTPConnection( );
call.setSOAPTransport(st);
resp = call.invoke(url, "");
call.setMethodName("getCount");
resp = call.invoke(url, "");
Parameter ret = resp.getReturnValue( );
Object value = ret.getValue( );
System.out.println("Result is " + value);
```

The lifetime of a server session is implementation dependent. The server platform you are using, the way it's configured, and the available configuration options all play a part in how long a session lasts. In most cases, the server terminates a session after some period of idle time has passed. GLUE manages sessions automatically, and lets you set the session lifetime by calling electric.server.http.HTTP.setSessionTimeout(). The parameter passed to this method is an integer that contains the number of seconds that the session can remain inactive before it is invalidated.

Passing Parameters

So far, the examples in this chapter have used methods that don't contain any parameters. We'll now spend a little time looking at how parameters are passed. Let's create a service called urn:StockPriceService, implemented by the javasoap.book.ch4.StockPrice class. The getPrice() method takes parameters for the stock symbol as well as the currency. The method always returns the float value of 75.33—not a very interesting stock, but at least it won't go down. Seriously though, we're just interested in how parameters are passed. The details of accessing a database or data feed to find a stock price are, for the moment, left to you.

```
package javasoap.book.ch4;
public class StockPrice {
    public float getPrice(String stock, String currency) {
        float result;
        // determine the price for stock and return it
        // in the specified currency
        result = (float)75.33;
        return result;
    }
}
```

We'll gloss over the deployment details, both for Apache SOAP and GLUE, since we've spent much of this chapter on that subject. Here's the Apache SOAP deployment descriptor for the StockPriceService implemented by the StockPrice class. The service uses application-level scope, and contains a single method called getPrice that retrieves the current trading price of a stock using a specified currency.

```
<isd:service
    xmlns:isd="http://xml.apache.org/xml-soap/deployment"
    id="urn:StockPriceService">

    <isd:provider type="java"
            scope="Application"
            methods="getPrice">
        <isd:java class="javasoap.book.ch4.StockPrice"
            static="false"/>
    </isd:provider>
    <isd:faultListener>
    org.apache.soap.server.DOMFaultListener
    </isd:faultListener>
    <isd:mappings>
```

```
    </isd:mappings>
  </isd:service>
```

This service can be deployed in Apache SOAP using the browser-based Admin tool or by putting this deployment descriptor into a file and using the service manager client. We'll use the latter approach. The file containing the deployment descriptor is *StockPriceService.dd*. Using that file, the following command will deploy the service on my local machine georgetown:

```
java org.apache.soap.server.ServiceManagerClient
   http://georgetown:8080/soap/servlet/rpcrouter deploy StockPriceService.dd
```

Here is a simple application using the Apache SOAP APIs to access the StockPriceService:

```
package javasoap.book.ch4;
import java.net.*;
import java.util.*;
import org.apache.soap.*;
import org.apache.soap.rpc.*;
public class StockPriceApp {
   public static void main(String[] args)
      throws Exception {

      URL url =
        new URL(
          "http://georgetown:8080/soap/servlet/rpcrouter");

      Call call = new Call( );
      call.setTargetObjectURI("urn:StockPriceService");

      call.setEncodingStyleURI(Constants.NS_URI_SOAP_ENC);
      String stock = "MINDSTRM";
      String currency = "USD";
      Vector params = new Vector( );
      params.addElement(new Parameter("stock",
                        String.class, stock, null));
      params.addElement(new Parameter("currency",
                        String.class, currency, null));
      call.setParams(params);

      try {
         call.setMethodName("getPrice");
         Response resp = call.invoke(url, "");
         Parameter ret = resp.getReturnValue( );
         Object value = ret.getValue( );
         System.out.println("Price is " + value);
      }
      catch (SOAPException e) {
         System.err.println("Caught SOAPException (" +
                        e.getFaultCode( ) + "): " +
                        e.getMessage( ));
      }
   }
}
```

The beginning of this application is similar to the applications we created earlier using the Apache SOAP APIs. The code for setting up parameters starts with a call to the setEncodingStyleURI( ) method of the Call object. The parameter passed to this method is a string that contains the URI of the encoding style that should be used to serialize the parameters. In this case, the encoding style is given by Constants.NS_ URI_SOAP_ENC, which is a constant defined by the org.apache.soap.Constants class. The value of this constant is "http://schemas.xmlsoap.org/soap/encoding/", which is the standard SOAP encoding namespace. The default value for the encoding style of a Call instance is null, so you must remember to call the setEncodingStyleURI( ) method. Without this, the server side will not understand the encoding scheme that should be used to deserialize the parameters.

Next, we set up two String variables that contain the stock symbol[*] and the currency to use when the getPrice( ) method is invoked. Now we create an instance of java. util.Vector, which will hold the parameters. Each parameter is held in an instance of org.apache.soap.rpc.Parameter. The constructor of this class takes the parameter's name, the class of the object that contains the parameter value, the object that contains the parameter value, and the encoding style URI for the parameter. For the first parameter of the org.apache.soap.rpc.Parameter constructor we pass the name stock, which is the name used for the first parameter of the getPrice method of the StockPrice class. The second parameter is String.class, which tells the constructor that the value is passed as a Java String instance. The third parameter is a String variable that contains the actual value we're passing: "MINDSTRM". We pass null for the last parameter, indicating that an encoding style URI should not be included for the XML element that will be serialized for this parameter. Remember that we've already set up the encoding style URI for the entire call when we called call.setEncodingStyleURI( ); unless you want to use some other encoding style for this particular parameter, just pass null. The org.apache.soap.rpc.Parameter instance is added to the vector using the params.addElement( ) method. We go through the same process for the currency parameter, adding it to the vector, params, as well.

Finally, we pass the vector containing the parameters to the Call object using the call.setParams( ) method. From here, the rest of the code is familiar. The getPrice( ) service method is invoked, and the result is printed for display. Here's the SOAP envelope that is sent to the server:

```
<SOAP-ENV:Envelope
 xmlns:SOAP-ENV="http://schemas.xmlsoap.org/soap/envelope/"
 xmlns:xsi="http://www.w3.org/2001/XMLSchema-instance"
 xmlns:xsd="http://www.w3.org/2001/XMLSchema">

<SOAP-ENV:Body>
 <ns1:getPrice
```

---

[*] MINDSTRM is not a real stock symbol.

```
        xmlns:ns1="urn:StockPriceService"
        SOAP-ENV:encodingStyle=
            "http://schemas.xmlsoap.org/soap/encoding/">
        <stock xsi:type="xsd:string">MINDSTRM</stock>
        <currency xsi:type="xsd:string">USD</currency>
      </ns1:getPrice>
    </SOAP-ENV:Body>
    </SOAP-ENV:Envelope>
```

As we've seen before, the name of the method we're calling is used for the child element of the SOAP Body, namespace-qualified by the name of the service itself. The SOAP-ENV:encodingStyle attribute on the getPrice element applies to all of its subelements, unless those elements include the SOAP-ENV:encodingStyle attribute themselves. (That's why we passed null to the org.apache.soap.rpc.Parameter constructor.) The two parameters are serialized as child elements of getPrice. Each one is explicitly typed using the xsi:type attribute with a value of xsd:string, and the parameter value is serialized as the element data value for the associated parameter.

Now let's take a look at what's required to pass parameters using the GLUE APIs. We've already seen that GLUE binds Java interfaces to services, and the methods of those interfaces are treated like any other Java instance. So there's really nothing profound about passing parameters in GLUE-based applications. But let's go through the steps anyway, just to reinforce the concepts.

Assuming that the CallCounterApp application is still running, we can use the GLUE console to deploy the new service on that GLUE server instance. Clicking the ADD button on the home page of your GLUE server brings you to an empty web service editor form. Fill in the appropriate service details, as shown in Figure 4-12.

In the figure, I've given the service a short description, as well as the service's URN (urn:StockPriceService). The Java class implementing the service is StockPrice, and the service activation mode is Application. Click SAVE to deploy the service.

Now we need a Java interface to bind to this service. You can use the one generated by the GLUE console, if you prefer; for this example, we'll use the interface IStockPriceService, listed below. In either case, remember that the names used by the GLUE console when it generates an interface are different from the names we use when creating the interfaces by hand.

```
package javasoap.book.ch4;
public interface IStockPriceService {
    float getPrice(String stock, String currency);
}
```

Writing an application that accesses the StockPriceService using the GLUE APIs is simple. We won't use the helper class by the GLUE console here, although there's certainly no reason why you couldn't. Here's the application for accessing the service:

```
package javasoap.book.ch4;
import electric.registry.Registry;
import electric.registry.RegistryException;
```

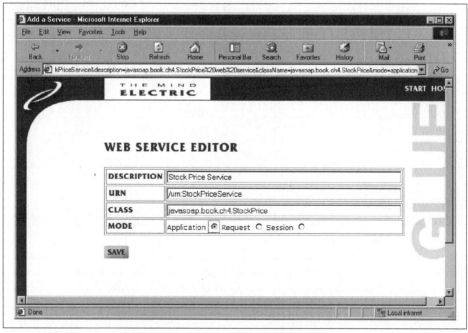

Figure 4-12. Specifying details with the web service editor

```java
public class StockPriceApp2 {
    public static void main(String[] args) throws Exception
    {
        try {
            IStockPriceService ctr =
              (IStockPriceService)Registry.bind(
                "http://georgetown:8004/glue/urn:StockPriceService.wsdl",
                IStockPriceService.class);
            String stock = "MINDSTRM";
            String currency = "USD";
            System.out.println("Price is " +
              ctr.getPrice(stock, currency));
        }
        catch (RegistryException e)
        {
            System.out.println(e);
        }
    }
}
```

Once you bind an interface to the service, you work directly with the Java interfaces as if the service objects were local. So all we need to do is call ctr.getPrice( ), passing the stock and currency variables as parameters. Run StockPriceApp2 and you'll get the following output:

```
Price is 75.33
```

We haven't yet looked at the SOAP messages transmitted by GLUE applications. Let's see how they differ from those transmitted by Apache SOAP. Here's the SOAP envelope that was transmitted by the GLUE APIs:

```
<soap:Envelope
  xmlns:xsi='http://www.w3.org/2001/XMLSchema-instance'
  xmlns:xsd='http://www.w3.org/2001/XMLSchema'
  xmlns:soap='http://schemas.xmlsoap.org/soap/envelope/'
  xmlns:soapenc='http://schemas.xmlsoap.org/soap/encoding/'
  soap:encodingStyle='http://schemas.xmlsoap.org/soap/encoding/'>
  <soap:Body>
    <n:getPrice
        xmlns:n='http://tempuri.org/javasoap.book.ch4.StockPrice'>
        <arg0 xsi:type='xsd:string'>MINDSTRM</arg0>
        <arg1 xsi:type='xsd:string'>USD</arg1>
    </n:getPrice>
  </soap:Body>
</soap:Envelope>
```

The GLUE-generated SOAP envelope sets up the xsi and xsd namespace identifiers the same way as Apache SOAP. Instead of using the SOAP-ENV identifier, GLUE uses the name soap, which is hardly a significant difference; this is just a name. It can be called anything, as long as it is assigned the value of http://schemas.xmlsoap.org/ soap/envelope. The encodingStyle attribute is the same as in the Apache SOAP examples as well. There seems to be an extra attribute, soapenc, that isn't referenced anywhere in the message, but that won't hurt anything. The getPrice element that represents the service method is not namespace-qualified by the service name, as is the case with Apache SOAP. The namespace is derived by appending the class name of the service implementation class to the address *http://tempuri.org/*, which is the default namespace generated by the GLUE server. Unlike the Apache SOAP examples, the parameters are named arg0, arg1, etc. Since the method parameters are listed in the order they appear, the names are not significant. They are explicitly typed, just as they are in the Apache examples.

I prefer to use the actual service name to qualify the service method name, rather than an artificial service name derived by default. This is easy to correct; just supply a namespace property to the context object used when the server is executed. We did the same thing to specify the service activation mode. Here's a modified version of the server application (originally CallCounterApp), only this time we specify the namespace to use by calling context.addProperty( ) with "namespace" as the first parameter and "urn:StockPriceService" as the second parameter. This new application publishes the urn:StockPriceService, so we don't need to go to the GLUE console.

```
package javasoap.book.ch4;
import electric.util.Context;
import electric.registry.Registry;
import electric.server.http.HTTP;
public class StockPriceApp3 {
    public static void main( String[] args )
        throws Exception {
```

```
        HTTP.startup("http://georgetown:8004/glue");
        Context context = new Context();
        context.addProperty("activation", "application");
        context.addProperty("namespace", "urn:StockPriceService");
        Registry.publish("urn:StockPriceService",
            javasoap.book.ch4.StockPrice.class, context );
    }
  }
```

If you still have an instance of CallCounterApp running, shut it down; it uses the same address and port number as this new application. Once you start StockPriceApp3, the namespace used to qualify the method name in SOAP messages will be urn: StockPriceService. Let's look at the response generated by the server for this request:

```
<soap:Envelope
 xmlns:xsi='http://www.w3.org/2001/XMLSchema-instance'
 xmlns:xsd='http://www.w3.org/2001/XMLSchema'
 xmlns:soap='http://schemas.xmlsoap.org/soap/envelope/'
 xmlns:soapenc='http://schemas.xmlsoap.org/soap/encoding/'
 soap:encodingStyle='http://schemas.xmlsoap.org/soap/encoding/'>
   <soap:Body>
     <n:getPriceResponse xmlns:n='urn:StockPriceService'>
       <Result xsi:type='xsd:float'>75.33</Result>
     </n:getPriceResponse>
   </soap:Body>
 </soap:Envelope>
```

The response envelope is pretty much the same as the envelope generated by Apache SOAP; the only real difference is that the return value is contained in an element named Result, whereas in Apache SOAP this element is named return. But it's the structure of the response that's important, and as you can see the structure is the same as that of an Apache SOAP server's response.

Using in, out, and in/out Parameters

All of the examples so far have assumed that method parameters contain values to be passed from the client to the service, and that the service does not change the value of the parameters before returning. That's the default behavior of SOAP RPC services; the parameters in this case are referred to as in parameters because the value is passed "in" to the service. But SOAP also supports the use of two other parameter styles. Service methods may contain parameters that do not contain any data to be passed from the client to the service, but do contain data (to be read by the client) when the method returns. These are known as out parameters: the value of the parameter is passed "out" of the service. Parameters may also be in/out, where a value is passed in to the service and another value is passed out.

Not all SOAP implementation support the use of out or in/out parameters (Apache SOAP doesn't; GLUE does). That, by itself, should sound an alarm for you. It's not really a good idea to use features that are not widely supported unless you are in control of the servers as well as the clients of those servers. You may be able to avoid the need for using out or in/out parameters by defining a custom type that contains the values you want returned, and then defining your service methods to return an instance of that custom type. This is the approach I take; it also avoids any confusion about the purpose of the method. On the other hand, most recent implementations do support in/out parameters. In fact, many of them use the same technique that we're about to explore.

Now that I've cautioned against using them, let's take a look at how out and in/out parameters can be used. GLUE uses holder classes that encapsulate data types when using out and in/out parameters. There are already holder classes for the Java primitives and common classes like java.lang.String. For custom data types, GLUE includes a holder utility that generates holder classes for you. (Keep in mind that this approach is specific to GLUE; SOAP doesn't dictate the API, only the XML encoding.) Here's a modified version of the StockPrice class that includes two new methods. The first method is getPriceOut( ); it returns a boolean value indicating whether the request was successful. The first two parameters are the same as those in the original getPrice( ) method: a stock symbol and the currency. The third parameter is called price; this is an out parameter that has no value when the method is invoked, and contains the resulting price when the method returns. So getOutPrice( ) uses an out parameter to return the price, which it computes using the original getPrice( ) method. The price parameter is an instance of electric.util.holder.floatOut, a holder class for floating-point out parameters.

The other new method is called correctSymbol( ), which converts a stock symbol to an appropriate format (all uppercase characters). It returns a boolean indicating success or failure, but more importantly uses a single in/out String parameter named symbol. This parameter contains a stock symbol when the method is called; when correctSymbol( ) returns, it contains the corrected stock symbol. To support this behavior, the symbol parameter is declared as an instance of electric.util.holder. java.lang.StringInOut, a holder class for String in/out parameters. The StockPriceApp3 can be used to publish the service without any modifications.

```
package javasoap.book.ch4;
import electric.util.holder.*;
import electric.util.holder.java.lang.*;
public class StockPrice {
    public float getPrice(String stock, String currency) {
        float result;
        // determine the price for stock and return it
        // in the specified currency
        result = (float)75.33;
        return result;
    }
    public boolean getOutPrice(String stock, String currency,
                    floatOut price) {
        try {
            price.value = getPrice(stock, currency);
            return true;
        }
```

```
        catch (Exception e) {
            return false;
        }
    }
    public boolean correctSymbol(StringInOut symbol) {
        symbol.value = symbol.value.toUpperCase();
        return true;
    }
}
```

Since we've modified the service by adding methods, we'll need to modify the javasoap.book.ch4.IStockPriceService interface in kind. Here's the new interface:

```
package javasoap.book.ch4;
import electric.util.holder.*;
import electric.util.holder.java.lang.*;
public interface IStockPriceService {
    float getPrice(String stock, String currency);
    public boolean getOutPrice(String stock, String currency,
                        floatOut price);
    public boolean correctSymbol(StringInOut symbol);
}
```

Now let's create an application to use this service. We'll call correctSymbol( ) first to convert a stock symbol to uppercase using an in/out parameter, and then call getOutPrice( ) to retrieve the price using an out parameter:

```
package javasoap.book.ch4;
import electric.registry.Registry;
import electric.registry.RegistryException;
import electric.util.holder.*;
import electric.util.holder.java.lang.*;
public class InOutApp {
    public static void main(String[] args) throws Exception
    {
        try {
            IStockPriceService ctr =
                (IStockPriceService)Registry.bind(
                  "http://georgetown:8004/glue/urn:StockPriceService.wsdl",
                  IStockPriceService.class);
            StringInOut stock = new StringInOut("MiNdStRm");
            boolean ok = ctr.correctSymbol(stock);
            if (ok) {
                System.out.println("Symbol converted to: "
                            + stock.value);
            }
            String currency = "USD";
            floatOut price = new floatOut( );
            ok = ctr.getOutPrice(stock.value, currency, price);
            System.out.println("Result is " + price.value);
        }
        catch (RegistryException e)
        {
            System.out.println(e);
        }
```

```
        }
    }
```

The stock symbol variable, stock, is instantiated with the symbol "MiNdStRm". We then pass that variable, which is an instance of electric.util.holder.java.lang .StringInOut, to the correctSymbol() method of the service interface. When the method call returns, we expect the symbol to have been converted to uppercase. Next we call getOutPrice(), passing stock.value as the first parameter. The currency is passed as before, and an instance of electric.holder.floatOut called price is passed as the last parameter. When the method returns, price contains the stock price. Running the example produces this output:

```
Symbol converted to: MINDSTRM
Result is 75.33
```

As you can see, both the out and in/out parameters were handled as expected. Before we finish up, let's take a look at the parts of the SOAP envelopes passed between client and server that were affected by our use of out and in/out parameters. The call to correctSymbol() results in a response envelope that looks a bit different from those we've seen before. The returned boolean value is immediately followed by the modified parameter value. Here's the SOAP body for that response:

```
<soap:Body>
  <n:correctSymbolResponse xmlns:n='urn:StockPriceService'>
    <Result xsi:type='xsd:boolean'>true</Result>
    <arg0 xsi:type='xsd:string'>MINDSTRM</arg0>
  </n:correctSymbolResponse>
</soap:Body>
```

The modified in/out parameter value in XML element arg0 comes right after the Result element. And, of course, you can see that the original value has been converted to uppercase. Now let's look at part of the envelope sent to the server when getOutPrice() was invoked. There are only two parameter values encoded, because the third parameter is an out parameter and so has no value at the time of the method invocation.

```
<n:getOutPrice xmlns:n='urn:StockPriceService'>
  <arg0 xsi:type='xsd:string'>MINDSTRM</arg0>
  <arg1 xsi:type='xsd:string'>USD</arg1>
</n:getOutPrice>
```

Finally, here's the response part of the SOAP body that was returned by the call to getOutPrice(). The value of the price parameter follows the result itself. The first two parameters don't have any values because they are both in parameters, and so don't have modified values.

```
<n:getOutPriceResponse xmlns:n='urn:StockPriceService'>
  <Result xsi:type='xsd:boolean'>true</Result>
  <arg2 xsi:type='xsd:float'>75.33</arg2>
</n:getOutPriceResponse>
```

In the next chapter, we'll begin investigating the more complex features and capabilities of SOAP and its implementations.

CHAPTER 5

Working with Complex Data Types

In the previous chapter, we created RPC-style services in Java. Those services dealt only with simple data types. Simple data types may suffice in many situations, but you'll eventually need to use more complex data types, like those you're familiar with in your day-to-day Java programming. In this chapter we'll look at creating services with method parameters and return values that are arrays and Java beans. We'll hold off on custom data types until the next chapter, since it's possible that any custom types you create would use the complex data types we'll be discussing here.

Passing Arrays as Parameters

Let's face it—arrays are probably the most common complex data type in programming. They're everywhere, so their use in SOAP is critical. We covered the details of SOAP arrays back in Chapter 3, so you should be aware of how arrays are encoded. So let's get right into writing some Java code for services that use arrays.

We've been working with stock market examples, so let's stick with that theme. It might be useful to have a service that returns information about a collection of stock symbols. It might provide the total volume of shares traded for the day, the average trading price of those stocks, the number of stocks trading higher for the day, etc. There are lots of possibilities. Let's start out with a service that returns the total number of shares traded for the day. The service is called urn:BasicTradingService, and it has a method called getTotalVolume. Here is the Java class that implements the service:

```
package javasoap.book.ch5;
public class BasicTradingService {

    public BasicTradingService() {}

    public int getTotalVolume(String[] stocks) {

        // get the volumes for each stock from some
        // data feed and return the total
```

```
        int total = 345000;
        return total;
    }
}
```

The `BasicTradingService` class contains the method `getTotalVolume( )`, which returns the total number of shares traded. Since we're not going to access a data feed, we'll just return a made-up value. The method returns an integer and takes a single parameter called `stocks` that is an array of `String` values. The strings in the array are the stock symbols; in a real application, we'd retrieve the volume for each stock from our data feed and return the total for all the stocks in the array.

Apache SOAP has built-in support for arrays, so you don't need to do anything special on the service side. This also means that there's nothing new in the deployment descriptor; it's built just like it was in the previous chapter. Here is the deployment descriptor for the `urn:BasicTradingService` service:

```
<isd:service
        xmlns:isd="http://xml.apache.org/xml-soap/deployment"
        id="urn:BasicTradingService">
    <isd:provider type="java"
        scope="Application"
        methods="getTotalVolume">
      <isd:java class="javasoap.book.ch5.BasicTradingService"
        static="false"/>
    </isd:provider>
    <isd:faultListener>org.apache.soap.server.DOMFaultListener
    </isd:faultListener>
    <isd:mappings>
    </isd:mappings>
</isd:service>
```

You can deploy the service using this deployment descriptor, or you can use the Apache SOAP Admin tool from your browser.

Now let's write a client application that accesses the service. This application is similar to some of the examples from the previous chapter; it differs only in that the parameter we're passing is an array of `String` instances, rather than a single object. Here is the code:

```
package javasoap.book.ch5;
import java.net.*;
import java.util.*;
import org.apache.soap.*;
import org.apache.soap.rpc.*;
public class VolumeClient {
    public static void main(String[] args) throws Exception {

        URL url = new URL("http://georgetown:8080/soap/servlet/rpcrouter");

        Call call = new Call();
        call.setTargetObjectURI("urn:BasicTradingService");
```

```
call.setEncodingStyleURI(Constants.NS_URI_SOAP_ENC);
String[] stocks = { "MINDSTRM", "MSFT", "SUN" };
Vector params = new Vector();
params.addElement(new Parameter("stocks",
                      String[].class, stocks, null));
call.setParams(params);

try {
    call.setMethodName("getTotalVolume");
    Response resp = call.invoke(url, "");
    Parameter ret = resp.getReturnValue();
    Object value = ret.getValue();
    System.out.println("Total Volume is " + value);
}
catch (SOAPException e) {
    System.err.println("Caught SOAPException (" +
                  e.getFaultCode() + "): " +
                  e.getMessage());
}
    }
}
```

We passed String[].class as the second parameter of the Parameter constructor. That identifies the stocks variable as an array of strings. That's it. Nothing else is required. If you run this example, the output should be:

```
Total Volume is 345000
```

Let's take a look at the SOAP envelope that was passed to the server for the invocation of the getTotalVolume service method:

```
<SOAP-ENV:Envelope
  xmlns:SOAP-ENV="http://schemas.xmlsoap.org/soap/envelope/"
  xmlns:xsi="http://www.w3.org/2001/XMLSchema-instance"
  xmlns:xsd="http://www.w3.org/2001/XMLSchema">

  <SOAP-ENV:Body>
    <ns1:getTotalVolume xmlns:ns1="urn:BasicTradingService"
      SOAP-ENV:encodingStyle=
          "http://schemas.xmlsoap.org/soap/encoding/">
      <stocks
        xmlns:ns2="http://schemas.xmlsoap.org/soap/encoding/"
        xsi:type="ns2:Array"
        ns2:arrayType="xsd:string[3]">
          <item xsi:type="xsd:string">MINDSTRM</item>
          <item xsi:type="xsd:string">MSFT</item>
          <item xsi:type="xsd:string">SUN</item>
      </stocks>
    </ns1:getTotalVolume>
  </SOAP-ENV:Body>
</SOAP-ENV:Envelope>
```

The stocks element represents the string array parameter that we passed to the service method. It is typed as an array by setting the xsi:type attribute to ns2:Array.

The ns2 namespace identifier was defined on the previous line. Next, the ns2:arrayType attribute is assigned a value of xsd:string[3]. This means that this is an array of size 3, and that each element of the array is an xsd:string. There are three child elements of stocks, each one named item. Remember that the name used for the array elements doesn't matter, and that different SOAP implementations use different schemes for naming these elements. Each element is explicitly typed by setting the xsi:type attribute to the value xsd:string.

This example uses a homogeneous array, i.e., all of the elements of the array are instances of the same type. You may have occasion to use heterogeneous arrays as well, so let's look at that possibility. In Java, arrays are often used as parameters to methods that, in other languages, would have a variable-length parameter list. For instance, the printf() function in the C language doesn't have a fixed number of parameters. Even though Java doesn't support this capability, you can simulate it by passing your parameter values in an array. An array can be of any size, and the array elements aren't required to have the same type.

Let's add a method to the urn:BasicTradingService that takes a single heterogeneous array as a parameter. The method is called executeTrade. Its parameter is an array containing the stock symbol, the number of shares to trade, and a flag indicating whether it's a buy or sell order (true means buy). The return value is a string that describes the trade.* Here is the modified BasicTradingService class:

```
package javasoap.book.ch5;
public class BasicTradingService {

    public BasicTradingService( ) {
    }
    public int getTotalVolume(String[] stocks) {

        // get the volumes for each stock from some
        // data feed and return the total

        int total = 345000;
        return total;
    }
    public String executeTrade(Object[] params) {
        String result;
        try {
            String stock = (String)params[0];
            Integer numShares = (Integer)params[1];
            Boolean buy = (Boolean)params[2];
            String orderType = "Buy";
            if (false == buy.booleanValue( )) {
```

---

* There are certainly other ways to design the interface to a method like this, and this is not the design I'd choose. This situation probably calls for using a custom class or Java bean. However, the approach I've used in this example demonstrates the use of heterogeneous arrays.

```
            orderType = "Sell";
        }
        result = (orderType + " " + numShares + " of " + stock);
    }
    catch (ClassCastException e) {
        result = "Bad Parameter Type Encountered";
    }
    return result;
    }
}
```

There is only one parameter for the executeTrade( ) method, an Object[] called params. The objects in this array must be cast to their corresponding types: a String, an Integer, and a Boolean. I like to put class casts inside a try/catch block in case the caller makes a mistake. That way I can do something useful if the method is called incorrectly, even if that means simply returning a description of the error. In Chapter 7, we'll look at generating SOAP faults for situations like this. The information passed in the array is used to generate a string that describes the parameters, and that string is stored in the result variable that is returned to the caller.

Now we can modify the client application so that it passes an appropriate Object[]as the parameter to the executeTrade service method. The multiParams variable is declared as an Object[], and is populated with the String MINDSTRM, an Integer with the value of 100, and a Boolean with the value of true. Since we're using an array of Java Object instances, we don't use Java primitives as elements of the array. Instead we wrap those primitive values in their Java object equivalents. The second parameter of the Parameter constructor is Object[].class, which is the class for an array of object instances.

```
package javasoap.book.ch5;
import java.net.*;
import java.util.*;
import org.apache.soap.*;
import org.apache.soap.rpc.*;
public class TradingClient {
    public static void main(String[] args)
        throws Exception {

        URL url =
          new URL(
            "http://georgetown:8080/soap/servlet/rpcrouter");

        Call call = new Call( );
        call.setTargetObjectURI("urn:BasicTradingService");

        call.setEncodingStyleURI(Constants.NS_URI_SOAP_ENC);
        Object[] multiParams = { "MINDSTRM", new Integer(100),
                                      new Boolean(true) };
        Vector params = new Vector( );
        params.addElement(new Parameter("params",
                          Object[].class, multiParams, null));
```

```
        call.setParams(params);

        try {
            call.setMethodName("executeTrade");
            Response resp = call.invoke(url, "");
            Parameter ret = resp.getReturnValue();
            Object value = ret.getValue();
            System.out.println("Trade Description: " + value);
        }
        catch (SOAPException e) {
            System.err.println("Caught SOAPException (" +
                        e.getFaultCode() + "): " +
                        e.getMessage());
        }
    }
}
```

If all goes well, the result of executing the executeTrade( ) service method is:

```
Trade Description: Buy 100 of MINDSTRM
```

We could force the service object down another path by changing the order of the parameters in the multiParams array. In this case, we would encounter a class cast exception, and the method would return an error string.

Here is the SOAP envelope for the proper invocation of the executeTrade( ) service method:

```
<SOAP-ENV:Envelope
    xmlns:SOAP-ENV="http://schemas.xmlsoap.org/soap/envelope/"
    xmlns:xsi="http://www.w3.org/2001/XMLSchema-instance"
    xmlns:xsd="http://www.w3.org/2001/XMLSchema">

    <SOAP-ENV:Body>
        <ns1:executeTrade xmlns:ns1="urn:BasicTradingService"
            SOAP-ENV:encodingStyle=
                "http://schemas.xmlsoap.org/soap/encoding/">

            <params
                xmlns:ns2="http://schemas.xmlsoap.org/soap/encoding/"
                xsi:type="ns2:Array" ns2:arrayType="xsd:anyType[3]">
            <item xsi:type="xsd:string">MINDSTRM</item>
            <item xsi:type="xsd:int">100</item>
            <item xsi:type="xsd:boolean">true</item>
            </params>
        </ns1:executeTrade>
    </SOAP-ENV:Body>
</SOAP-ENV:Envelope>
```

The params element is typed by assigning the xsi:type attribute the value of ns2:
Array. The only difference from the homogeneous case is that every array element has a different value assigned to the ns2:arrayType attribute. The value xsd:anyType[3]

indicates that the array contains 3 elements, each of which can be of any valid data type.[*]

Now let's take a look at passing arrays as parameters using GLUE. The BasicTradingService class can be deployed in GLUE without modification. We'll use a simple Java application to get this service started:

```
package javasoap.book.ch5;
import electric.util.Context;
import electric.registry.Registry;
import electric.server.http.HTTP;
public class BasicTradingApp {
    public static void main( String[] args )
        throws Exception {

        HTTP.startup("http://georgetown:8004/glue");
        Context context = new Context();
        context.addProperty("activation", "application");
        context.addProperty("namespace",
                            "urn:BasicTradingService");
        Registry.publish("urn:BasicTradingService",
            javasoap.book.ch5.BasicTradingService.class, context );
    }
}
```

Compile and execute the application, and the service is deployed. Now let's write a simple example to access the service using the GLUE API. First let's look at the interface to the service, IBasicTradingService:

```
package javasoap.book.ch5;
public interface IBasicTradingService {
  int getTotalVolume(String[] symbols);
  String executeTrade(Object[] params);
}
```

Now we can write an application that binds to the service and calls both its methods:

```
package javasoap.book.ch5;
import electric.registry.RegistryException;
import electric.registry.Registry;
public class BasicTradingClient {
    public static void main(String[] args) throws Exception
    {
        try {
          IBasicTradingService srv =
            (IBasicTradingService)Registry.bind(
              "http://georgetown:8004/glue/urn:BasicTradingService.wsdl",
              IBasicTradingService.class);
```

---

[*] In Chapter 3, we talked about using ur-type to represent any possible data type. Here we see the use of anyType for that purpose. The XML Schema Part 0 recommendation, dated May 2, 2001, explains this in section 2.5.4 as follows: "The anyType represents an abstraction called the ur-type which is the base type from which all simple and complex types are derived. An anyType type does not constrain its content in any way."

```
            String[] stocks = { "MINDSTRM", "MSFT", "SUN" };
            int total = srv.getTotalVolume(stocks);
            System.out.println("Total Volume is " + total);
            Object[] multiParams = { "MINDSTRM", new Integer(100),
                                     new Boolean(true) };
            String desc = srv.executeTrade(multiParams);
            System.out.println("Trade Description: " + desc);
        }
        catch (RegistryException e)
        {
            System.out.println(e);
        }
    }
}
```

As we've seen before, GLUE allows us to use familiar Java programming syntax without having to think about the underlying SOAP constructs. This holds true for the passing of array parameters as well. Everything is pretty much handled for us after the interface is bound to the service.

There are some interesting things to see in the SOAP request envelopes generated by this example. Here is the SOAP envelope for the getTotalVolume( ) method invocation:

```
<soap:Envelope
  xmlns:xsi='http://www.w3.org/2001/XMLSchema-instance'
  xmlns:xsd='http://www.w3.org/2001/XMLSchema'
  xmlns:soap='http://schemas.xmlsoap.org/soap/envelope/'
  xmlns:soapenc='http://schemas.xmlsoap.org/soap/encoding/'
  soap:encodingStyle='http://schemas.xmlsoap.org/soap/encoding/'>
    <soap:Body>
        <n:getTotalVolume xmlns:n='urn:BasicTradingService'>
          <arg0 href='#id0'/>
        </n:getTotalVolume>
        <id0 id='id0' soapenc:root='0'
          xmlns:ns2='http://www.themindelectric.com/package/java.lang/'
          xsi:type='soapenc:Array' soapenc:arrayType='xsd:string[3]'>
          <i xsi:type='xsd:string'>MINDSTRM</i>
          <i xsi:type='xsd:string'>MSFT</i>
          <i xsi:type='xsd:string'>SUN</i>
        </id0>
    </soap:Body>
</soap:Envelope>
```

The Body element starts off like we've seen before; the envelope is qualified by a namespace identifier, soap, which represents the namespace of the SOAP envelope. The first child element of the SOAP body is getTotalVolume, which of course is the name of the service method being invoked. getTotalVolume is namespace-qualified using the name of the service. The only child element of getTotalVolume is arg0, which represents the parameter passed to the method. But this isn't the array we passed; it's a reference to the array. This is a significant difference between the ways that GLUE and the Apache SOAP API generate this call. Apache SOAP puts the array in the envelope as a child element of getTotalVolume, and GLUE uses a reference and serializes the array after the getTotalVolume element terminates. So the parameter is serialized as arg0, and includes an href attribute with the value #id0. No data is included, as the array resides elsewhere.

The array that we passed as a parameter follows the getTotalVolume element. It's named id0, although the element name itself, which is generated by GLUE, is not important. The id attribute is assigned a value of id0, which coincides with the href value used in the getTotalVolume element. GLUE generates the soapenc:root attribute with a value of 0, meaning that this element is not considered the root of an object graph. (GLUE seems to include that attribute automatically.) Next we see a declaration of a namespace identifier called ns2 that seems to identify the internal GLUE package for java.lang; however, the ns2 namespace identifier is never used. The xsi:type and soapenc:arrayType attributes are set up in the same way as in the Apache SOAP examples. Finally, the elements of the array are serialized. The only difference between this example and the one generated by Apache SOAP is in the name of the array elements themselves. Apache SOAP named these elements item, and GLUE named them i. The names don't matter; the result is the same.

This example gives us a good opportunity to see two equally valid ways to serialize arrays. It's important that SOAP implementations understand these different styles if they are to interoperate. This is one of the reasons we keep showing the SOAP envelopes generated by the examples. Becoming familiar with the various styles of serialization will help you down the road if you run into problems getting applications based on different implementations to communicate correctly. (Did I say *if*?)

Let's take a look at the SOAP envelope for the call to the executeTrade service method. This method takes a heterogeneous array as a parameter. It too uses a reference to a separately serialized array, this time encoded as xsd:anyType:

```
<soap:Envelope
   xmlns:xsi='http://www.w3.org/2001/XMLSchema-instance'
   xmlns:xsd='http://www.w3.org/2001/XMLSchema'
   xmlns:soap='http://schemas.xmlsoap.org/soap/envelope/'
   xmlns:soapenc='http://schemas.xmlsoap.org/soap/encoding/'
   soap:encodingStyle='http://schemas.xmlsoap.org/soap/encoding/'>
   <soap:Body>
      <n:executeTrade xmlns:n='urn:BasicTradingService'>
         <arg0 href='#id0'/>
      </n:executeTrade>
      <id0 id='id0' soapenc:root='0'
         xmlns:ns2='http://www.themindelectric.com/package/java.lang/'
         xsi:type='soapenc:Array' soapenc:arrayType='xsd:anyType[3]'>
         <i xsi:type='xsd:string'>MINDSTRM</i>
         <i xsi:type='xsd:int'>100</i>
         <i xsi:type='xsd:boolean'>true</i>
      </id0>
   </soap:Body>
</soap:Envelope>
```

Returning Arrays

So far we've been passing arrays as parameters. Now let's use an array as the return value of a service method. We'll add a method to our service called getMostActive( ), which returns a String[] that contains the symbols for the most actively traded stocks of the day. Here's the new version of the BasicTradingService class:

```java
package javasoap.book.ch5;
public class BasicTradingService {

    public BasicTradingService( ) {
    }
    public String[] getMostActive( ) {

        // get the most actively traded stocks
        String[] actives = { "ABC", "DEF", "GHI", "JKL" };
        return actives;
    }
    public int getTotalVolume(String[] stocks) {

        // get the volumes for each stock from some
        // data feed and return the total
        int total = 345000;
        return total;
    }
    public String executeTrade(Object[] params) {
        String result;
        try {
            String stock = (String)params[0];
            Integer numShares = (Integer)params[1];
            Boolean buy = (Boolean)params[2];
            String orderType = "Buy";
            if (false == buy.booleanValue( )) {
                orderType = "Sell";
            }
            result = (orderType + " " + numShares + " of " + stock);
        }
        catch (ClassCastException e) {
            result = "Bad Parameter Type Encountered";
        }
        return result;
    }
}
```

Since we're not really calling a data feed, we just stuff a few phony stock symbols into an array and return it. Go ahead and redeploy the service now. Calling this service method from an Apache SOAP client is simple. There are no parameters to the service method, so we just have to set up the call and invoke it:

```java
package javasoap.book.ch5;
import java.net.*;
import org.apache.soap.*;
import org.apache.soap.rpc.*;
public class MostActiveClient
```

```
{
  public static void main(String[] args) throws Exception
  {
    URL url = new
      URL("http://georgetown:8080/soap/servlet/rpcrouter");
    Call call = new Call();
    call.setTargetObjectURI("urn:BasicTradingService");
    call.setMethodName("getMostActive");
    Response resp;
    try {
      resp = call.invoke(url, "");
      Parameter ret = resp.getReturnValue();
      String[] value = (String[])ret.getValue();
      int cnt = value.length;
      for (int i = 0; i < cnt; i++) {
        System.out.println(value[i]);
      }
    }
    catch (SOAPException e) {
      System.err.println("Caught SOAPException (" +
                          e.getFaultCode() + "): " +
                          e.getMessage());
    }
  }
}
```

We cast the return value of ret.getValue to a String[], since that's the return type we're expecting. In past examples we were able to leave the value as an Object instance because we relied on the object's toString() method to display the value. In this case we need to iterate over the array, so it's necessary to cast the value to the appropriate array type. After that, we just find the array length and then loop over the array values, printing each one as we get to it. If you run this example you should see the following output:

```
ABC
DEF
GHI
JKL
```

The SOAP envelope returned by this method invocation is pretty straightforward:

```
<SOAP-ENV:Envelope
  xmlns:SOAP-ENV="http://schemas.xmlsoap.org/soap/envelope/"
  xmlns:xsi="http://www.w3.org/2001/XMLSchema-instance"
  xmlns:xsd="http://www.w3.org/2001/XMLSchema">
  <SOAP-ENV:Body>
    <ns1:getMostActiveResponse
        xmlns:ns1="urn:BasicTradingService"
        SOAP-ENV:encodingStyle=
          "http://schemas.xmlsoap.org/soap/encoding/">

      <return
        xmlns:ns2="http://schemas.xmlsoap.org/soap/encoding/"
        xsi:type="ns2:Array" ns2:arrayType="xsd:string[4]">
```

```
          <item xsi:type="xsd:string">ABC</item>
          <item xsi:type="xsd:string">DEF</item>
          <item xsi:type="xsd:string">GHI</item>
          <item xsi:type="xsd:string">JKL</item>
        </return>
      </ns1:getMostActiveResponse>
    </SOAP-ENV:Body>
  </SOAP-ENV:Envelope>
```

To deploy this version of the BasicTradingService class in GLUE, we can use our old BasicTradingApp class. We can modify the Java interface, IBasicTradingService, to include the new method:

```
package javasoap.book.ch5;
public interface IBasicTradingService {
  int getTotalVolume(String[] symbols);
  String executeTrade(Object[] params);
  String[] getMostActive();
}
```

Now we modify the application BasicTradingClient to include a call to the getMostActive() method, and then iterate over the values in the array and print them out. When using GLUE we don't have to cast the return value to a String[] because, unlike the Apache SOAP example, the getMostActive() method of the interface is defined to return the proper type. Here's the modified code:

```
package javasoap.book.ch5;
import electric.registry.RegistryException;
import electric.registry.Registry;
public class BasicTradingClient {
   public static void main(String[] args) throws Exception
   {
      try {
        IBasicTradingService srv = (IBasicTradingService)Registry.bind(
          "http://georgetown:8004/glue/urn:BasicTradingService.wsdl",
          IBasicTradingService.class);
        String[] stocks = { "MINDSTRM", "MSFT", "SUN" };
        int total = srv.getTotalVolume(stocks);
        System.out.println("Total Volume is " + total);
        Object[] multiParams = { "MINDSTRM", new Integer(100),
                                 new Boolean(true) };
        String desc = srv.executeTrade(multiParams);
        System.out.println("Trade Description: " + desc);
        String[] actives = srv.getMostActive();
        int cnt = actives.length;
        for (int i = 0; i < cnt; i++) {
           System.out.println(actives[i]);
        }
      }
      catch (RegistryException e)
      {
         System.out.println(e);
      }
   }
}
```

If you run this example, you'll get the following output:

```
Total Volume is 345000
Trade Description: Buy 100 of MINDSTRM
ABC
DEF
GHI
JKL
```

GLUE uses the same serialization technique for arrays as return values that we saw earlier for array parameters; it uses a reference to a separately serialized array as the actual return value, and it references the actual array data. The SOAP envelope returned when invoking the getMostActive( ) method is:

```
<soap:Envelope
   xmlns:xsi='http://www.w3.org/2001/XMLSchema-instance'
   xmlns:xsd='http://www.w3.org/2001/XMLSchema'
   xmlns:soap='http://schemas.xmlsoap.org/soap/envelope/'
   xmlns:soapenc='http://schemas.xmlsoap.org/soap/encoding/'
   soap:encodingStyle='http://schemas.xmlsoap.org/soap/encoding/'>
     <soap:Body>
       <n:getMostActiveResponse
         xmlns:n='urn:BasicTradingService'>
         <Result href='#id0'/>
       </n:getMostActiveResponse>
       <id0 id='id0' soapenc:root='0'
         xmlns:ns2='http://www.themindelectric.com/package/java.lang/'
         xsi:type='soapenc:Array' soapenc:arrayType='xsd:string[4]'>
           <i xsi:type='xsd:string'>ABC</i>
           <i xsi:type='xsd:string'>DEF</i>
           <i xsi:type='xsd:string'>GHI</i>
           <i xsi:type='xsd:string'>JKL</i>
       </id0>
     </soap:Body>
</soap:Envelope>
```

Passing Custom Types as Parameters

As Java programmers, we certainly don't restrict ourselves to the classes found in the standard Java packages. A substantial part of our code exists as custom types, Java classes of our own creation that embody the functionality and characteristics of the systems we're building.

Consider the design of a Java class that contains all of the data necessary to specify a stock trade. This new class might contain the symbol for the stock being traded, the number of shares to trade, and an indication of the order type (buy or sell). When designing such a class, it's important to view it in the context of the larger system. That kind of analysis yields clues that can lead to decisions regarding the properties and behaviors to be given to the class. We all do this kind of work all the time; it's called software design. The result is a Java class that contains methods for accessing properties and behavior. Since SOAP is a data transport, we're interested in the properties of the class. That's what we want to transmit over the wire.

One common way to express the properties of a Java class is to use the JavaBeans design patterns. These patterns specify a naming convention to be used for the class's access methods. You may not be familiar with JavaBeans, but I bet you've seen this pattern many times. Here's how the property accessor pattern is described in the O'Reilly book *Developing Java Beans*:

> The methods used for getting and setting property values should conform to the standard design pattern for properties. These methods are allowed to throw checked exceptions if desired, but this is optional. The method signatures are as follows:
>
> ```
> public void set<PropertyName>(<PropertyType> value);
> public <PropertyType> get<PropertyName>( );
> ```
>
> The existence of a matching pair of methods that conform to this pattern represents a read/write property with the name <PropertyName> of the type <PropertyType>. If only the get method exists, the property is considered to be read only, and if only the set method exists the property is considered to be write only. In the case where the <PropertyType> is boolean, the get method can be replaced or augmented with a method that uses the following signature:
>
> ```
> public boolean is<PropertyName>( );
> ```

If you follow this pattern for naming property accessors, the accessor methods can be determined at runtime by using the Java reflection mechanism.* This is a convenient way for SOAP implementations to access the data values of a Java class instance in order to serialize the data in a SOAP message. It turns out that both Apache SOAP and GLUE take advantage of reflection. This means that all you need to do is follow a well-established naming convention, and you'll be well on your way to using custom classes in SOAP. Of course, there's a little more to it than that, so let's dig in.

First let's define a stock trade in terms of data that we want it to contain. It needs to have a stock symbol to represent the stock being traded; the symbol should be a string type element. It needs a boolean indicator that specifies whether the order is buy or sell. Lastly, it needs an integer that contains the number of shares to be traded. (In a real-world application, it might also contain various security credentials, the names of the purchaser and the broker, and many other things. Alternatively, this ancillary data could be represented in other objects.) Here's what an XML schema snippet for the stock trade might look like:

```
<element name="StockTrade" type="StockTrade"/>
<complexType name="StockTrade">
    <element name="symbol" type="xsd:string"/>
    <element name="buy" type="xsd:boolean"/>
    <element name="numshares" type="xsd:int"/>
</complexType>
```

---

* JavaBeans provides for other ways to accomplish this, but those are not within the scope of this book.

Let's create a custom Java class for specifying a stock trade called StockTrade_ClientSide. Normally I'd name this class StockTrade, but I want to make it clear that I'll be using this class on the client side of the example. We'll be writing a similar class to be used on the server side that will have a corresponding name. I'm doing this to point out that you are not required to use the same Java class on both sides of the message transaction. In fact, it probably won't make sense to use the same class, and it often won't even be possible.

StockTrade_ClientSide has three read/write properties named Symbol, Buy, and NumShares that represent the stock symbol, the buy/sell indicator, and the number of shares to trade, respectively.

```java
package javasoap.book.ch5;
public class StockTrade_ClientSide {
    String   _symbol;
    boolean  _buy;
    int      _numShares;
    public StockTrade_ClientSide( ) {
    }
    public StockTrade_ClientSide(String symbol,
                          boolean buy, int numShares) {
        _symbol = symbol;
        _buy = buy;
        _numShares = numShares;
    }
    public String getSymbol( ) {
        return _symbol;
    }
    public void setSymbol(String symbol) {
        _symbol = symbol;
    }
    public boolean isBuy( ) {
        return _buy;
    }
    public void setBuy(boolean buy) {
        _buy = buy;
    }
    public int getNumShares( ) {
        return _numShares;
    }
    public void setNumShares(int numShares) {
        _numShares = numShares;
    }
}
```

Now let's create a StockTrade_ServerSide class to represent the stock trade on the server side. Just to be sure that this class is different from its client-side counterpart, let's eliminate the constructor that takes parameters. And for good measure, let's also change the names of the class variables and the order in which they appear.

```java
package javasoap.book.ch5;
public class StockTrade_ServerSide {
```

```
int      _shares;
boolean  _buyOrder;
String   _stock;
public StockTrade_ServerSide( ) {
}
public String getSymbol( ) {
   return _stock;
}
public void setSymbol(String stock) {
   _stock = stock;
}
public boolean isBuy( ) {
   return _buyOrder;
}
public void setBuy(boolean buyOrder) {
   _buyOrder = buyOrder;
}
public int getNumShares( ) {
   return _shares;
}
public void setNumShares(int shares) {
   _shares = shares;
}
}
```

We can add a new method to the urn:BasicTradingService service called
executeStockTrade( ), which takes a stock trade as a parameter. The return value
from this method is a string that describes the order. Here's the modified
BasicTradingService class. We can take advantage of the executeTrade( ) method
that already exists in this class. In the new method, executeStockTrade( ), we build
an Object array from the three properties of the trade parameter, and we pass that
array to the executeTrade( ) method.

```
package javasoap.book.ch5;
public class BasicTradingService {

    public BasicTradingService( ) {
    }
    public String executeStockTrade(StockTrade_ServerSide trade) {
        Object[] params = new Object[3];
        params[0] = trade.getSymbol( );
        params[1] = new Integer(trade.getNumShares( ));
        params[2] = new Boolean(trade.isBuy( ));
        return executeTrade(params);
    }
    public String[] getMostActive( ) {

        // get the most actively traded stocks
        String[] actives = { "ABC", "DEF", "GHI", "JKL" };
        return actives;
    }
    public int getTotalVolume(String[] stocks) {
```

```
        // get the volumes for each stock from some
        // data feed and return the total

        int total = 345000;
        return total;
    }
    public String executeTrade(Object[] params) {
        String result;
        try {
            String stock = (String)params[0];
            Integer numShares = (Integer)params[1];
            Boolean buy = (Boolean)params[2];
            String orderType = "Buy";
            if (false == buy.booleanValue()) {
                orderType = "Sell";
            }
            result = (orderType + " " + numShares + " of " + stock);
        }
        catch (ClassCastException e) {
            result = "Bad Parameter Type Encountered";
        }
        return result;
    }
}
```

To deploy the service, we need to map the custom type to the Java class that implements that type. We need to give the custom type a name and qualify it with an appropriate namespace. This is not unlike the process we'd use to declare a service. This mapping takes place in the deployment descriptor, within the isd:mappings section. Here's the deployment descriptor we'll use to deploy the service in Apache SOAP:

```
<isd:service
    xmlns:isd="http://xml.apache.org/xml-soap/deployment"
    id="urn:BasicTradingService">
  <isd:provider
    type="java"
    scope="Application"
    methods="getTotalVolume getMostActive executeTrade executeStockTrade">
    <isd:java
        class="javasoap.book.ch5.BasicTradingService"
        static="false"/>
  </isd:provider>

  <isd:faultListener>org.apache.soap.server.DOMFaultListener
  </isd:faultListener>
  <isd:mappings>
    <isd:map
        encodingStyle="http://schemas.xmlsoap.org/soap/encoding/"
        xmlns:x="urn:BasicTradingService" qname="x:StockTrade"
        javaType="javasoap.book.ch5.StockTrade_ServerSide"
        java2XMLClassName="org.apache.soap.encoding.soapenc.BeanSerializer"
        xml2JavaClassName="org.apache.soap.encoding.soapenc.BeanSerializer"/>
  </isd:mappings>
</isd:service>
```

This is important, so let's summarize the mapping before we go any further. The mapping of a custom type to a Java class is associated with an encoding style as well as a fully qualified type name. A Java class that implements the custom type is specified, as well as the utility classes used to perform serialization and deserialization. Now let's look at the details of the example.

Most of the deployment descriptor should look familiar; it's similar to the ones shown in Chapter 4. The difference is that we now have an entry in the isd:mappings section. There is one entry, isd:map, that describes the mapping of the stock trade type to the StockTrade_ServerSide class. The isd:map element has no data; all the information is supplied as attributes. The first attribute, encodingStyle, specifies the encoding style associated with the serialization of the type. Next, a namespace identifier, x, is assigned the value urn:BasicTradingService. I'm using the name of the service as the namespace qualifier for the custom type; however, you don't have to do this, and in fact may not want to in many instances. For example, if you have custom types that are used by multiple services, or if you're using custom types whose definitions are specified by a third party, then you'd certainly want to qualify the custom type using the appropriate namespace. The next attribute, qname, specifies the fully qualified name of the type being mapped. The value assigned is x:StockTrade, which is the same StockTrade namespace qualified using the service name. The javaType attribute specifies the server-local Java class used to implement the type; on the server side we're using javasoap.book.ch5.StockTrade_ServerSide. The last two attributes, java2XMLClassName and xml2JavaClassName, tell Apache SOAP which local Java classes to use to perform the serialization and deserialization, respectively. Apache SOAP comes with a custom serializer/deserializer class that can convert between custom XML types and Java classes that conform to the JavaBeans property accessor pattern. It can handle both serialization and deserialization, which is why we use it for both attributes. In the next chapter we'll look at creating custom type serializers.

Now that we have a deployment descriptor, we can go ahead and redeploy the urn:BasicTradingService. Once we do that, our service is ready to accept executeStockTrade method invocations. However, we need to do some setup work in the client application as well. Let's take a look at the client application:

```
package javasoap.book.ch5;
import java.net.*;
import java.util.*;
import org.apache.soap.*;
import org.apache.soap.rpc.*;
import org.apache.soap.encoding.*;
import org.apache.soap.encoding.soapenc.*;
import org.apache.soap.util.xml.*;
public class StockTradeClient
{
  public static void main(String[] args) throws Exception
  {
    URL url = new
      URL("http://georgetown:8080/soap/servlet/rpcrouter");
```

```
            Call call = new Call();
            SOAPMappingRegistry smr = new SOAPMappingRegistry();
            call.setSOAPMappingRegistry(smr);
            call.setEncodingStyleURI(Constants.NS_URI_SOAP_ENC);
            call.setTargetObjectURI("urn:BasicTradingService");
            call.setMethodName("executeStockTrade");
            BeanSerializer beanSer = new BeanSerializer();
            // Map the Stock Trade type
            smr.mapTypes(Constants.NS_URI_SOAP_ENC,
                new QName("urn:BasicTradingService", "StockTrade"),
                StockTrade_ClientSide.class, beanSer, beanSer);
            // create an instance of the stock trade
            StockTrade_ClientSide trade =
                    new StockTrade_ClientSide("XYZ", false, 350);
            Vector params = new Vector();
            params.addElement(new Parameter("trade",
                                    StockTrade_ClientSide.class, trade, null));
            call.setParams(params);
            Response resp;
            try {
              resp = call.invoke(url, "");
              Parameter ret = resp.getReturnValue();
              Object desc = ret.getValue();
              System.out.println("Trade Description: " + desc);
            }
            catch (SOAPException e) {
              System.err.println("Caught SOAPException (" +
                                    e.getFaultCode() + "): " +
                                    e.getMessage());
            }
        }
    }
}
```

After the Call object is created, we create an instance of org.apache.soap.encoding.
SOAPMappingRegistry called smr. This class holds the mappings of custom types to
Java classes, and gets passed to the Call object using the setSOAPMappingRegistry()
method of our Call object. We haven't had to do this in previous examples because
the Call object creates a mapping registry for itself if one isn't passed to it. The
SOAPMappingRegistry() contains all of the predefined mappings, such as those we
took advantage of for arrays. We'll add our mapping to it shortly.

Next we call the call.setEncodingStyleURI() method. This method specifies the
overall encoding style to be used for the custom type parameters. The constant
NS_URI_SOAP_ENC, from the org.apache.soap.Constants class, represents the http://
schemas.xmlsoap.org/soap/encoding/ namespace that we've been using thus far. This
should be the same encoding style namespace that we specified in the deployment
descriptor for the StockTrade type. The setTargetObjectURI() and setMethodName()
methods are used in the same way as in previous examples. The next step is to create
an instance of org.apache.soap.encoding.soapenc.BeanSerializer; we can use this
standard serializer because our custom type conforms to the JavaBeans property accessor pattern. Now we can establish the mapping by calling smr.mapTypes(). The first

parameter is `Constants.NS_URI_SOAP_ENC`, which specifies that the encoding style used for this mapping is the standard SOAP encoding. You may be wondering why we need to do this if we've already specified the encoding style for the entire call earlier. The reason is simple: this parameter gives you the opportunity to override the encoding style used for this particular mapping. However, if you use `null` as the parameter value, you'll end up with a mapping that attempts to use the `null` namespace for the encoding style, which is not correct. When we look at the SOAP envelope for this message, you'll see that since the encoding style is the same as that of the overall call, the `encodingStyle` attribute will not be repeated for this serialized parameter. If the encoding style were not the same as that of the `Call`, it would appear as an attribute of the parameter.

The next parameter of `smr.mapTypes()` is an instance of `org.apache.soap.util.xml.Qname`, which represents a fully qualified name (one that includes a namespace qualifier followed by a name). We use `urn:BasicTradingService` as the namespace and `StockTrade` as the name. The third parameter is `StockTrade_ClientSide.class`, the Java class that implements the custom type. The next two parameters are instances of the serializer and deserializer that will be used for this type. We use the `beanSer` object that we created earlier for both, as the `org.apache.soap.encoding.soapenc.BeanSerializer` class implements both serialization and deserialization.

The rest is pretty simple. We create an instance of `StockTrade_ClientSide`, taking advantage of the parameterized constructor to set its property values. Then we set up a `Vector` of parameters, just as we've done in earlier examples. If you run this example, you should see the following output:

```
Trade Description: Sell 350 of XYZ
```

Let's take a look at the SOAP envelope that was transmitted. The relevant part of the envelope begins with the trade element, representing the custom type parameter passed to the executeStockTrade service method. The value assigned to `xsi:type` is `ns1:StockTrade`. The `ns1` namespace identifier is declared to be `urn:BasicTradingService` in the parent executeStockTrade element. And `StockTrade` is the name we specified for our custom type. There are three child elements of the trade element, each one corresponding to the properties of the `StockTrade` custom type. The name of each element corresponds exactly to the property name. This is crucial, as Apache SOAP is going to use Java reflection to find the set methods of the associated Java class. Therefore, the names in the envelope must match the names used by the class. Each one of these property elements is explicitly typed, and those types have to coincide with the types of the corresponding properties as well.

```
<SOAP-ENV:Envelope
  xmlns:SOAP-ENV="http://schemas.xmlsoap.org/soap/envelope/"
  xmlns:xsi="http://www.w3.org/2001/XMLSchema-instance"
  xmlns:xsd="http://www.w3.org/2001/XMLSchema">
  <SOAP-ENV:Body>
    <ns1:executeStockTrade xmlns:ns1="urn:BasicTradingService"
```

```
    SOAP-ENV:encodingStyle="http://schemas.xmlsoap.org/soap/encoding/">
      <trade xsi:type="ns1:StockTrade">
        <numShares xsi:type="xsd:int">350</numShares>
        <buy xsi:type="xsd:boolean">false</buy>
        <symbol xsi:type="xsd:string">XYZ</symbol>
      </trade>
    </ns1:executeStockTrade>
  </SOAP-ENV:Body>
</SOAP-ENV:Envelope>
```

Now let's see how custom types are handled in GLUE, using the BasicTradingService class without modification. We need to add the executeStockTrade( ) method to the IBasicTradingService interface. We can deploy the service as we did before. Here's the new version of IBasicTradingService:

```
package javasoap.book.ch5;
public interface IBasicTradingService {
   int getTotalVolume(String[] symbols);
   String executeTrade(Object[] params);
   String[] getMostActive( );
   String executeStockTrade(StockTrade_ClientSide trade);
}
```

Writing applications that access services has been easy using the GLUE API because we haven't dealt directly with the SOAP constructs. We should be able to follow that same pattern here, but there's a problem. The executeStockTrade( ) method of the IBasicTradingInterface interface says that the parameter is an instance of StockTrade_ClientSide. But the executeStockTrade method of the BasicTradingService class that implements the service uses a parameter of StockTrade_ServerSide. So there's a mismatch, albeit by design. By default, GLUE looks for the same class on the client and server sides. If we had used the StockTrade_ServerSide class in our client application instead of the StockTrade_ClientSide class, all would work perfectly. We're not going to do that, so just take my word for it that it works (or better yet, try it for yourself). We'll have to take another approach.

Whenever I develop distributed systems, I'm happy to share Java interfaces between both client and server code bases. However, I don't like to share Java classes, especially if those classes contain code that is specific to either the client or the server. In this example, we could rework the design of our stock trade classes to come up with something that contains the relevant data without any of the functionality of either the client or the server. We would want both the client and the server to use the class from the same package, so as the implementer of the basic trading web service, we'd have to distribute the package containing such a class to the developers' client applications. That would work, and it's not uncommon in practice. Getting back to the notion of sharing Java interfaces instead of classes, we could create an interface for the trade data, and have both the server and client classes implement that interface. That's a nice clean way to share between server and client code bases without sharing any actual executable code. Again, this interface would reside in a package available to both server and client systems. This mechanism is expected to be supported in a future version of GLUE (which might already be available by the time you read this).

GLUE does support another mechanism for making this stuff work. This mechanism doesn't require you to modify the server side, and the work involved on the client side is trivial. We're going to create a new package for this client example, because our work will create some files that have the same names as those we created earlier. The new package prevents us from overwriting files when running both client and server on the same machine. So be aware that this example is part of a new package called javasoap.book.ch5.client, and the files we'll be developing need to be in the corresponding directory for that package.

I've purposely avoided discussion of WSDL so far, even though GLUE is based entirely on WSDL. However, the first step in this process makes use of GLUE's wsdl2java utility, which generates Java code based on a WSDL file. So where does the WSDL come from? The GLUE server generates it automatically. The client-side applications based on the GLUE API have been taking advantage of this all along. wsdl2java generates the Java interface for binding to the service, a helper class, a Java data structure class that represents the data fields of the custom type we're working with, and a map file. The map file is essentially a schema definition for the custom type; it tells GLUE how to map the fields of the Java data structure class to the fields of the custom type. GLUE uses a number of mechanisms for handling custom type mapping; in this case, the map file defines the mapping explicitly, rather than basing the mapping on Java reflection.

So let's go ahead and generate the files for the client application. Enter the following command, making sure you are in the directory for the javasoap.book.ch5.client package:

```
wsdl2java http://georgetown:8004/glue/urn:BasicTradingService.wsdl
    -p javasoap.book.ch5.client
```

The parameter to the wsdl2java utility is the full URL of the service WSDL, just like we've been using in the bind( ) methods in previous examples. The -p option tells the utility the name of the local package for which code should be generated: javasoap.book.ch5.client. The output from wsdl2java consists of four files. The first one is *IBasicTradingService.java*, which contains the Java interface for binding to the service. We've been writing this one by hand up until now; let's take a look at the one generated by wsdl2java:

```
// generated by GLUE
package javasoap.book.ch5.client;
public interface IBasicTradingService
  {
  String executeStockTrade( StockTrade_ServerSide arg0 );
  String[] getMostActive();
  int getTotalVolume( String[] arg0 );
  String executeTrade( Object[] arg0 );
  }
```

The only differences between this interface definition and the one we wrote our-selves are a different package declaration, the naming of the method parameters, and the executeStockTrade taking a parameter of StockTrade_ServerSide instead of StockTrade_ClientSide. Remember that the earlier version of IBasicTradingService won't work for us because GLUE defaults to using the same class on both client and server. At first glance, the use of the StockTrade_ServerSide class here seems to vio-late our desire to completely decouple the server code from the client code. But remember that the package declaration is javasoap.book.ch5.client, so this Java interface is not referencing the same StockTrade_ServerSide class being used by our server, which belongs to a different package. Let's take a look at the StockTrade_ ServerSide class generated by wsdl2java and placed in the file named *StockTrade_ ServerSide.java*:

```
// generated by GLUE
package javasoap.book.ch5.client;
public class StockTrade_ServerSide
   {
   public int _shares;
   public boolean _buyOrder;
   public String _stock;
   }
```

This is only a shadow of the corresponding class in the javasoap.book.ch5 package that the server side uses. It does, however, properly reflect the data values. We'll be creating an instance of this class in our client application to pass to the service, as this is the type expected by the executeStockTrade() method of the IBasicTradingService interface that was generated.

The third file generated by wsdl2java is *BasicTradingService.map*, which contains the mapping schema mentioned earlier. You can take a look at the contents of the map-ping file on your own; suffice it to say that it contains XML entries that define field mappings between the client-side and server-side Java. The last generated file is *BasicTradingServiceHelper.java*, which contains a helper class for performing the bind() operation. I don't use that helper class, so we'll ignore it here.

It's taken far longer to describe the process than it takes to perform it. Now let's move on to writing the client application:

```
package javasoap.book.ch5.client;
import electric.registry.RegistryException;
import electric.registry.Registry;
import electric.xml.io.Mappings;
public class StockTradeClient2 {
   public static void main(String[] args) throws Exception
   {
      try {
        Mappings.readMappings("BasicTradingService.map");
        IBasicTradingService srv =
          (IBasicTradingService)Registry.bind(
          "http://georgetown:8004/glue/urn:BasicTradingService.wsdl",
```

```
            IBasicTradingService.class);
        StockTrade_ServerSide trade =
                      new StockTrade_ServerSide( );
        trade._stock = "MINDSTRM";
        trade._buyOrder = true;
        trade._shares = 500;
        String desc = srv.executeStockTrade(trade);
        System.out.println("Trade Description is: " + desc);
    }
    catch (RegistryException e)
    {
        System.out.println(e);
    }
  }
}
```

The critical step is to read the mappings before you perform the bind operation. This is done by calling the readMappings( ) method of the electric.xml.io.Mappings class provided as part of GLUE. After the bind( ) call, we simply create an instance of StockTrade_ServerSide, set its field values, and call the executeStockTrade method. The output from running this application should be:

```
Trade Description is: Buy 500 of MINDSTRM
```

Now let's look at the SOAP envelope generated by this application. As we've come to expect, the executeStockTrade element is namespace-qualified using the name of the service. The child element arg0 is a reference to a separately serialized element named id0, just as GLUE generated for an array parameter. This example shows us why GLUE has been generating the ns2 namespace identifier that seems to reference the package where the implementing server-side class resides. Here that namespace is used to qualify the value of the xsi:type attribute, with a value corresponding to the name of the implementing class StockTrade_ServerSide. The child elements of the id0 element contain the data fields for the custom type.

```
<soap:Envelope
  xmlns:xsi='http://www.w3.org/2001/XMLSchema-instance'
  xmlns:xsd='http://www.w3.org/2001/XMLSchema'
  xmlns:soap='http://schemas.xmlsoap.org/soap/envelope/'
  xmlns:soapenc='http://schemas.xmlsoap.org/soap/encoding/'
  soap:encodingStyle='http://schemas.xmlsoap.org/soap/encoding/'>
    <soap:Body>
      <n:executeStockTrade xmlns:n='urn:BasicTradingService'>
        <arg0 href='#id0'/>
      </n:executeStockTrade>
      <id0 id='id0' soapenc:root='0'
        xmlns:ns2='http://www.themindelectric.com/package/javasoap.book.ch5/'
        xsi:type='ns2:StockTrade_ServerSide'>
        <_shares xsi:type='xsd:int'>500</_shares>
        <_buyOrder xsi:type='xsd:boolean'>true</_buyOrder>
        <_stock xsi:type='xsd:string'>MINDSTRM</_stock>
      </id0>
    </soap:Body>
</soap:Envelope>
```

Returning Custom Types

It's equally useful (and equally common) to return custom types from service method calls. We can enhance our trading service by offering a method that takes a single stock symbol as a parameter and returns its high and low trading prices for the day. The classes HighLow_ServerSide and HighLow_ClientSide represent the high/low prices on the server and client, respectively.

```java
package javasoap.book.ch5;
public class HighLow_ServerSide {
    public float _high;
    public float _low;
    public HighLow_ServerSide( ) {
    }
    public HighLow_ServerSide (float high, float low) {
        setHigh(high);
        setLow(low);
    }
    public float getHigh( ) {
        return _high;
    }
    public void setHigh(float high) {
        _high = high;
    }
    public float getLow( ) {
        return _low;
    }
    public void setLow(float low) {
        _low = low;
    }
}

package javasoap.book.ch5;
public class HighLow_ClientSide {
    public float _high;
    public float _low;
    public String toString( ) {
        return "High: " + _high +
          " Low: " + _low;
    }
    public HighLow_ClientSide( ) {
    }
    public float getHigh( ) {
        return _high;
    }
    public void setHigh(float high) {
        _high = high;
    }
    public float getLow( ) {
        return _low;
    }
    public void setLow(float low) {
```

```
    _low = low;
    }
}
```

The server-side class includes a parameterized constructor as a convenience for creating the return value; the client-side class includes a toString( ) method to make it easy for our client application to display the contents of the object after it's returned from the server. Let's add a new method to the BasicTradingService class called getHighLow( ). That method takes a single string parameter for the stock symbol and returns an instance of HighLow_ServerSide. Here's the class with its new method, with the unchanged code omitted:

```
package javasoap.book.ch5;
public class BasicTradingService {
    public BasicTradingService( ) {
    }
    . . .

    . . .
    public HighLow_ServerSide getHighLow(String stock) {

        // retrieve the high and low for the specified stock
        return new HighLow_ServerSide((float)110.375,
                    (float)109.5);
    }
}
```

In order to make this new method available in Apache SOAP, we'll need to redeploy the service using a modified deployment descriptor. We need to add getHighLow to the list of methods, and add an entry in the mappings section for the high/low object. The second mapping entry defines the HighLow custom type, namespace-qualified using the service name urn:BasicTradingService. Here is the modified deployment descriptor:

```
<isd:service
    xmlns:isd="http://xml.apache.org/xml-soap/deployment"
    id="urn:BasicTradingService">
  <isd:provider
    type="java"
    scope="Application"
    methods="getTotalVolume getMostActive executeTrade executeStockTrade
            getHighLow">
    <isd:java
        class="javasoap.book.ch5.BasicTradingService"
        static="false"/>
  </isd:provider>

  <isd:faultListener>org.apache.soap.server.DOMFaultListener
  </isd:faultListener>
  <isd:mappings>
    <isd:map
        encodingStyle="http://schemas.xmlsoap.org/soap/encoding/"
        xmlns:x="urn:BasicTradingService" qname="x:StockTrade"
```

```
        javaType="javasoap.book.ch5.StockTradeServer"
        java2XMLClassName="org.apache.soap.encoding.soapenc.BeanSerializer"
        xml2JavaClassName="org.apache.soap.encoding.soapenc.BeanSerializer"/>
    <isd:map
        encodingStyle="http://schemas.xmlsoap.org/soap/encoding/"
        xmlns:x="urn:BasicTradingService" qname="x:HighLow"
        javaType="javasoap.book.ch5.HighLow_ServerSide"
        java2XMLClassName="org.apache.soap.encoding.soapenc.BeanSerializer"
        xml2JavaClassName="org.apache.soap.encoding.soapenc.BeanSerializer"/>
  </isd:mappings>
</isd:service>
```

Now we can create a client application that invokes the getHighLow service method
and receives a high/low object in return. For the Apache SOAP client, we'll use the
HighLow_ClientSide class to represent the return value. Here's the new application:

```
package javasoap.book.ch5;
import java.net.*;
import java.util.*;
import org.apache.soap.*;
import org.apache.soap.rpc.*;
import org.apache.soap.encoding.*;
import org.apache.soap.encoding.soapenc.*;
import org.apache.soap.util.xml.*;
public class HighLowClient
{
  public static void main(String[] args) throws Exception
  {
    URL url = new
        URL("http://georgetown:8080/soap/servlet/rpcrouter");
    Call call = new Call();
    SOAPMappingRegistry smr = new SOAPMappingRegistry();
    call.setTargetObjectURI("urn:BasicTradingService");
    call.setMethodName("getHighLow");
    call.setEncodingStyleURI(Constants.NS_URI_SOAP_ENC);
    call.setSOAPMappingRegistry(smr);
    BeanSerializer beanSer = new BeanSerializer();
    // Map the High/Low type
    smr.mapTypes(Constants.NS_URI_SOAP_ENC,
            new QName("urn:BasicTradingService", "HighLow"),
            HighLow_ClientSide.class, beanSer, beanSer);
    String stock = "XYZ";
    Vector params = new Vector();
    params.addElement(new Parameter("stock",
                        String.class, stock, null));
    call.setParams(params);
    Response resp;
    try {
      resp = call.invoke(url, "");
      Parameter ret = resp.getReturnValue();
      HighLow_ClientSide hilo =
            (HighLow_ClientSide)ret.getValue();
      System.out.println(hilo);
    }
```

```
            catch (SOAPException e) {
              System.err.println("Caught SOAPException (" +
                                 e.getFaultCode( ) + "): " +
                                 e.getMessage( ));
            }
          }
        }
```

smr.MapTypes( ) maps the HighLow custom type to the HighLow_ClientSide Java class. Just as before, we can use Apache's BeanSerializer to convert between XML and Java, since our class conforms to the JavaBeans property accessor pattern. We set up a single String parameter called stock to pass to the getHighLow method (although we don't actually make use of it in the server code). After the method is invoked, we cast the return value of resp.getReturnValue( ) to an instance of HighLow_ClientSide. Then we pass the return parameter variable, ret, to the System.out.println( ) method for display. This is all we need, since we implemented the toString( ) method in our HighLow_ClientSide class. When you run this example, you'll get the following output:

```
High: 110.375 Low: 109.5
```

Here's the SOAP envelope returned from this method invocation. The return element is typed as a HighLow that is namespace-qualified by the urnBasicTradingService namespace. The properties, which are child elements of the return element, are typed as floats and appear along with their corresponding values.

```
<SOAP-ENV:Envelope
   xmlns:SOAP-ENV="http://schemas.xmlsoap.org/soap/envelope/"
   xmlns:xsi="http://www.w3.org/2001/XMLSchema-instance"
   xmlns:xsd="http://www.w3.org/2001/XMLSchema">
 <SOAP-ENV:Body>
    <ns1:getHighLowResponse
      xmlns:ns1="urn:BasicTradingService"
      SOAP-ENV:encodingStyle="http://schemas.xmlsoap.org/soap/encoding/">
      <return xsi:type="ns1:HighLow">
         <low xsi:type="xsd:float">109.5</low>
         <high xsi:type="xsd:float">110.375</high>
      </return>
    </ns1:getHighLowResponse>
 </SOAP-ENV:Body>
</SOAP-ENV:Envelope>
```

To return a HighLow using GLUE, we'll take the same steps we did for passing custom types. Again we'll separate our client-side work into another package, javasoap. book.ch5.client. Just restart the application of BasicTradingApp to get the service deployed. Now run the wsdl2java utility from the directory corresponding to the javasoap.book.ch5.client package:

```
wsdl2java http://georgetown:8004/glue/urn:BasicTradingService.wsdl
    -p javasoap.book.ch5.client
```

The following code is the new IBasicTradingService interface generated by wsdl2java. The getHighLow() method returns an instance of HighLow_ServerSide; remember that this class is the new one generated by GLUE as part of the javasoap. book.ch5.client package, not the one being used by our server class, BasicTradingApp.

```
// generated by GLUE
package javasoap.book.ch5.client;
public interface IBasicTradingService
    {
    HighLow_ServerSide getHighLow( String arg0 );
    String executeStockTrade( StockTradeServer arg0 );
    String[] getMostActive();
    int getTotalVolume( String[] arg0 );
    String executeTrade( Object[] arg0 );
    }
```

The next class, HighLow_ServerSide, is simply a Java data structure reflecting the data fields that will be mapped to the HighLow custom type. I added the toString() method by hand to make it simpler to display the results.

```
package javasoap.book.ch5.client;
public class HighLow_ServerSide {
    public float _high;
    public float _low;
    public String toString() {
        return "High: " + _high +
            " Low: " + _low;
    }
}
```

Now let's create a client application using GLUE that invokes the getHighLow service method and displays the contents of the resulting return value. There's not much to this, really; we simply read the map file, perform the bind, and then call the getHighLow method on the bound interface. The resulting instance of javasoap.book. ch5.client.HighLow_ServerSide is passed to System.out.println() for display. Just as in the Apache SOAP example, the toString() method of the class handles the creation of the display string.

```
package javasoap.book.ch5.client;
import electric.registry.RegistryException;
import electric.registry.Registry;
import electric.xml.io.Mappings;
public class HighLowClient2 {
    public static void main(String[] args) throws Exception
    {
        try {
            Mappings.readMappings("BasicTradingService.map");
            IBasicTradingService srv = (IBasicTradingService)Registry.bind(
                "http://georgetown:8004/glue/urn:BasicTradingService.wsdl",
                IBasicTradingService.class);
            HighLow_ServerSide hilo = srv.getHighLow("ANY");
```

```
            System.out.println(hilo);
        }
        catch (RegistryException e)
        {
            System.out.println(e);
        }
    }
}
```

Here's the SOAP envelope returned from the server. You should be able to follow this by now. GLUE uses a reference to a separately serialized instance of the custom type, just as it did when returning an array.

```
<soap:Envelope
 xmlns:xsi='http://www.w3.org/2001/XMLSchema-instance'
 xmlns:xsd='http://www.w3.org/2001/XMLSchema'
 xmlns:soap='http://schemas.xmlsoap.org/soap/envelope/'
 xmlns:soapenc='http://schemas.xmlsoap.org/soap/encoding/'
 soap:encodingStyle='http://schemas.xmlsoap.org/soap/encoding/'>
    <soap:Body>
        <n:getHighLowResponse xmlns:n='urn:BasicTradingService'>
          <Result href='#id0'/>
        </n:getHighLowResponse>
        <id0 id='id0' soapenc:root='0'
          xmlns:ns2='http://www.themindelectric.com/package/javasoap.book.ch5/'
          xsi:type='ns2:HighLow_ServerSide'>
          <_high xsi:type='xsd:float'>110.375</_high>
          <_low xsi:type='xsd:float'>109.5</_low>
        </id0>
    </soap:Body>
</soap:Envelope>
```

In this chapter, we've taken an in-depth look at the use of arrays and custom data types, and discussed how these structures are supported by Apache SOAP and GLUE. There are other useful types that you may find support for in these, or other, SOAP implementations. These types might include Java `Vector` and `Hashtable` classes, Java collections, and a variety of other commonly used Java classes.

We've seen that Apache SOAP and GLUE approach complex types in different ways, and both do a good job of supporting them. However, there may be times when you need to work with a custom type that either can't, or shouldn't, be serialized in the way provided by your SOAP implementation. This situation may arise because there simply is no support for a particular type of data, as is the case with multidimensional or sparse arrays, or perhaps for some other reason related to your application. We'll tackle this issue in the next chapter.

CHAPTER 6

Custom Serialization

You may find that your web services and client applications work perfectly well using the set of data types supported by your SOAP implementation. After all, the technologies we're looking at provide a great deal of flexibility with their support for arrays and custom types. On the other hand, somewhere along the line you may need to serialize something that simply isn't possible using the techniques we've covered up to this point. Maybe you want to serialize the data for a Java class in a way that is more consistent with your existing applications, even if the encoding is not industry standard. Or maybe you want to add support for constructs that are described in the SOAP specification but are not supported in the available SOAP implementations.

The implementation of SOAP that you use may force you to write custom serializers for certain types of objects. For example, Apache provides the Bean serializer; it could provide other special case serializers, and it's not required to provide that one. So the conditions under which you need to supply a custom serializer are implementation dependent.

It's also important to consider the usefulness of the data being serialized. Many of Java's rules about what implements the Serializable interface make sense here as well. For example, SOAP or not, serializing an I/O stream is not likely a sensible thing to do. This is true for any kind of distributed system. You have to understand the semantics of the data before blindly sending it to another party.

We'll tackle a few examples of custom serialization in this chapter, exploring the techniques and APIs available in both Apache SOAP and GLUE. Unlike in previous chapters, we won't repeat the examples using both technologies. By now, you should be sufficiently familiar with both Apache SOAP and GLUE to have an idea of how to work with each.

Custom Type Encoding

Let's start off by working with a custom data type that uses a nonstandard serialization. We'll develop this example using Apache SOAP. Imagine that we're developing a web service that acts as a pass-thru proxy to a proprietary stock market data feed. We want to send the data to the service already serialized in the form used by the feed. Yep, another contrived example! But by the time we finish it, I bet you'll have thought of a few uses for this technique. The service is designed to allow client applications to pass agreed-upon formats to the downstream data feed service without having to modify the web service itself. So the serialized data format is not known to the web service; it's understood only by the client application and the data feed. Figure 6-1 shows what this architecture might look like. Both of the client applications use the same service and invoke the same methods. However, they may or may not be using the same serialization format for the data to be sent to the data feed.

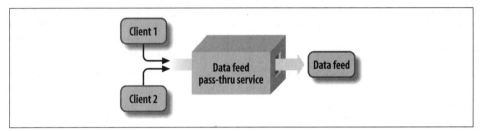

Figure 6-1. A pass-thru service

Let's say that the default data format for the feed is a linear self-describing format. This format is an arbitrary-length string that contains a variable number of named data fields and their string values. The format can accept from 1 to 9 fields. The first character of the message contains the number of fields, and can be any ASCII character between 1 and 9. Each field consists of the name of the field followed by a colon, then the field value, followed by another colon. Here's an example of a message that contains two fields named SYMBOL and PRICE, with corresponding values of ZZ and 110.5:

```
2SYMBOL:ZZ:PRICE:110.5:
```

This is the format we want to use to serialize messages. But first, let's create a new service called urn:DataFeedService that contains a method called sendMessage. This method takes a single message parameter and returns a message parameter. So before we begin to define the Java class for the service, we need to define the Java class for the message. The DataFeedMessage class represents a message to be used for this service. It contains a list of name/value pairs for keeping track of the field names and their data values.

```
package javasoap.book.ch6;
import java.util.*;
public class DataFeedMessage {
```

```java
Hashtable _fields = new Hashtable();
public DataFeedMessage() {
}
public void addField(String name, String value) {
    _fields.put(name, value);
}
public Enumeration getFieldNames() {
    return _fields.keys();
}
public String getFieldValue(String name) {
    return (String)_fields.get(name);
}
public String toString() {
    String cnt = String.valueOf(_fields.size());
    StringBuffer msg = new StringBuffer();
    msg.append(cnt);
    msg.append(":");
    for (Enumeration e =_fields.keys(); e.hasMoreElements();) {
        String name = (String)e.nextElement();
        String value = (String)_fields.get(name);
        String section = name + ":" + value + ":";
        msg.append(section);
    }
    return msg.toString();
}
public void parseFormattedMessage(String msg) {
    _fields.clear();
    StringTokenizer st = new StringTokenizer(msg, ":");
    String token = st.nextToken();
    int cnt = new Integer(token).intValue();
    for (int i = 0; i < cnt; i++) {
        String name = st.nextToken();
        String value = st.nextToken();
        addField(name, value);
    }
}
}
```

The fields are stored in the _fields variable, which is an instance of java.util. Hashtable. The addField() method allows you to add a field by providing its name and value as parameters, which are then added to the hash table using the name as the key. The getFieldNames() and getFieldValue() methods provide access to the hash table element names and values without exposing the fact that the class uses a java.util.Hashtable internally. The last two methods are the most interesting. The toString() method returns a string containing all of the fields and their data values in the message format we defined earlier. The parseFormattedMessage() method takes a string parameter in the described format and populates the internal hash table with the contents. These two methods will be helpful when we want to serialize and deserialize our custom message type.

Now we can create the Java class for this new service. We'll call the class DataFeedService, and we'll include a method called sendMessage() that takes an instance of DataFeedMessage as its parameter. This method returns an instance of DataFeedMessage as well. Here is the DataFeedService class:

```
package javasoap.book.ch6;
public class DataFeedService {
    public DataFeedService() {
    }
    public DataFeedMessage sendMessage(DataFeedMessage msg) {
        // we could pull the formatted message here
        // by calling msg.toString();
        String stock = msg.getFieldValue("SYMBOL");
        String request = msg.getFieldValue("REQUEST");
        DataFeedMessage res = new DataFeedMessage();
        res.addField("SYMBOL", stock);
        if (request.equals("PRICE"))
            res.addField("PRICE", "123.5");
        return res;
    }
}
```

All we're doing in the example is grabbing the stock symbol from the data feed message, using it as the stock symbol for the return value, and adding a price field to the return value as if the field named REQUEST has a value of PRICE. So the sendMessage() method uses some of the data from the input parameter to create a return value of type DataFeedMessage.

Because this class doesn't obey the JavaBeans method naming patterns, we can't use the BeanSerializer provided by Apache SOAP to serialize and deserialize instances of the data feed message we've created. So we'll create a serializer of our own. A custom Java class for serializing objects must implement the org.apache.soap.util.xml. Serializer interface; to implement this interface, we must write a marshall() method. Similarly, a Java class for deserializing objects must implement the org. apache.soap.util.xml.Deserializer interface and provide the unmarshall() method. It's perfectly reasonable to create one class that handles both functions, so we'll take that approach. Let's call our custom serializer class DataFeedMessageSerializer.

```
package javasoap.book.ch6;
import org.apache.soap.encoding.soapenc.*;
import org.apache.soap.util.xml.*;
import org.apache.soap.util.*;
import org.apache.soap.rpc.SOAPContext;
import org.w3c.dom.*;
import java.io.*;
import java.util.*;
public class DataFeedMessageSerializer
                implements Serializer, Deserializer {

    public DataFeedMessageSerializer() {
    }
    public void marshall(String inScopeEncStyle, Class javaType,
                Object src, Object context, Writer sink,
                NSStack nsStack, XMLJavaMappingRegistry xjmr,
```

```
                SOAPContext ctx)
        throws IllegalArgumentException, IOException  {

    if(!javaType.equals(DataFeedMessage.class)) {
      throw new IllegalArgumentException(
        "Can only serialize javasoap.book.ch6.DataFeedMessage instances");
    }

    nsStack.pushScope();

    if (src != null)
    {
      SoapEncUtils.generateStructureHeader(inScopeEncStyle,
                                           javaType, context,
                                           sink, nsStack, xjmr);
      DataFeedMessage msg = (DataFeedMessage)src;
      String data = msg.toString();
      sink.write(data);
      sink.write("</" + context + '>');
    }
    else
    {
      SoapEncUtils.generateNullStructure(inScopeEncStyle,
                                         javaType, context,
                                         sink, nsStack, xjmr);
    }
    nsStack.popScope();
  }
  public Bean unmarshall(String inScopeEncStyle, QName
               elementType, Node src,
               XMLJavaMappingRegistry xjmr, SOAPContext ctx)
        throws IllegalArgumentException {

    Element elem = (Element)src;
    String value = DOMUtils.getChildCharacterData(elem);

    DataFeedMessage msg = null;
    if(value!=null && !((value=value.trim()).equals(""))) {
       msg = new DataFeedMessage();
       msg.parseFormattedMessage(value);
    }
    return new Bean(DataFeedMessage.class, msg);
  }
}
```

Let's look first at the `marshall()` method, which serializes an instance of
`DataFeedMessage`. It first verifies that the `javaType` parameter value is `DataFeedMessage`.
`class`, because this custom serializer can't serialize an instance of any other object. If
the class is wrong, `marshall()` throws an `IllegalArgumentException` with an appropriate description. (We haven't discussed exceptions yet, so you may be wondering what
the result of throwing one would be. Hold that thought until Chapter 7, which delves
into that subject.) Next, we call `nsStack.pushScope()`. The `nsStack` variable that was

passed as a parameter represents the hierarchical namespace of the SOAP message being serialized. This object serves as a stack of namespace definitions. Each time the marshall( ) method of a serializer is called, we push the namespace scope. This technique allows us to make namespace declarations at our level of the hierarchy. Before returning from the marshall( ) method, we must be sure to pop the stack. If we don't, we run the risk of overriding the namespace declarations of the XML elements above us in the hierarchy.

Now that we've pushed the namespace scope, we make sure that the object that we're supposed to serialize isn't null. If src is null, we call the SoapEncUtils. generateNullStructure( ) method, which handles the creation of a null element for us. If src is not null (the more interesting case), we call SoapEncUtils. generateStructureHeader( ) as the first step in creating a SOAP message. This method creates the element tag, and writes any attributes and associated values that are needed. We don't have to handle any of that; our job is to deal with the serialization of the actual data, not the XML tag details. Well, that's almost the truth. We do some cleanup work at the end, as you'll see shortly.

Since we know that src is the right type, we cast it to DataFeedMessage and save a reference to it in the msg variable. All we have to do now is call the msg.toString( ) method, which returns the data of the data feed message in the required format. The properly formatted message is now stored in the data variable. The marshall( ) method takes a parameter called sink, which is an instance of java.io.Writer. This is where all of the serialization for the SOAP envelope takes place. At this point, sink is positioned at the point where the actual serialized data belongs. Calling the sink. write( ) method using data as the parameter writes the formatted data feed message to the sink. The last step is to write the terminating tag for this element, even though writing the element tag was handled for us. We'll need the name of the element to write its closing tag; that's available in the context object passed as one of the parameters to marshall( ). We call sink.write( ) one more time to close the element. This works because context implements the toString( ) method, which returns the name of the element being serialized. That's all there is to it. Pop the namespace stack by calling nsStack.popStack( ), and we're done.

Now let's look at the process of deserializing: turning the encoded data into an instance of a Java class. This process is handled by the unmarshall( ) method of the serializer. Deserialization requires the use of some XML processing APIs provided by Apache SOAP. We cast the src parameter into an instance of org.w3c.dom.Element, which is a class used to represent an XML element. Next, we want to get at the formatted data of the element. That's the data feed message in the format described at the start of this section. This is accomplished by passing the elem variable to the getChildCharacterData( ) method of the org.apache.soap.util.xml.DOMUtils class. The string value returned from that call, saved in value, contains the formatted data feed message. Of course, it's a good idea to make sure there is actually data in the message, which is why we check for a null or empty string first. If there is data, a new instance of DataFeedMessage is created and the data is passed to its parseFormattedMessage( ) method. At this point, we've successfully deserialized the data and used it to populate an instance of DataFeedMessage. The unmarshall( ) method needs to return an instance of org.apache.soap.util.Bean;* this class is used to associate a Java object with its Java class. You may be wondering why this is necessary when you can determine the class of an object by calling its getClass( ) method. However, calling getClass( ) is problematic if the object is implemented using a subclass of the mapped class, and it is impossible if the object is null. So the last step is creating an instance of org.apache.soap.util.Bean, using DataFeedMessage. class as the first constructor parameter and msg as the second.

We've now implemented the serialization and deserialization capabilities of our custom serializer. Now we can go ahead and deploy urn:DataFeedService. Deploying the service requires that we include an appropriate mapping entry in the deployment descriptor so that instances of our custom type are mapped to the correct Java class, and associated with the custom serializer we just created. Here's the deployment descriptor:

```
<isd:service
    xmlns:isd="http://xml.apache.org/xml-soap/deployment"
    id="urn:DataFeedService">
  <isd:provider
    type="java"
    scope="Application"
    methods="sendMessage">
    <isd:java
      class="javasoap.book.ch6.DataFeedService"
      static="false"/>
  </isd:provider>

  <isd:faultListener>org.apache.soap.server.DOMFaultListener
  </isd:faultListener>
  <isd:mappings>
    <isd:map
      encodingStyle="http://schemas.xmlsoap.org/soap/encoding/"
      xmlns:x="urn:DataFeedService" qname="x:DataFeedMessage"
      javaType="javasoap.book.ch6.DataFeedMessage"
        java2XMLClassName="javasoap.book.ch6.DataFeedMessageSerializer"
        xml2JavaClassName="javasoap.book.ch6.DataFeedMessageSerializer"/>
  </isd:mappings>
</isd:service>
```

The mapping section has an entry for DataFeedMessage, namespace-qualified using the name of the service itself. We assign the value javasoap.book.ch6. DataFeedMessageSerializer to both the java2XMLClassName and the xml2JavaClassName

---

* Don't be confused by the fact that this class is called a Bean. It's not specifically related to the BeanSerializer class we worked with in the previous chapter; it's just a name left over from some other project.

attributes, which tells the system about our custom serializer class. The service can now be deployed.

Here's a client application that accesses this service. The process is similar to the one we used in the last chapter: we map our custom types as beans and use the DataFeedMessageSerializer to serialize and deserialize the object.

```java
package javasoap.book.ch6;
import java.net.*;
import java.util.*;
import org.apache.soap.*;
import org.apache.soap.rpc.*;
import org.apache.soap.encoding.*;
import org.apache.soap.util.xml.*;
public class DataFeedClient {
    public static void main(String[] args)
        throws Exception {

        URL url =
          new URL(
            "http://georgetown:8080/soap/servlet/rpcrouter");

        Call call = new Call();

        SOAPMappingRegistry smr = new SOAPMappingRegistry();
        call.setTargetObjectURI("urn:DataFeedService");
        call.setMethodName("sendMessage");
        call.setEncodingStyleURI(Constants.NS_URI_SOAP_ENC);
        call.setSOAPMappingRegistry(smr);
        DataFeedMessageSerializer msgSer =
                    new DataFeedMessageSerializer();
        // Map the data feed message type
        smr.mapTypes(Constants.NS_URI_SOAP_ENC,
            new QName("urn:DataFeedService", "DataFeedMessage"),
            DataFeedMessage.class, msgSer, msgSer);
        DataFeedMessage msg = new DataFeedMessage();
        msg.addField("SYMBOL", "XYZ");
        msg.addField("REQUEST", "PRICE");
        Vector params = new Vector();
        params.addElement(new Parameter("msg",
                    DataFeedMessage.class, msg, null));
        call.setParams(params);

        try {
            Response resp = call.invoke(url, "");
            Parameter ret = resp.getReturnValue();
            Object value = ret.getValue();
            System.out.println(value);
        }
        catch (SOAPException e) {
            System.err.println("Caught SOAPException (" +
                        e.getFaultCode() + "): " +
                        e.getMessage());
```

```
            }
        }
    }
```

We create an instance of `DataFeedMessageSerializer` in the variable called `msgSer`. When we call `smr.mapTypes()` to map our custom type to the `DataFeedMessage` class, we pass `msgSer` as both the serializer and the deserializer. So when we invoke the `sendMessage` service method, the `DataFeedMessageSerializer` is used to serialize the data feed message, and also to deserialize the return value from the service method. An instance of `DataFeedMessage` is created, and fields are added named SYMBOL and REQUEST, with data values of XYZ and PRICE, respectively. Now we set up the service method parameters and invoke the method. The return value from the `sendMessage` service method is also a data feed message, so it is deserialized into an instance of `DataFeedMessage`. We don't bother to cast the return of `ret.getValue()`, because we can take advantage of the `toString()` method to display its contents. When you run this example you should get the following output:

```
2:SYMBOL:XYZ:PRICE:123.5:
```

This is the formatted data from the returned instance of `DataFeedMessage`; the server put the symbol that was passed to it into the return value, along with a price field with a value of 123.5. Let's take a look at the SOAP envelope that was sent to the server:

```
<SOAP-ENV:Envelope
    xmlns:SOAP-ENV="http://schemas.xmlsoap.org/soap/envelope/"
    xmlns:xsi="http://www.w3.org/2001/XMLSchema-instance"
    xmlns:xsd="http://www.w3.org/2001/XMLSchema">
    <SOAP-ENV:Body>
        <ns1:sendMessage
            xmlns:ns1="urn:DataFeedService"
            SOAP-ENV:encodingStyle=
                "http://schemas.xmlsoap.org/soap/encoding/">
            <msg
            xsi:type="ns1:DataFeedMessage">2:REQUEST:PRICE:SYMBOL:XYZ:
            </msg>
        </ns1:sendMessage>
    </SOAP-ENV:Body>
</SOAP-ENV:Envelope>
```

The `msg` element is typed as `DataFeedMessage`, namespace-qualified with `urn:DataFeedService`. You can see that the data is formatted according to our specification. Now let's look at the SOAP envelope returned by the service method, which also types the returned data as a `DataFeedMessage` using the `urn:DataFeedService` namespace. So we've been able to use our custom serialization classes to handle the marshalling and unmarshalling of our data feed message on both the server and the client.

```
<SOAP-ENV:Envelope
    xmlns:SOAP-ENV="http://schemas.xmlsoap.org/soap/envelope/"
    xmlns:xsi="http://www.w3.org/2001/XMLSchema-instance"
    xmlns:xsd="http://www.w3.org/2001/XMLSchema">
```

```
<SOAP-ENV:Body>
  <ns1:sendMessageResponse
    xmlns:ns1="urn:DataFeedService"
    SOAP-ENV:encodingStyle=
      "http://schemas.xmlsoap.org/soap/encoding/">
      <return
      xsi:type="ns1:DataFeedMessage">2:PRICE:123.5:SYMBOL:XYZ:
      </return>
  </ns1:sendMessageResponse>
  </SOAP-ENV:Body>
</SOAP-ENV:Envelope>
```

Serializing Sparse Arrays

We discussed sparse arrays back in Chapter 3. However, neither Apache SOAP nor GLUE supports them. So let's do it ourselves.

Writing a sparse array serializer from scratch could be a lot of work, so we start by grabbing the source code for org.apache.soap.encoding.soapenc.ArraySerializer from the Apache SOAP distribution. We'll modify the ArraySerializer code to create a new class called javasoap.book.ch6.SparseArraySerializer. Here's the code for the entire class, but don't be overwhelmed. Most of it came from the ArraySerializer class. We'll just walk through the modifications for handling sparse arrays.

```
package javasoap.book.ch6;
import org.apache.soap.encoding.soapenc.*;
import java.beans.*;
import java.io.*;
import java.util.*;
import java.lang.reflect.*;
import org.w3c.dom.*;
import org.apache.soap.util.*;
import org.apache.soap.util.xml.*;
import org.apache.soap.*;
import org.apache.soap.rpc.*;
public class SparseArraySerializer implements Serializer, Deserializer
{
    public SparseArraySerializer() {
    }
    public void marshall(String inScopeEncStyle,
                Class javaType, Object src,
                Object context, Writer sink, NSStack nsStack,
                XMLJavaMappingRegistry xjmr, SOAPContext ctx)
        throws IllegalArgumentException, IOException {
        nsStack.pushScope();
        String lengthStr = src != null
                        ? Array.getLength(src) + ""
                        : "";
        Class componentType = javaType.getComponentType();
        QName elementType = xjmr.queryElementType(componentType,
                        Constants.NS_URI_SOAP_ENC);
        if (src == null) {
```

```
            SoapEncUtils.generateNullArray(inScopeEncStyle,
                                javaType,
                                context,
                                sink,
                                nsStack,
                                xjmr,
                                elementType,
                                lengthStr);
    }
    else {

        SoapEncUtils.generateArrayHeader(inScopeEncStyle,
                                javaType,
                                context,
                                sink,
                                nsStack,
                                xjmr,
                                elementType,
                                lengthStr);
        sink.write(StringUtils.lineSeparator);
        int length = Array.getLength(src);
        for (int i = 0; i < length; i++) {

            nsStack.pushScope();
            Object value = Array.get(src, i);
            // we only want to serialize if the
            // element exists, since
            // this is a sparse array serializer
            if (value != null) {
             Class actualComponentType = value.getClass();
              // use a temporary sink so that we can
              // modify it before writing it out
              StringWriter sw = new StringWriter();
              xjmr.marshall(inScopeEncStyle,
                        actualComponentType, value, "item",
                    sw, nsStack, ctx);

             sink.write("<item ");
             sink.write(nsStack.getPrefixFromURI(
                 Constants.NS_URI_SOAP_ENC) +
                 ":position=\"[" + i + "]\" ");
            sink.write(sw.toString().substring(6));
            sink.write(StringUtils.lineSeparator);
           }
          nsStack.popScope();
        }
        sink.write("</" + context + '>');
    }
    nsStack.popScope();
}
public Bean unmarshall(String inScopeEncStyle,
                QName elementType, Node src,
                XMLJavaMappingRegistry xjmr, SOAPContext ctx)
        throws IllegalArgumentException {
```

```
Element root = (Element)src;
String name = root.getTagName( );
QName arrayItemType = new QName("", "");
Object array = getNewArray(inScopeEncStyle, root,
                           arrayItemType, xjmr);
if (SoapEncUtils.isNull(root)) {
    return new Bean(array.getClass( ), null);
}
Element tempEl = DOMUtils.getFirstChildElement(root);
while (tempEl != null) {
    String declEncStyle = DOMUtils.getAttributeNS(tempEl,
            Constants.NS_URI_SOAP_ENV,
            Constants.ATTR_ENCODING_STYLE);
    String actualEncStyle = declEncStyle != null
                      ? declEncStyle
                      : inScopeEncStyle;
    QName declItemType =
            SoapEncUtils.getAttributeValue(tempEl,
            Constants.NS_URI_CURRENT_SCHEMA_XSI,
            Constants.ATTR_TYPE,
            "array item", false);
    QName actualItemType = declItemType != null
                      ? declItemType
                      : arrayItemType;
    Bean itemBean = xjmr.unmarshall(actualEncStyle,
                      actualItemType,
                      tempEl, ctx);
    // get the position in the array
    String pos = DOMUtils.getAttributeNS(tempEl,
                      inScopeEncStyle, "position");

    int right = pos.indexOf(']');
    String substr = pos.substring(1, right);
    int idx = Integer.parseInt(substr);
    Array.set(array, idx, itemBean.value);
    tempEl = DOMUtils.getNextSiblingElement(tempEl);
}
    return new Bean(array.getClass( ), array);
}
public static Object getNewArray(String inScopeEncStyle,
                Element arrayEl,
                QName arrayItemType,
                XMLJavaMappingRegistry xjmr)
        throws IllegalArgumentException {
    QName arrayTypeValue =
        SoapEncUtils.getAttributeValue(arrayEl,
        Constants.NS_URI_SOAP_ENC,
        Constants.ATTR_ARRAY_TYPE,
        "array", true);
    String arrayTypeValueNamespaceURI =
        arrayTypeValue.getNamespaceURI( );
    String arrayTypeValueLocalPart =
        arrayTypeValue.getLocalPart( );
    int leftBracketIndex =
```

```
                    arrayTypeValueLocalPart.lastIndexOf('[');
            int rightBracketIndex =
                    arrayTypeValueLocalPart.lastIndexOf(']');
            if (leftBracketIndex == -1
              || rightBracketIndex == -1
              || rightBracketIndex < leftBracketIndex) {
                throw new IllegalArgumentException(
                        "Malformed arrayTypeValue '" +
                        arrayTypeValue + "'.");
            }
            String componentTypeName =
                    arrayTypeValueLocalPart.substring(0,
                    leftBracketIndex);
            if (componentTypeName.endsWith("]")) {
                throw new IllegalArgumentException(
                    "Arrays of arrays are not " +
                    "supported '" + arrayTypeValue + "'.");
            }
            arrayItemType.setNamespaceURI(arrayTypeValueNamespaceURI);
            arrayItemType.setLocalPart(componentTypeName);
            int length = DOMUtils.countKids(arrayEl,
                Node.ELEMENT_NODE);
            String lengthStr =
                arrayTypeValueLocalPart.substring(leftBracketIndex + 1,
                                        rightBracketIndex);
            if (lengthStr.length() > 0) {
                if (lengthStr.indexOf(',') != -1) {
                    throw new IllegalArgumentException(
                            "Multi-dimensional arrays are " +
                            "not supported '" + lengthStr + "'.");
                }
                try {
                    int explicitLength = Integer.parseInt(lengthStr);
                    length = explicitLength;
                }
                catch (NumberFormatException e) {
                    throw new IllegalArgumentException(
                            "Explicit array length is not a " +
                            "valid integer '" + lengthStr + "'.");
                }
            }
            Class componentType = xjmr.queryJavaType(arrayItemType,
                        inScopeEncStyle);
            return Array.newInstance(componentType, length);
        }
    }
```

Let's look at the code for the marshall( ) method first. This method is called when
the array is serialized. The serialization of a sparse array doesn't require that the
array elements be treated differently. There are no additional attributes, and the
attribute values used are identical to those used for a regularly serialized array. The
only change is that each item in the array requires a position attribute that indicates
where in the array that element is located. The position element needs to be

namespace-qualified using http://schemas.xmlsoap.org/soap/encoding/. We also want the serializer to skip over any array items that are null, instead of including them in the serialization.

Look at the marshall( ) code where the array length is determined by calling Array. getLength( ). The value is returned in the integer variable length, which is used in the subsequent for loop. Inside this loop, the code works with each item of the array.* We get a reference to each element as an Object named value, and check whether the object is null. If it is, we don't care about it and we loop around for the next item. If it's not null, we start by determining the runtime class of the value object. Next, we want to start writing out the element tag for the array item, but Apache SOAP doesn't provide a mechanism for serializing element attributes. This presents a problem, since we have to include a position attribute for every item element of a sparse array. However, we still want to take advantage of all the Apache SOAP code that handles the writing of elements and their values.

Let's take care of the latter part first. An instance of java.io.StringWriter called sw is created. Normally we'd pass the sink to the xjmr.marshall( ) method, which serializes the item and writes it to the sink. Instead of passing the sink, we pass the StringWriter instance, sw. This stores the serialized form of the array item, which we'll use shortly. The fourth parameter passed to xjmr.marshall( ) is "item", which is the tag name for the element. Since that's the next thing we really want written to the sink, we do it ourselves by calling sink.write with a parameter of "<item ". Here's our chance to stuff an attribute/value pair into the sink, because we're positioned exactly where we want to be after writing the item tag. We need to namespace-qualify the attribute, so nsStatck.getPrefixFromURI( ) is used to find the namespace ID being used for the SOAP encoding namespace. The constant Constants.NS_URI_ SOAP_ENC represents that namespace, so that is passed as the parameter to getPrefixFromURI( ). We start the process of building the entire attribute/value pair for the position attribute using the namespace ID that we just retrieved. We know the attribute name is position, and that the array item index corresponds to the value of the loop variable i. All this is formatted by concatenating these values and passing the result to sink.write( ). Since the value of the position attribute gets enclosed in quotes, we used escape sequences to get those quotes into the string.

Next, we want to get the serialized data from the temporary StringWriter into the sink. But we don't want the element tag at the beginning because we've already written the tag and its attributes to the sink. Since we used the same tag name, item, we can skip the first six characters of the data in the StringWriter instance and grab the rest. (The six characters that we want to skip are the opening <, plus item, plus the

---

* In practice, this is probably not the best way to represent a sparse array in Java, as it still requires you to loop over the entire array. Very large sparse arrays with very few actual entries should be implemented using a more intelligent representation.

trailing space that follows.) So we call sw.toString( ).substring(6) and pass that to sink.write( ). We've managed to get the attribute into the item element and still take advantage of the Apache SOAP API to do most of the work. The remainder of the code in marshall( ) adds a line break and the closing tag to the sink to finish off the serialization of the array element.

Next let's look at the unmarshall( ) method used to deserialize a sparse array. In this case, we don't have much work to do. Almost all the code centers around determining the array size and type, and allocating an appropriate array instance. We just want to determine the value of the position attribute so that we can put the deserialized item instance into the proper position of the array. We can get the string value of the attribute by calling DOMUtils.getAttributeNS. We pass the method the element of the XML document, the encoding style that is currently in-scope, and the name of the attribute. The element is in the variable tempEl, which was handled earlier in the method. The encoding style is found in the inScopeEncStyle parameter that was passed to the unmarshall( ) method. And, of course, we know that the attribute name is position. The value of the attribute will be an integer enclosed in square brackets. So we pull out the substring between the brackets and pass it to Integer.parseInt( ) to get an int value that represents the array position. This value is passed as the second parameter to the Array.set( ) method, which places the item into the array at the specified position. The rest was already written for us.

Now that we've got a sparse array serializer, we need a way to use it. After all, Apache SOAP, by default, wants to use the ArraySerializer class to handle the serialization and deserialization of arrays. So we need to find a way to override that behavior. My first inclination would be to modify the org.apache.soap.encoding. SOAPMappingRegistry class provided as part of Apache SOAP to force it to use the SparseArraySerializer instead of the ArraySerializer. However, one problem with this approach is that it renders invalid any arrays serialized without position parameters. That doesn't sound good. We could have made the SparseArraySerializer smart enough to handle both possibilities, but that would have meant a highly complex serializer with a lot more code. If you'd like to take that on, I bet the Apache folks would be happy to consider including it. A simpler approach would be to map the sparse array serializer in the mapping section of those services that use sparse arrays. This means that we don't have to modify the Apache SOAP source code, which could become a real pain if changes in future versions of the Apache code are inconsistent with our modified version. So we'll use the service-specific approach.

Let's add a method called echoStocks to the urn:DataFeedService service. This method takes a string array as a parameter and uses that same array as the return value. Here's the new version of the DataFeedService class with the Java implementation, echoStocks( ), added:

```
package javasoap.book.ch6;
public class DataFeedService {
    public DataFeedService() {
```

```
    }
    public String[] echoStocks(String[] stocks) {
        return stocks;
    }
    public DataFeedMessage sendMessage(DataFeedMessage msg) {
        // we could pull the formatted message here
        // by calling msg.toString( );
        String stock = msg.getFieldValue("SYMBOL");
        String request = msg.getFieldValue("REQUEST");
        DataFeedMessage res = new DataFeedMessage( );
        res.addField("SYMBOL", stock);
        if (request.equals("PRICE"))
            res.addField("PRICE", "123.5");
        return res;
    }
}
```

We need to add a mapping entry to the deployment descriptor so that the sparse array serializer is used for arrays. The type that we want to map is Array, namespace-qualified by http://schemas.xmlsoap.org/soap/encoding/. That's the standard SOAP array using standard SOAP encoding. This mapping entry overrides the default classes for serializing and deserializing arrays. We already know that the SparseArraySerializer class will be used as the value for both the java2XMLClassName and the xml2JavaClassName attributes. That tells the system to use our new serializer for arrays. Now we need to specify the Java class that's used to instantiate a Java array. That class comes from the Java reflection API, and is named java.lang.reflect.Array. We use this value for the javaType attribute of the mapping entry. The echoStocks method name is added to the methods attribute of the service tag.

We still need to work around a problem, however. The Apache SOAP Java code doesn't expect you to override the standard serializers, and makes some assumptions about the serializers and mapping registry. Even though we've specified the SparseArraySerializer for the java2xmlClassName in the mapping entry, it doesn't get used when our service attempts to return an array from echoStocks. The workaround is to write our own mapping registry, which is easier than it sounds. We'll do this shortly; the new registry will be named javasoap.book.ch6. BetterSOAPMappingRegistry. We need to specify this registry in the deployment descriptor by including the defaultRegistryClass attribute in the isd:mappings element, using the class name of our new registry as the value. Here's the modified deployment descriptor:

```
<isd:service
    xmlns:isd="http://xml.apache.org/xml-soap/deployment"
    id="urn:DataFeedService">
  <isd:provider
    type="java"
    scope="Application"
    methods="sendMessage echoStocks">
    <isd:java
        class="javasoap.book.ch6.DataFeedService"
```

```
              static="false"/>
      </isd:provider>

      <isd:faultListener>org.apache.soap.server.DOMFaultListener
      </isd:faultListener>

      <isd:mappings defaultRegistryClass="javasoap.book.ch6.BetterSOAPMappingRegistry" >
          <isd:map
            encodingStyle="http://schemas.xmlsoap.org/soap/encoding/"
            xmlns:x="http://schemas.xmlsoap.org/soap/encoding/" qname="x:Array"
            javaType="java.lang.reflect.Array"
            java2XMLClassName="javasoap.book.ch6.SparseArraySerializer"
            xml2JavaClassName="javasoap.book.ch6.SparseArraySerializer"/>
          <isd:map
            encodingStyle="http://schemas.xmlsoap.org/soap/encoding/"
            xmlns:x="urn:DataFeedService" qname="x:DataFeedMessage"
            javaType="javasoap.book.ch6.DataFeedMessage"
            java2XMLClassName="javasoap.book.ch6.DataFeedMessageSerializer"
            xml2JavaClassName="javasoap.book.ch6.DataFeedMessageSerializer"/>
      </isd:mappings>
  </isd:service>
```

All our new mapping registry needs to do is return an instance of the
SparseArraySerializer instead of ArraySerializer when it gets queried for an array
serializer. The BetterSOAPMappingRegistry extends the SOAPMappingRegistry class provided by Apache SOAP. To solve the problem, we override the querySerializer
method so that it returns the SparseArraySerializer when needed. The base class is
doing most of the work, but if it wants to return an ArraySerializer, we return a
SparseArraySerializer instead. Here's the new registry class:

```
package javasoap.book.ch6;
import org.apache.soap.util.xml.*;
import org.apache.soap.*;
import org.apache.soap.encoding.soapenc.*;
public class BetterSOAPMappingRegistry
        extends org.apache.soap.encoding.SOAPMappingRegistry {
    SparseArraySerializer sparseSer = new SparseArraySerializer();
    public BetterSOAPMappingRegistry() {
        super();
    }
    public Serializer querySerializer(Class javaType,
                    String encodingStyleURI)
            throws IllegalArgumentException {

      Serializer s;
      try {
        s = super.querySerializer(javaType, encodingStyleURI);
        if (s instanceof ArraySerializer)
          return sparseSer;
      }
      catch (IllegalArgumentException e) {
        if (javaType != null
          && encodingStyleURI != null
```

```
           && encodingStyleURI.equals(Constants.NS_URI_SOAP_ENC)) {
               if (javaType.isArray()) {
                 return sparseSer;
               }
             }
             throw e;
           }
         return s;
       }
     }
```

Why do we need a mapping entry in the deployment descriptor if we're using the defaultRegistryClass attribute of the isd:service element? Well, because the attribute by itself doesn't seem to work either, but the combination of the attribute and the mapping entry does. The workaround is fairly simple, and saves you from going deeply into the Apache source code. Go ahead and deploy the service.

Now, let's see what has to be done in a client application. We actually need to do the same thing, but it's accomplished in a different way. We specify the mapping, and use the BetterSOAPMappingRegistry class instead of the SOAPMappingRegistry class. Here's the client code:

```
package javasoap.book.ch6;
import java.net.*;
import java.util.*;
import org.apache.soap.*;
import org.apache.soap.rpc.*;
import org.apache.soap.encoding.*;
import org.apache.soap.util.xml.*;
public class DataFeedClient2 {
    public static void main(String[] args)
        throws Exception {

        URL url =
          new URL(
            "http://georgetown:8080/soap/servlet/rpcrouter");

        Call call = new Call();

        BetterSOAPMappingRegistry smr =
                    new BetterSOAPMappingRegistry();
        call.setTargetObjectURI("urn:DataFeedService");
        call.setMethodName("echoStocks");
        call.setEncodingStyleURI(Constants.NS_URI_SOAP_ENC);
        call.setSOAPMappingRegistry(smr);
        SparseArraySerializer arraySer =
                    new SparseArraySerializer();
        // Map the array
        smr.mapTypes(Constants.NS_URI_SOAP_ENC,
                new QName(Constants.NS_URI_SOAP_ENC, "Array"),
                java.lang.reflect.Array.class, arraySer,
                arraySer);
        String[] stocks = new String[10];
```

```
        stocks[2] = "XYZ";
        stocks[5] = "ABC";
        Vector params = new Vector();
        params.addElement(new Parameter("msg", String[].class,
                                stocks, null));
        call.setParams(params);

        try {
            Response resp = call.invoke(url, "");
            Parameter ret = resp.getReturnValue();
            String[] value = (String[])ret.getValue();
            int cnt = value.length;
            for (int i = 0; i < cnt; i++) {
                if (value[i] != null) {
                    System.out.println("Item " + i + ": " + value[i]);
                }
            }
        }
        catch (SOAPException e) {
            System.err.println("Caught SOAPException (" +
                        e.getFaultCode() + "): " +
                        e.getMessage());
        }
    }
}
```

The smr variable is now an instance of BetterSOAPMappingRegistry, but from that point on we use it just as in the previous examples. We create an instance of SparseArraySerializer to use for the mapping process; then we call smr.mapTypes(), giving it the previously instantiated SparseArraySerializer as the object to use for both serializing and deserializing, and java.lang.reflect.Array.class as the class to use for the object that implements the array. Take note of the parameters used for the Qname constructor. The first parameter is the standard SOAP encoding namespace, and the second is "Array". So this should override the default mapping.

Now we create an empty string array of size 10, and assign values to positions 2 and 5. The rest of the items in the array are null. Don't assign empty strings here, because an empty string is not the same as a null value. (Although there's actually no harm in trying empty strings; you will get a serialized element for all 10 items in the array.) The echoStocks service method is invoked the same way as we've done before. The return value is cast to a String[] so that we can iterate through it looking for the values. If all is correct, we should find objects only at positions 2 and 5, since the server echoed back the same array we sent to it. Running this application results in the following output:

```
Item 2: XYZ
Item 5: ABC
```

And here's the SOAP envelope for this example. If nothing else, this shows that only the non-null elements were actually serialized.

```
<SOAP-ENV:Envelope
    xmlns:SOAP-ENV="http://schemas.xmlsoap.org/soap/envelope/"
    xmlns:xsi="http://www.w3.org/2001/XMLSchema-instance"
    xmlns:xsd="http://www.w3.org/2001/XMLSchema">
<SOAP-ENV:Body>
 <ns1:echoStocks
    xmlns:ns1="urn:DataFeedService"
    SOAP-ENV:encodingStyle="http://schemas.xmlsoap.org/soap/encoding/">
      <msg
        xmlns:ns2="http://schemas.xmlsoap.org/soap/encoding/"
        xsi:type="ns2:Array" ns2:arrayType="xsd:string[10]">
          <item ns2:position="[2]" xsi:type="xsd:string">XYZ</item>
          <item ns2:position="[5]" xsi:type="xsd:string">ABC</item>
      </msg>
 </ns1:echoStocks>
</SOAP-ENV:Body>
</SOAP-ENV:Envelope>
```

The msg element is typed as an array of 10 strings, no different from any other array. Each item element is explicitly typed as an xsd:string, and includes a position attribute that indicates its position in the array. That's exactly what we were shooting for.

Serializing Collections

Arrays aren't the only collection types commonly used in Java programming. It would also be nice to be able to serialize hash tables, linked lists, and other collection types. GLUE provides a custom implementation for a hash table that's worth looking at. This example uses just one of the many mechanisms that GLUE provides for custom serialization. It requires you to write the custom type schema on the fly, which of course means you'll need to understand schemas. That's not the subject of this book, but it's still worth looking at that part of the code.

To write a custom serializer in GLUE, start with a Java class that extends electric. xml.io.Type, the base class for SOAP types in GLUE. All we need to do is override the methods writeSchema(), writeObject(), and readObject(). Here is GLUE's implementation of the HashtableType class:

```
// copyright 2001 by The Mind Electric
package electric.xml.io.collections;
import java.io.*;
import java.util.*;
import electric.xml.*;
import electric.xml.io.*;
import electric.util.Value;
public class HashtableType extends Type
  {
  /**
   * @param schema
   */
  public void writeSchema( Element schema )
```

```java
    {
    Element complexType = schema.addElement( "complexType" );
    complexType.setAttribute( "name", "Map" );
    Element sequence = complexType.addElement( "sequence" );
    Element element = sequence.addElement( "element" );
    element.setAttribute( "name", "item" );
    element.setAttribute( "minOccurs", "0" );
    element.setAttribute( "maxOccurs", "unbounded" );
    Element subType = element.addElement( "complexType" );
    Element subSequence = subType.addElement( "sequence" );
    Element key = subSequence.addElement( "element" );
    key.setAttribute( "name", "key" );
    key.setAttribute( "type", getName( key, Object.class ) );
    Element value = subSequence.addElement( "element" );
    value.setAttribute( "name", "value" );
    value.setAttribute( "type", getName( key, Object.class ) );
    }
/**
 * @param writer
 * @param object
 * @throws IOException
 */
public void writeObject( IWriter writer, Object object )
  throws IOException
  {
  writer.writeType( this );
  Hashtable hashtable = (Hashtable) object;
  for( Enumeration enum = hashtable.keys();
                          enum.hasMoreElements(); )
    {
    Object key = enum.nextElement();
    Object value = hashtable.get( key );
    IWriter itemWriter = writer.writeElement( "item" );
    itemWriter.writeObject( "key", key );
    itemWriter.writeObject( "value", value );
    }
  }
/**
 * @param reader
 * @param value
 * @throws IOException
 */
public void readObject( IReader reader, Value value )
  throws IOException
  {
  Hashtable hashtable = new Hashtable();
  value.setObject( hashtable );
  IReader[] readers = reader.getReaders( "item" );
  for( int i = 0; i < readers.length; i++ )
    {
    IReader itemReader = readers[ i ];
    Object key = itemReader.readObject( "key" );
    Object theValue = itemReader.readObject( "value" );
    hashtable.put( key, theValue );
```

```
            }
        }
    }
```

GLUE provides built-in support for this class, so we won't have to register it when we write the service and client application code. If you want to develop your own custom type serializers in GLUE, you must use one of the `mapClass()` methods from the `electric.xml.io.Mappings` class. These methods tell the GLUE system how to map your custom types to serializers.

The code in the `writeSchema()` method writes a schema definition for the hash table. Instead of looking at each class and method used to accomplish this, let's look at the resulting schema:

```
<complexType name="Map">
  <sequence>
    <element name="item" minOccurs="0" maxOccurs="unbounded">
      <complexType>
        <sequence>
          <element name="key" type="KEYTYPE"/>
          <element name="value" type="VALUETYPE"/>
        </sequence>
      </complexType>
    </element>
  </sequence>
</complexType>
```

This is a schema definition for a hash table, otherwise known as a map. Remember that each entry in a map contains a key/value pair. It's defined as a `complexType` with the name `Map`, containing a sequence of 0 or more elements. Each element is, in turn, also a complex type containing a sequence of two elements, key and value. These two elements are typed using the appropriate type names for the key and value elements; I used `KEYTYPE` and `VALUETYPE` as placeholders. In the code, those types are determined from the class of the corresponding Java object instance. We'll see this shortly when we run an example using this custom serializer.

The `writeObject()` method is where the contents of the custom type are serialized. The first parameter of the method is an instance of the `electric.xml.io.IWriter` interface. We use this interface to write the contents of the object being serialized. The second parameter is the Java object to be serialized. The method first writes the object's type to the stream, passing `this` to the `writeType()` method of the `writer`. This identifies the type of the object being serialized as a `Map`. Then the object is cast to a `Hashtable` instance so that we can access the key/value pairs. All we need to do is iterate over the elements of the table, using the `Enumeration` returned from the `hashtable.keys()` method. For each element, we retrieve the `Object` instances for the key and the value. To write each item, we call `writer.writeElement()`, which returns a new instance of `IWriter` called `itemWriter`. This instance is used for writing out the key and value data for that item using `itemWriter.writeObject()`, which is given the element name and the associated `Object` instance as parameters.

readObject( ) performs the deserialization. Its first parameter is an instance of the electric.xml.io.IReader interface, which we use to read the contents to be deserialized. The other parameter is an instance of electric.util.Value, which contains a java.lang.Object instance and its associated type (an instance of java.lang.Class). The first step is to create a new instance of java.util.Hashtable and pass it as a parameter to value.setObject( ). Next we call reader.getReaders( ), which returns an array of IReader instances, one for each key/value pair in the map. For each IReader, we call getObject( ) to retrieve the key and value objects for the element. These two objects are now added to the hash table using the hashtable.put( ) method.

That's all there is to it. So we'll now build a service and a client application that use hash tables to see how the custom serializer gets registered. Let's create a new service called urn:AnotherFeedService. This one, like the data feed service from before, contains a method called sendMessage( ). But this time the method takes a hash table as the parameter, where the elements of the hash table contain the field names and their associated values. This means that the new service must format the data as specified at the beginning of this chapter. We won't bother with that, since it doesn't have any real impact on what we're doing. We'll just concentrate on the custom serialization of hash tables. The javasoap.book.ch6.AnotherFeedService class implements the service.

```java
package javasoap.book.ch6;
import java.util.Hashtable;
public class AnotherFeedService {
    public AnotherFeedService() {
    }
    public Hashtable sendMessage(Hashtable msg) {
        String stock = (String)msg.get("SYMBOL");
        String request = (String)msg.get("REQUEST");
        Hashtable res = new Hashtable();
        res.put("SYMBOL", stock);
        if (request.equals("PRICE"))
            res.put("PRICE", "123.5");
        return res;
    }
}
```

The sendMessage( ) method performs essentially the same function as it did in the earlier DataFeedService class. The difference is that the messages are passed using hash tables instead of instances of DataFeedMessage. To deploy the service, we use the class FeedServiceApp:

```java
package javasoap.book.ch6;
import electric.util.Context;
import electric.registry.Registry;
import electric.server.http.HTTP;
import java.util.Hashtable;
public class FeedServiceApp {

    public static void main( String[] args )
                throws Exception {
```

```
        String ns = "urn:AnotherFeedService";
        HTTP.startup("http://georgetown:8004/glue");
        Context context = new Context();
        context.addProperty("activation", "application");
        context.addProperty("namespace", ns);
        Registry.publish(ns,
            javasoap.book.ch6.AnotherFeedService.class, context );
    }
}
```

Let's write the interface for binding to the service by hand, since we're taking advantage of a custom type that's already built in to GLUE. Here's the javasoap.book.ch6. IAnotherDataFeed interface. It contains the sendMessage( ) method that we defined for the service, which takes a Hashtable as a parameter and also returns one.

```
package javasoap.book.ch6;
public interface IAnotherFeedService {
   java.util.Hashtable sendMessage(java.util.Hashtable msg);
}
```

FeedServiceClient is an application that binds to the urn:AnotherFeedService service and passes a hash table to the sendMessage( ) method.

```
package javasoap.book.ch6;

import electric.registry.RegistryException;
import electric.registry.Registry;
import java.util.*;

public class FeedServiceClient {
    public static void main(String[] args) throws Exception
    {
        try {

            IAnotherFeedService srv = (IAnotherFeedService)Registry.bind(
              "http://georgetown:8004/glue/urn:AnotherFeedService.wsdl",
              IAnotherFeedService.class);

            Hashtable msg = new Hashtable();
            msg.put("SYMBOL", "XYZ");
            msg.put("REQUEST", "PRICE");

            Hashtable result = srv.sendMessage(msg);

            for (Enumeration e = result.keys(); e.hasMoreElements(); ) {
                String key = (String)e.nextElement();
                String value = (String)result.get(key);
                System.out.println(key + ": " + value);
            }
        }
        catch (RegistryException e) {
            System.out.println(e);
        }
    }
}
```

The returned hash table is enumerated, and the key/value pairs are printed for display. The result is:

```
SYMBOL: XYZ
PRICE: 123.5
```

Let's take a look at the SOAP envelope that was sent to the service when sendMessage( ) was invoked. This gives us a chance to see the serialized hash table.

```
<soap:Envelope
  xmlns:xsi='http://www.w3.org/2001/XMLSchema-instance'
  xmlns:xsd='http://www.w3.org/2001/XMLSchema'
  xmlns:soap='http://schemas.xmlsoap.org/soap/envelope/'
  xmlns:soapenc='http://schemas.xmlsoap.org/soap/encoding/'
  soap:encodingStyle='http://schemas.xmlsoap.org/soap/encoding/'>
    <soap:Body>
      <n:sendMessageResponse xmlns:n='urn:AnotherFeedService'>
        <Result href='#id0'/>
      </n:sendMessageResponse>
      <id0 id='id0' soapenc:root='0'
            xmlns:ns2='http://xml.apache.org/xml-soap'
            xsi:type='ns2:Map'>
        <item>
          <key xsi:type='xsd:string'>PRICE</key>
          <value xsi:type='xsd:string'>123.5</value>
        </item>
        <item>
          <key xsi:type='xsd:string'>SYMBOL</key>
          <value xsi:type='xsd:string'>XYZ</value>
        </item>
      </id0>
    </soap:Body>
</soap:Envelope>
```

Just as we've seen in all the other GLUE examples using complex types, the actual data is serialized separately, and the parameter references that data. The hash table we sent can be found in the id0 element. It is typed as a Map, qualified by the http://xml.apache.org/xml-soap namespace. This namespace is used because the Apache group actually created the schema for encoding a map, or hash table, type. The GLUE implementation is consistent with the Apache work in this area. Each item child element contains key and value elements that in turn contain the key/value pair for the map entry. In this case, all the keys and values are strings because that's the type we used in the example.

In this chapter, we looked at how to create serializers for our own custom types. Using these techniques combined with the built-in support for many types, there is virtually no limit to the data that can be transmitted using SOAP. In some cases you may find that you're designing your classes with SOAP in mind, or least with the capabilities and restrictions of your chosen SOAP implementation in mind. Whether or not designing around the limitations of your SOAP implementation makes sense for your project, custom serialization opens up a lot of possibilities when you need to go beyond the basics.

CHAPTER 7

Faults and Exceptions

The difference between good software and bad software is often the way in which errors and problems are handled. It's much easier to deal with processes when everything is working properly than it is to deal with failures. Structured and object-oriented programming provide lots of techniques for handling errors. Methods often return a special value, like null or -1, to indicate an error of some kind. In Java, methods frequently throw an exception indicating that something unusual has occurred. Good software is written to expect certain types of errors, and is prepared to take appropriate action. In SOAP terminology, these unusual, or exceptional, circumstances are called *faults*. Faults occur whenever a service method is not able to process input parameters and return results properly. There are endless reasons why this may occur. Common problems that result in faults are bad method parameter values, back-end problems, and improperly formatted SOAP request messages. I'm sure you can think of plenty of others, and have probably had to write code to deal with them. In this chapter we'll look at the mechanisms for generating and handling faults in SOAP.

Throwing Server-Side Exceptions in Apache SOAP

The most common way for a service to generate a fault is to throw an exception. Apache SOAP has a mechanism for handling exceptions thrown from the Java class methods that implement service methods. The information in the exception is used to generate corresponding SOAP faults to be sent back to the caller.

The contents of a SOAP fault were covered back in Chapter 2. In that section we discovered that four fault codes could be used in a fault. One of those possibilities is SOAP-ENV:Server, which indicates that a problem occurred while processing the message that was not related to the contents of the request. This fault code could be used if, for example, the back-end server needed to properly process the message was not available. Let's create a simple service that generates the simplest of faults so that we can see the basic mechanism used in Apache SOAP. Here's the javasoap.book.ch7. SampleFaultService class that implements the service urn:SampleFaultService:

```
package javasoap.book.ch7;
import org.apache.soap.SOAPException;
public class SampleFaultService {
    public SampleFaultService() {
    }
    public int generateFault()
        throws Exception {
        // something bad must have happened...
        throw new Exception();
    }
}
```

The declaration of the generateFault() method indicates that it may throw an instance of java.lang.Exception. In fact, that's all it does. We're simulating what would happen if the service method received a call that could not be processed because of a back-end problem.

Now let's look at a client application that calls the generateFault service. Up until now, we've always gotten the result from a web service by calling the getReturnValue() method of the Response object. However, this approach assumes that the service was invoked successfully, and doesn't handle the possibility that a fault was generated. To take faults into account, we need to ask the Response object if a fault was generated by calling its faultGenerated() method, which returns true if a fault was generated and false otherwise. If a fault wasn't generated, we can proceed as before. If a fault was generated, we retrieve the fault from the Response object by calling its getFault() method. This returns an instance of org.apache.soap.Fault, a class used to encapsulate the contents of a SOAP fault.

```
package javasoap.book.ch7;
import java.net.*;
import java.util.*;
import org.apache.soap.*;
import org.apache.soap.rpc.*;
import org.apache.soap.encoding.*;
import org.apache.soap.util.xml.*;
public class SampleClient {
    public static void main(String[] args)
        throws Exception {

        URL url =
          new URL(
            "http://georgetown:8080/soap/servlet/rpcrouter");

        Call call = new Call();

        call.setTargetObjectURI("urn:SampleFaultService");
        call.setMethodName("generateFault");
        try {
            Response resp = call.invoke(url, "");
```

```
            if (resp.generatedFault()) {
                String code = resp.getFault().getFaultCode();
                String desc = resp.getFault().getFaultString();
                System.out.println(code + ": " + desc);          }
            else {
                Parameter ret = resp.getReturnValue();
                Object value = ret.getValue();
                System.out.println(value);
            }
        }
        catch (SOAPException e) {
            System.err.println("Caught SOAPException (" +
                        e.getFaultCode() + "): " +
                        e.getMessage());
        }
    }
}
```

If you run this example you'll get the following output:

```
SOAP-ENV:Server: Exception from service object: null
```

Doing nothing more than throwing an instance of java.lang.Exception from our service method results in a properly formed SOAP fault with a fault code of SOAP-ENV: Server. The fault also contains a default value for the fault string and fault actor elements. Here's the SOAP fault returned from the generateFault service method:

```
<SOAP-ENV:Envelope
    xmlns:SOAP-ENV="http://schemas.xmlsoap.org/soap/envelope/"
    xmlns:xsi="http://www.w3.org/2001/XMLSchema-instance"
    xmlns:xsd="http://www.w3.org/2001/XMLSchema">
<SOAP-ENV:Body>
<SOAP-ENV:Fault>
<faultcode>SOAP-ENV:Server</faultcode>
<faultstring>Exception from service object: null</faultstring>
<faultactor>/soap/servlet/rpcrouter</faultactor>
</SOAP-ENV:Fault>
</SOAP-ENV:Body>
</SOAP-ENV:Envelope>
```

But where did the fault get generated? The answer can be found in any of the deployment descriptors we've used in prior examples. Every one of those descriptors contains an isd:faultListener element entry that looks like this:

```
<isd:faultListener>org.apache.soap.server.DOMFaultListener
</isd:faultListener>
```

This element specifies the Java class that handles fault processing for your service. This class handles the exception that your service throws, and converts it into a SOAP fault. Unfortunately, the information that can be extracted from an instance of java.lang.Exception isn't all that useful. Apache SOAP includes a class called org.apache.soap.SOAPException that extends java.lang.Exception and includes methods for setting and getting the SOAP fault code and fault string. This is certainly more useful, so let's modify the service class to make use of the SOAPException:

```
package javasoap.book.ch7;
import org.apache.soap.SOAPException;
public class SampleFaultService {
    public SampleFaultService( ) {
    }
    public int generateFault( )
        throws SOAPException {
      throw new SOAPException("SOAP-ENV:Server",
                         "Data Feed Unavailable");
    }
}
```

Now the generateFault( ) method throws an instance of SOAPException. Let's say that the fault occurs because the underlying data feed used by this service is not available. In this case we're required to use the SOAP-ENV:Server fault code, which is the first parameter of the SOAPException constructor. The second parameter describes the fault. These two values are used to populate the faultcode and faultstring elements of the SOAP fault. This approach also allows us to generate faults using the SOAP-ENV:Client fault code, which indicates that the service method encountered an improperly formatted request or some other information within the SOAP body that prevents successful processing. Think back to the stock market data feed service examples from earlier chapters. A few of those examples used attribute/value pairs as message fields. If a particular required field were missing, such as a SYMBOL field that provides a stock symbol, the server could generate a fault using the SOAP-ENV:Client fault code as follows:

```
throw new SOAPException("SOAP-ENV:Client", "Missing SYMBOL");
```

This may be all you ever need to generate adequate faults. However, in some cases, you can return much more meaningful information in SOAP faults by using the detail element. This element is allowed only when describing faults associated with the body of the request message. Therefore, it's not useful for describing something like an unavailable data feed, but it can certainly be useful for many other fault conditions. (Actually, I find this short-sighted because there are many situations where it would be helpful to provide details of a fault not related to the body of the request. For example, let's say the data feed is unavailable, but there is another data feed willing to accept requests. You might want the fault to include the necessary information for the client to make use of the alternative service. Of course, you could design your service to use alternative back-end resources automatically, but that's not always desirable.) In the next section, we'll look at providing fault details in the context of a SOAP-ENV:Client fault code.

Creating a Fault Listener in Apache SOAP

To populate a fault with a detail element, we need to create a new class for fault listening by implementing the org.apache.soap.server.SOAPFaultListener interface. This interface defines a method called fault( ), which is called by the Apache SOAP framework when a fault needs to be generated. The only parameter passed to this method is an instance of org.apache.soap.server.SOAPFaultEvent,* which carries an instance of org.apache.soap.Fault and the SOAPException that was thrown by the service method. The fault object contains methods for getting and setting the fault code, fault string, fault actor, and details. This is the object we want to manipulate to provide detail information.

But before we create the fault listener, we need a mechanism for providing it with the detail data. We don't have a direct path from our service methods to the fault listener, but we can take advantage of the exception mechanism. Since we've seen that the SOAPException that gets thrown by the service method is available to the fault listener, we can inherit from SOAPException and create a new class that meets our needs. But before we do that, we need a class to carry our detail information. Let's use a java.util.Hashtable. That way we can set up any number of attribute/value pairs to represent the fault detail information. With all this in mind, let's create a new exception type with a property called Detail that's an instance of Hashtable.

```
package javasoap.book.ch7;
import org.apache.soap.*;
import java.util.Hashtable;
public class FeedException extends SOAPException {
    Hashtable _detail;
    public FeedException(String fcode, String fstring) {
        super(fcode, fstring);
    }
    public void setDetail(Hashtable detail) {
        _detail = detail;
    }
    public Hashtable getDetail() {
        return _detail;
    }
}
```

The code is pretty simple. Since FeedException extends SOAPException, we can use an instance of this new class in place of the SOAPException instance we used earlier. The constructor takes the fault code and fault string as parameters and passes them along to the superclass constructor. We have set and get accessors for the Detail property, defined as an instance of Hashtable.

Now we can modify the service class to throw an instance of FeedException and populate it with some detail information. Here's the new SampleFaultService code with the changes. We've included reasonCode, reasonDescription, alternateProvider, and alternateContact fields in the details with appropriate values. Those details, contained in a hash table, are passed to the FeedException instance using the setDetail( )

---

* If you're familiar with the JavaBeans patterns for events you should recognize this naming convention. The event that has taken place is a SOAPFault. The listener interface is named by appending Listener to the event name, and the object carrying the event information is named by appending Event.

---

method. We can throw the FeedException successfully because it's a subclass of SOAPException. Alternately, we could modify the method definition to specify that it throws a FeedException.

```
package javasoap.book.ch7;
import org.apache.soap.SOAPException;
import java.util.Hashtable;
public class SampleFaultService {
   public SampleFaultService( ) {
   }
   public int generateFault( )
         throws SOAPException {
      FeedException e = new FeedException("SOAP-ENV:Server",
                             "Data Feed Unavailable");
      Hashtable detail = new Hashtable( );
      detail.put("reasonCode", "199");
      detail.put("reasonDescription", "Power Outage");
      detail.put("alternateProvider", "www.mindstrm.com");
      detail.put("alternateContact", "rob@mindstrm.com");
      e.setDetail(detail);
      throw e;
   }
}
```

Now we can work on the new fault listener class. Let's call it javasoap.book.ch7. FeedFaultListener. It implements the org.apache.soap.server.SOAPFaultListener interface and implements the required fault( ) method.

```
package javasoap.book.ch7;
import org.apache.soap.*;
import org.apache.soap.server.*;
import java.util.*;
import org.w3c.dom.*;
import org.apache.soap.util.xml.*;
import javax.xml.parsers.DocumentBuilder;

public class FeedFaultListener
        implements SOAPFaultListener {
   public FeedFaultListener( ) {
   }
   public void fault(SOAPFaultEvent event) {

      FeedException ex = (FeedException)event.getSOAPException( );
      Vector v = new Vector( );
      DocumentBuilder builder =
              XMLParserUtils.getXMLDocBuilder( );
      Document doc = builder.newDocument( );
      Hashtable detail = ex.getDetail( );
      Enumeration e = detail.keys( );
      while (e.hasMoreElements( )) {
         String name = (String)e.nextElement( );
         String value = (String)detail.get(name);
         Element elem = doc.createElement(name);
         Text txt = doc.createTextNode("");
```

```
            txt.setData(value);
            elem.appendChild(txt);
            v.addElement(elem);
        }

        event.getFault( ).setDetailEntries(v);
    }
}
```

Before describing the logic in detail, let's look at a high level at what the fault( ) method has to do. It receives a SOAPFaultEvent in response to the FeedException thrown by the service method. This event includes references to both the FeedException and the actual Fault that will be sent to the caller. So we need to extract the detailed information we stuck into the FeedException, turn it into a group of XML elements that can be added to the Fault, and then stick these entries into the Fault so that they'll be in the SOAP document sent back to the caller.

The fault( ) method starts by getting the FeedException that was thrown by the service method. To get the exception, we call the getSOAPException( ) method on the event. The result is cast to a FeedException, since that's where we'll find the details of the fault. An instance of java.util.Vector is created to store the elements of the detail section as we create them.

Now we need to create XML child elements of the detail element, making use of APIs for manipulating XML that are in no way specific to SOAP. If you want to learn about manipulating XML in Java, see Brett McLaughlin's book, *Java and XML* (O'Reilly). We're not doing anything complicated, though, so you should be able to follow along without much trouble. We call XMLParserUtils.getXMLDocBuilder to get an instance of a DocumentBuilder interface, which in turn is used to create a new document. This Document is an XML document that we'll use to populate our detail entries.

The details are retrieved using the getDetail( ) method of the FeedException. The next step is to enumerate the hash table entries, pulling out the name/value pairs that constitute the detail data. For each pair, we create a new XML element by calling doc.createElement( ) using the name as the element name. We then create a text node and set its value using the value retrieved from the hash table. Now the text node is appended to the element, and the element is added to the vector we created earlier. When we've done this for all of the pairs, the vector of detail elements is added to the Fault object by passing it as a parameter to its setDetailEntries( ) method.

We now need to redeploy the service, this time using the FeedFaultListener class as the value of the isd:FaultListener element in the deployment descriptor:

```
<isd:faultListener>
javasoap.book.ch7.FeedFaultListener
</isd:faultListener>
```

If you run the client application, the fault returned from the server will now include a detail section. The client doesn't look for a detail section, but we can see the result of our work by looking at the SOAP envelope returned from the server:

```
<SOAP-ENV:Envelope
 xmlns:SOAP-ENV="http://schemas.xmlsoap.org/soap/envelope/"
 xmlns:xsi="http://www.w3.org/2001/XMLSchema-instance"
 xmlns:xsd="http://www.w3.org/2001/XMLSchema">
<SOAP-ENV:Body>
 <SOAP-ENV:Fault>
  <faultcode>SOAP-ENV:Server</faultcode>
  <faultstring>Data Feed Unavailable</faultstring>
  <faultactor>/soap/servlet/rpcrouter</faultactor>
  <detail>
    <alternateProvider>www.mindstrm.com</alternateProvider>
    <reasonDescription>Power Outage</reasonDescription>
    <alternateContact>rob@mindstrm.com</alternateContact>
    <reasonCode>199</reasonCode>
  </detail>
 </SOAP-ENV:Fault>
</SOAP-ENV:Body>
</SOAP-ENV:Envelope>
```

The four detail fields are included as children of the detail element. For this information to be useful, we want to get at the details from our client application, so let's do that now. Here is a modified version of the client application that extracts the details we sent with the fault:

```
package javasoap.book.ch7;
import java.net.*;
import java.util.*;
import org.apache.soap.*;
import org.apache.soap.rpc.*;
import org.apache.soap.encoding.*;
import org.apache.soap.util.xml.*;
import org.w3c.dom.*;
public class SampleClient {
    public static void main(String[] args)
        throws Exception {

        URL url =
          new URL(
            "http://georgetown:8080/soap/servlet/rpcrouter");

        Call call = new Call();

        call.setTargetObjectURI("urn:SampleFaultService");
        call.setMethodName("generateFault");
        try {
           Response resp = call.invoke(url, "");
           if (resp.generatedFault()) {
              Fault fault = resp.getFault();
              String code = fault.getFaultCode();
```

```
            String desc = fault.getFaultString();
            System.out.println(code + ": " + desc);
            Vector v = fault.getDetailEntries();
            int cnt = v.size();
            for (int i = 0; i < cnt; i++) {
                Element n = (Element)v.elementAt(i);
                Node nd = n.getFirstChild();
                System.out.println(n.getNodeName() + ": " +
                                        nd.getNodeValue());
            }
        }
        else {
            Parameter ret = resp.getReturnValue();
            Object value = ret.getValue();
            System.out.println(value);
        }
    }
    catch (SOAPException e) {
        System.err.println("Caught SOAPException (" +
                        e.getFaultCode() + "): " +
                        e.getMessage());
    }
    }
}
```

If resp.generatedFault( ) returns true, we print out the fault code and fault string
values just as we did before. Next, we call fault.getDetailEntries( ), which returns
a vector containing the detail elements. We simply iterate over the vector, casting
each object retrieved to an instance of org.w3c.dom.Element and calling the
getFirstChild( ) method on the resulting element. Now we display the element name
and the node data. If you run the example you should see the following output:

```
SOAP-ENV:Server: Data Feed Unavailable
alternateProvider: www.mindstrm.com
reasonDescription: Power Outage
alternateContact: rob@mindstrm.com
reasonCode: 199
```

Throwing and Catching Exceptions in GLUE

The concepts covered for faults and exceptions in Apache SOAP are similar to those
used in GLUE, although some of the techniques are different. Actually, GLUE has a
few ways of dealing with exceptions, so if you're interested in all the possibilities, I
encourage you to read the GLUE user's guide; we're going to cover only one
technique here.

Let's skip the basics and get right into an example that returns faults with a detail
section. GLUE includes its own SOAP exception class called electric.net.soap.
SOAPException. It's not the same as the Apache SOAPException, so don't confuse the
two. GLUE's SOAPException allows you to set the fault code, fault string, fault actor,

and details, and has several constructors using a variety of combinations of these fault element values. Therefore, you don't have to write a fault handler to get the detail information into the fault; just throw an instance of SOAPException with the appropriate values. Let's create a service called urn:AnotherFaultService and implement it with the AnotherFaultService class:

```
package javasoap.book.ch7;
import electric.net.soap.SOAPException;
import electric.xml.*;
public class AnotherFaultService {
    public int generateFault( )
            throws SOAPException {
        Element elem = new Element("detail");
        Element sub = elem.addElement("reasonCode");
        sub.addText("199");
        sub = elem.addElement("reasonDescription");
        sub.addText("Power Outage");
        sub = elem.addElement("alternateProvider");
        sub.addText("www.mindstrm.com");
        sub = elem.addElement("alternateContact");
        sub.addText("rob@mindstrm.com");
        SOAPException e = new SOAPException(
                        "Data Feed Unavailable",
                        SOAPException.SERVER,
                        "urn:AnotherFaultService",
                        elem);
        throw e;
    }
}
```

In this class, we generate the detail section before creating an instance of SOAPException. GLUE includes a simple XML API, which I've used here to create the detail element. The first step is to create an instance of electric.xml.Element with a tag name of "detail". Following that, I add new elements to the detail element by calling elem.addElement( ), with the tag name of the added element as the parameter. The data is set by calling the addText( ) method of the element returned from elem.addElement( ). Once we have the detail element, we're ready to create the SOAPException. The parameters to the constructor are the fault string, the fault code, the fault actor, and the XML element containing the details. Here's the code used to deploy urn:AnotherFaultService:

```
package javasoap.book.ch7;
import electric.util.Context;
import electric.server.http.HTTP;
import electric.registry.Registry;
public class FaultServiceApp {

    public static void main( String[] args )
                throws Exception {
        String ns = "urn:AnotherFaultService";
        HTTP.startup("http://georgetown:8004/glue");
```

```
            Context context = new Context( );
            context.addProperty("activation", "application");
            context.addProperty("namespace", ns);
            Registry.publish(ns,
                javasoap.book.ch7.AnotherFaultService.class, context );
        }
    }
```

The Java interface for binding to this service contains the generateFault( ) method, which is declared to throw an instance of electric.net.soap.SOAPException:

```
package javasoap.book.ch7;
import electric.net.soap.SOAPException;
public interface IAnotherFaultService {
  int generateFault( ) throws SOAPException;
}
```

GLUE will handle the details of putting the fault on the wire, as well as turning that fault back into an instance of electric.net.soap.SOAPException on the client side. Here's the client application that invokes the generateFault( ) method of urn: AnotherFaultService:

```
package javasoap.book.ch7;
import electric.registry.RegistryException;
import electric.registry.Registry;
import electric.net.soap.SOAPException;
import electric.xml.*;
public class FaultServiceClient {
    public static void main(String[] args) throws Exception
    {
        try {
            IAnotherFaultService srv =
              (IAnotherFaultService)Registry.bind(
                "http://georgetown:8004/glue/urn:AnotherFaultService.wsdl",
                IAnotherFaultService.class);
            srv.generateFault( );

        }
        catch (SOAPException se) {
            System.out.println(se.getSOAPCode( ));
            System.out.println(se.getMessage( ));
            System.out.println(se.getSOAPActor( ));
            System.out.println(se.getSOAPDetailElement( ));
        }
        catch (RegistryException e) {
            System.out.println(e);
        }
    }
}
```

We print the contents of the fault in the catch block for SOAPException. The fault code, fault string, and fault actor are retrieved using the SOAPException method calls getSOAPCode( ), getMessage( ), and getSOAPActor( ), and the details can be retrieved as an XML element by calling getSOAPDetailElement( ). If we wanted to process the fields of the detail section, we could look at the subelements and their values individually. In this case, we're just displaying its contents by taking advantage of the toString( ) method of the detail Element. If you run this example you'll get the following output:

```
Server
Data Feed Unavailable
urn:AnotherFaultService
<detail>
   <reasonCode>199</reasonCode>
   <reasonDescription>Power Outage</reasonDescription>
   <alternateProvider>www.mindstrm.com</alternateProvider>
   <alternateContact>rob@mindstrm.com</alternateContact>
</detail>
```

The only thing that may look unusual is that the fault code, displayed on the first line, does not include its namespace qualifier; the SOAPException implementation apparently strips it off. That's probably a good idea, since the qualifier is meaningless unless you know its value as well. You can see what I mean by looking at the SOAP envelope returned by the server:

```
<soap:Envelope
   xmlns:xsi='http://www.w3.org/2001/XMLSchema-instance'
   xmlns:xsd='http://www.w3.org/2001/XMLSchema'
   xmlns:soap='http://schemas.xmlsoap.org/soap/envelope/'
   xmlns:soapenc='http://schemas.xmlsoap.org/soap/encoding/'
   soap:encodingStyle='http://schemas.xmlsoap.org/soap/encoding/'>
     <soap:Body>
       <soap:Fault>
         <faultcode>soap:Server</faultcode>
         <faultstring>Data Feed Unavailable</faultstring>
         <faultactor>urn:AnotherFaultService</faultactor>
         <detail>
            <reasonCode>199</reasonCode>
            <reasonDescription>Power Outage</reasonDescription>
            <alternateProvider>www.mindstrm.com</alternateProvider>
            <alternateContact>rob@mindstrm.com</alternateContact>
         </detail>
       </soap:Fault>
     </soap:Body>
</soap:Envelope>
```

Generating and handling SOAP faults is an integral part of writing applications using SOAP. You can't ignore it any more than you can ignore exceptions and exception handling in Java. Luckily, the techniques for working with faults are straightforward, and with a little extra work an endless amount of detail can be included.

The best software always expects faults to take place. The trick is to design for them ahead of time, and not be surprised by faults that you didn't plan for. That's not SOAP; that's software design. Get your fault processing design right, and you'll have no trouble implementing it using SOAP.

CHAPTER 8

Alternative Techniques

Although SOAP is most commonly used for RPC, there are other possibilities as well. SOAP can also be used to create message-style services in which a SOAP envelope is sent to a server without the requirement that anything be returned to the caller. The message can contain any payload that is appropriate for the service—it doesn't have to look like a procedure call. This is similar to the way email systems work. When you send an email, you don't get anything back from the server, and there aren't any rules about what the email can contain. The server accepts your message and does its job without any more involvement from the sender. This is in sharp contrast to RPC services, where a return value is an integral part of the method invocation process.

Not all SOAP implementations support message-style services, but these services can be a useful model and are well worth investigating. GLUE doesn't support message services, but Apache SOAP does, so we'll use Apache SOAP to develop some examples.

The Apache SOAP API for message-style services is a lower level API than the one we've been using for RPC. This shouldn't be surprising, since RPC works by sending messages back and forth. The RPC API is built on top of the message API and includes some useful abstractions that make writing RPC services and service clients relatively easy. You won't find any such convenience in the Apache SOAP message service world. Instead you'll have to work with the lower level APIs that deal directly with envelope marshalling and unmarshalling, XML structures, and a variety of other things that were handled automatically in the RPC world. The upside is that you have more control over the process, although in most cases I prefer better abstractions.

In most of the examples so far, we've used the SOAP encoding style, but that's not the only way to encode data. Literal encoding is another important and useful mechanism, especially when you're trying to pass existing XML documents using SOAP. So let's look at an example using literal encoding to see how this option is used.

We'll also take a look at SOAP with attachments. The idea behind this is simple: just as you can attach a file to an email message, you can attach external data to a SOAP message, using MIME. This technique is useful when you need to pass data that has no business being encoded or decoded as part of your SOAP message, such as an image or sound file. Using attachments lets you send large binary data objects along with your SOAP messages without having to include the data within the SOAP envelope. For many systems, using attachments results in a significant performance improvement over encoding the data within the envelope.

SOAP Messaging

The format of the SOAP envelope for messaging services differs from the format used for RPC services. There is no concept of a method signature, method parameters, or return values in the messaging model. Basically, you're just sending some XML to a service. However, there are some requirements that allow you to direct the message to the correct service and service method. The name of the first child element of the SOAP Body must correspond to the name of the service method to be used, and the xmlns namespace attribute on that element specifies the name of the service. Here's a simple SOAP message that is directed to the recordTemperature method of the urn:WeatherDiary service for processing:

```
<SOAP_ENV:Envelope
  xmlns:SOAP-ENV="http://schemas.xmlsoap.org/soap/envelope/">
    <SOAP-ENV:Body>
        <recordTemperature xmlns="urn:WeatherDiary"/>
        <temperature>75.5</temperature>
        <zipcode>50328</zipcode>
    </SOAP-ENV:Body>
</SOAP-ENV:Envelope>
```

The recordTemperature service method records the current temperature associated with a zip code. Notice that there's no data in the recordTemperature element, although it's perfectly valid for that element to contain data and child elements. The point is that it isn't required. In fact, I could have made the temperature and zipcode elements children of recordTemperature instead of siblings. Either way is fine; as far as SOAP is concerned, this is just a message that is delivered to a method, not an RPC with arguments that need to be handled correctly. As you'll see shortly, we're going to have to write some code to get at these elements either way.

So as long as you've got that first element set up properly, the rest of the XML is up to you. You don't have any parameters to encode or any strict syntax requirements. This doesn't mean you can just send any message to any message service endpoint, however. On the contrary, the absence of strict syntax requirements makes it harder to interoperate with services and service clients not under your control. You have to make sure your messages conform to the formats required by various other services. That doesn't make this service model bad; it makes it more flexible, with all of the problems associated with that level of flexibility.

Writing a Message Service

Writing a message-style service is not all that different from writing an RPC service: you have to write a method that is called when a message is received. The difference is in the method signatures. With RPC, we had the luxury of defining the service method's parameters and their types, as well as the return value type. In the messaging model, all service methods have the same signature. There are three parameters. The first is an instance of org.apache.soap.Envelope, which encapsulates the contents of the SOAP envelope that was received by the service method. The other two parameters are instances of org.apache.soap.rpc.SOAPContext,* a class that encapsulates a MIME multipart message. One is for the input, and the other is for the output. Yes, that's right—the output! Even though SOAP messaging services are not required to provide a response, they are permitted to do so if the underlying transport supports it. HTTP certainly allows content to be returned to the caller, so a message service built on top of HTTP can provide a response. Actually, the Apache SOAP framework requires a message service to provide a response.

Let's write a Java class for the urn:WeatherDiary service. We'll need a method called recordTemperature so that client applications can send their current temperature to the service. Here is the javasoap.book.ch8.WeatherDiary class that implements the service:

```
package javasoap.book.ch8;
import java.io.*;
import java.util.*;
import org.apache.soap.*;
import org.apache.soap.rpc.SOAPContext;
import javax.mail.MessagingException;
import org.w3c.dom.*;
public class WeatherDiary {
    Hashtable _diary = new Hashtable();
    public void recordTemperature (Envelope env, SOAPContext
                    reqCtx, SOAPContext resCtx)
        throws Exception {

        Vector v = env.getBody().getBodyEntries();
        int cnt = v.size();
        String zipcode = null;
        String temperature = null;
        for (int i = 0; i < cnt; i++) {
            Element e = (Element)v.elementAt(i);
            String name = e.getTagName();
            if (name.equals("zipcode")) {
                zipcode = e.getFirstChild().getNodeValue();
            }
            else if (name.equals("temperature")) {
                temperature = e.getFirstChild().getNodeValue();
```

---

* It's interesting that this class resides in the SOAP RPC package. That's not an indication that its intended use is only in RPC-style services; it probably should be in a different package.

```
        }
    }
    if (zipcode == null || temperature == null) {
        throw new IllegalArgumentException(
                "ZIPCODE and/or TEMPERATURE Not Specified");
    }
    _diary.put(zipcode, temperature);
    resCtx.setRootPart("OK", "text/xml");
    }
}
```

We want to get at the elements contained within the SOAP body. We do this by call-ing the getBody( ) method of the env parameter, which returns an instance of org. apache.soap.Body. Then we call the body object's getBodyEntries( ) method, which returns a java.util.Vector containing instances of org.w3c.dom.Element. Each Element in the vector encapsulates one of the direct child elements of the SOAP body. If you look at the SOAP envelope that we're sending to the service, you'll see that we used three direct child elements of the body: recordTemperature, zipcode, and temperature. That's the format we'll use for the recordTemperature method of the urn: WeatherDiary service. We iterate over the Vector to get at each Element of the body. To find out what kind of element we got, we call the getTagName( ) method and check the result to see if it's the zipcode or temperature element. (We'll also get the recordTemperature element used to specify the service and method name, but we don't have any use for that element in this example.) When we find an element tag that we're interested in, we get its first (and only) child node, where we'll find the data for that element. The data is stored in the local variables zipcode and temperature. After falling out of the loop, we look to see whether either of the variables is still null. If so, at least one of the required elements did not appear in the message, so we throw an exception. That exception causes Apache SOAP to return a SOAP fault to the caller. Otherwise, the data is stored in the _diary hash table with the zip code as the key and the temperature as the value. We're going to deploy this service using appli-cation scope, so the contents of the hash table will be intact across invocations.

The last step is to set a return value. This is a bit confusing—why should a message-style service have a return value? However, you'll get an exception from the Apache framework if you don't supply one. As I said earlier, the Apache framework insists on supplying a response message, and wants something to put in the message. The easi-est way to set the return value is to supply a simple text message as the root part of the response context by calling the resCtx.setRootPart( ) method. The first parameter is the text to be sent; the second part is the MIME type of the data, in this case text/xml. All I'm doing is sending back the string "OK" to indicate that the data was received.

Now let's deploy the service. Here's the deployment descriptor:

```
<isd:service
    xmlns:isd="http://xml.apache.org/xml-soap/deployment"
    id="urn:WeatherDiary" type="message">
    <isd:provider
```

```
        type="java"
        scope="Application"
        methods="recordTemperature">
      <isd:java
          class="javasoap.book.ch8.WeatherDiary"
          static="false"/>
    </isd:provider>

    <isd:faultListener>org.apache.soap.server.DOMFaultListener
    </isd:faultListener>
    <isd:mappings>
    </isd:mappings>
  </isd:service>
```

The only difference between this deployment descriptor and those we created for RPC-style services is the use of the type attribute on the isd:service element. The value of this attribute is now set to "message", which indicates that the service being deployed is a message service, rather than an RPC service.

So this service can go along happily receiving temperature updates from client applications that supply readings at various locations. Let's take a look at a client application that sends the updates. We'll build the XML for the SOAP envelope and then send it to the urn:WeatherDiary service.

```java
package javasoap.book.ch8;
import java.io.*;
import java.net.*;
import javax.xml.parsers.*;
import org.w3c.dom.*;
import org.xml.sax.*;
import org.apache.soap.*;
import org.apache.soap.messaging.*;
import org.apache.soap.transport.*;
import org.apache.soap.util.xml.*;
public class WeatherClient {
    public static void main (String[] args) throws Exception {
        DocumentBuilder xdb = XMLParserUtils.getXMLDocBuilder();
        Document doc = xdb.newDocument();

        Element elem =
                doc.createElementNS(Constants.NS_URI_SOAP_ENV,
                "SOAP-ENV:Envelope");
        doc.appendChild(elem);

        Element sub =
                doc.createElementNS(Constants.NS_URI_SOAP_ENV,
                "SOAP-ENV:Body");
        elem.appendChild(sub);
        elem = sub;
        sub = doc.createElement("recordTemperature");
        sub.setAttribute("xmlns", "urn:WeatherDiary");
        elem.appendChild(sub);
        sub = doc.createElement("zipcode");
```

```
            Text txt = doc.createTextNode("");
            txt.setData("12345");
            sub.appendChild(txt);
            elem.appendChild(sub);
            sub = doc.createElement("temperature");
            txt = doc.createTextNode("");
            txt.setData("52.3");
            sub.appendChild(txt);
            elem.appendChild(sub);
            Envelope msgEnv = Envelope.unmarshall(
                              doc.getDocumentElement());
            URL url = new URL(
              "http://georgetown:8080/soap/servlet/messagerouter");
            Message msg = new Message();
            msg.send(url, "", msgEnv);

            SOAPTransport st = msg.getSOAPTransport();
            BufferedReader br = st.receive();
            String line;
            while ((line = br.readLine()) != null) {
                System.out.println(line);
            }
        }
    }
```

Most of this code is not really about SOAP; it's about building an XML document that happens to be a SOAP envelope. However, it seems to me that if you're going to use the Apache message-style services, then you may also be creating your SOAP envelope on the fly.* So let's take a quick look at how it's done.

The first step is to get an instance of org.w3c.dom.Document, which encapsulates the entire XML document starting with the root element. We get the initial Document by calling XMLParserUtils.getXMLDocBuilder() to get a DocumentBuilder, and then calling its newDocument() method. Now we can work on the envelope element, which we will use as the root of our document. The doc.createElementNS() method creates an element along with a qualifying namespace identifier. The first parameter is the standard SOAP envelope namespace http://schemas.xmlsoap.org/soap/envelope/, which we get from Constants.NS_URI_SOAP_ENV. The second parameter is a qualified name, i.e., a qualifier and element name separated by a colon (:). In this case we're using the qualifier SOAP-ENV to be consistent with earlier examples, but the qualifier is nothing more than a namespace identifier; you can use any name. The name of the element itself is Envelope. Now that we've created the SOAP envelope, we need to add it to the document by calling doc.appendChild(). We use the same technique to create the Body element, only this time we append it to the Envelope element rather than to the document itself, because the SOAP Body is a child element of the SOAP Envelope.

---

* If you won't be creating your own envelope on the fly, you might want to look at the messaging example provided with Apache SOAP. That example assumes that the envelope was generated by some other system and shows you how to load it into your application to be sent to a service.

Now that we've set up the Envelope and the Body, we need to create elements for our specific content and add them to the body. So we set the elem variable to the Body element, and use the sub variable to create the child elements of the body. To invoke the correct service method, the first child element of the body must be named recordTemperature. This element is created by calling doc.createElement( ) and passing the name of the element as the parameter. The resulting element is saved in the sub variable. To invoke the proper service, we need to set the xmlns attribute value to the name of the service. We do this by calling sub.setAttribute( ), where the first parameter is the name of the attribute and the second parameter is the value. The recordTemperature element doesn't have any data or child elements, so we just append it to the body by calling elem.appendChild(sub).

Next we create the zipcode element, again using the doc.createElement( ) method. No attributes are necessary for this element, but we need to add a data node for the zip code. We create an instance of org.w3c.dom.Text by calling the doc.createTextNode( ) method. The Text class is used to represent textual data, which is perfect for our purpose. The zip code data is set by calling txt.setData( ), and the text node is appended to the zipcode element by the sub.appendChild( ) method. In turn, the zipcode element is appended to the Body element. We create the temperature element in exactly the same way, and then it too is appended to the Body element.

We're going to send this message to the server using an instance of org.apache.soap.messaging.Message, but first we need to turn the XML document into an instance of org.apache.soap.Envelope. We accomplish this by calling the Envelope.unmarshall( ) method, passing it the root document element. This seems like it's going to add some overhead; you can bet that the resulting Envelope object will be marshalled all over again to be sent to the server. In any case, the result of this method call is an Envelope instance called msgEnv. Next we create an instance of java.net.URL with the address of the SOAP router that handles routing for message services. For RPC services, we've been sending SOAP requests to *http://georgetown:8080/soap/servlet/rpcrouter*; for message services, we send to *http://georgetown:8080/soap/servlet/messagerouter*. Now we can create an instance of Message and call its send( ) method. The URL is the first parameter, and the envelope is the last. The second parameter is an empty string representing the SOAP actor; since we don't have any use for a SOAP actor here, an empty string is good enough.

Because we know that our service transport is HTTP and that our service responds with either a fault or a simple "OK", it's a good idea to look at the response before the application terminates. To view the response, we start by calling msg.getSOAPTransport( ), which gives us an instance of the transport used to send the message. This method returns an instance of org.apache.soap.transport.SOAPTransport. If the transport supports responses, like HTTP does, you can call the transport's receive( ) method, which returns a BufferedReader object. If the transport doesn't support responses, the receive( ) method returns null. Once we have the BufferedReader, all we do is grab each line of the response and print it to the console.

If the service was happy with the message, the only thing that will be printed is the string "OK". Otherwise, you'll see the entire SOAP fault document.

Now that we've put the client together, let's look at the SOAP envelope that it sends:

```
<SOAP-ENV:Envelope
  xmlns:SOAP-ENV="http://schemas.xmlsoap.org/soap/envelope/">
  <SOAP-ENV:Body>
    <recordTemperature xmlns="urn:WeatherDiary"/>
    <zipcode>12345</zipcode>
    <temperature>52.3</temperature>
  </SOAP-ENV:Body>
</SOAP-ENV:Envelope>
```

Now we have a service that can collect information and a client that can send information, but we still don't have a mechanism that allows someone to retrieve the data that has been collected. We should really extend the service by adding a method for querying the temperature at a specified zip code. But wait…that sounds more like an RPC-style service than a messaging service. It's one thing to have a message service respond with something general like "OK, I got your message," but it's quite another to have it respond with a specific result based on the content of the message received. Why should you use RPC-style services when working with a request/response model? Many developers hold strong opinions about what kind of service is appropriate for each application, but other than the fact that not all messaging transports support a response, there aren't any good reasons not to use a message service in this situation. It's easy to fall into the trap of thinking only in a procedural model. Some systems could benefit from the freedom provided by the messaging model, where you're not bound by the rules of specific parameter passing like you are in the RPC world. For example, you might want to send a purchase order document to a message service and receive a confirmation document with a delivery schedule in return. This exchange could be implemented as an RPC, but it's a lot easier to think of it in terms of a message exchange. Although the structure of SOAP RPC doesn't prevent you from developing open-ended parameter passing models, the messaging model may fit your designs better. So let's expand our service with a getTemperature( ) method that returns an XML document.

```
package javasoap.book.ch8;
import java.io.*;
import java.util.*;
import org.apache.soap.*;
import org.apache.soap.rpc.SOAPContext;
import javax.mail.MessagingException;
import org.w3c.dom.*;
import org.apache.soap.util.xml.*;
public class WeatherDiary {
    Hashtable _diary = new Hashtable( );
    Hashtable _times = new Hashtable( );
    public void getTemperature(Envelope env, SOAPContext reqCtx,
                               SOAPContext resCtx)
            throws Exception {
```

```
        Vector v = env.getBody().getBodyEntries( );
        int cnt = v.size( );
        String zipcode = null;
        for (int i = 0; i < cnt; i++) {
            Element e = (Element)v.elementAt(i);
            String name = e.getTagName( );
            if (name.equals("zipcode")) {
                zipcode = e.getFirstChild().getNodeValue( );
            }
        }
        if (zipcode == null) {
            throw new IllegalArgumentException(
                    "ZIPCODE Not Specified");
        }
        String temperature = (String)_diary.get(zipcode);
        String rectime = (String)_times.get(zipcode);
        String response = "<WeatherDiaryResponse>" +
                        (char)10 +
                        "    <temperature>" + temperature +
                        "</temperature>" +
                        (char)10 +
                        "    <recordTime>" + rectime +
                        "</recordTime>" +
                        (char)10 +
                        "</WeatherDiaryResponse>";
        resCtx.setRootPart(response, "text/xml");
    }
    public void recordTemperature (Envelope env, SOAPContext
                    reqCtx, SOAPContext resCtx)
        throws Exception {

        Vector v = env.getBody().getBodyEntries( );
        int cnt = v.size( );
        String zipcode = null;
        String temperature = null;
        for (int i = 0; i < cnt; i++) {
            Element e = (Element)v.elementAt(i);
            String name = e.getTagName( );
            if (name.equals("zipcode")) {
                zipcode = e.getFirstChild().getNodeValue( );
            }
            else if (name.equals("temperature")) {
                temperature = e.getFirstChild().getNodeValue( );
            }
        }
        if (zipcode == null || temperature == null) {
            throw new IllegalArgumentException(
                    "ZIPCODE and/or TEMPERATURE Not Specified");
        }
        _diary.put(zipcode, temperature);
        _times.put(zipcode, new Date().toString( ));
        resCtx.setRootPart("OK", "text/xml");
    }
}
```

To make the response from the service method more interesting, we modified the recordTemperature( ) method to store the time the temperature was recorded in another hash table called _times, which uses the zip code as the key and the current time as the value. But the most important addition is the getTemperature( ) service method. This method starts by looking through the child elements of the SOAP body for an element called zipcode, which tells the method which zip code is being requested. If a zipcode element isn't found, the method throws an exception, resulting in a SOAP fault. Once we have a zip code, we retrieve the temperature and the time it was recorded from the _diary and _times hash tables, respectively. Next, we build an XML document in the String variable called response. This document is simple. Its root is an element named WeatherDiaryResponse, which contains two child elements named temperature and recordTime. These elements contain the temperature and the time it was recorded for the specified zip code. The response string is used as the first parameter of the resCtx.setRootPart( ) method. The result is that we've responded to the incoming message with an XML document that contains the requested data. You'll need to redeploy the service, adding the getTemperature( ) method to the deployment descriptor.

Now let's create a client application that requests temperature data. The client goes through the same process that we've demonstrated in other examples. This time, we include only the zipcode element and its data, and the first element is named getTemperature to invoke the correct service method. Here's the code for the client:

```
package javasoap.book.ch8;
import java.io.*;
import java.net.*;
import javax.xml.parsers.*;
import org.w3c.dom.*;
import org.xml.sax.*;
import org.apache.soap.*;
import org.apache.soap.messaging.*;
import org.apache.soap.transport.*;
import org.apache.soap.util.xml.*;
public class TemperatureClient {
    public static void main (String[] args) throws Exception {
        DocumentBuilder xdb = XMLParserUtils.getXMLDocBuilder( );
        Document doc = xdb.newDocument( );

        Element elem =
                doc.createElementNS(Constants.NS_URI_SOAP_ENV,
                "SOAP-ENV:Envelope");
        doc.appendChild(elem);

        Element sub =
                doc.createElementNS(Constants.NS_URI_SOAP_ENV,
                "SOAP-ENV:Body");
        elem.appendChild(sub);
        elem = sub;
        sub = doc.createElement("getTemperature");
```

```
sub.setAttribute("xmlns", "urn:WeatherDiary");
elem.appendChild(sub);
sub = doc.createElement("zipcode");
Text txt = doc.createTextNode("");
txt.setData("12345");
sub.appendChild(txt);
elem.appendChild(sub);
Envelope msgEnv = Envelope.unmarshall
                     (doc.getDocumentElement ());
URL url = new URL(
    "http://georgetown:8080/soap/servlet/messagerouter");
Message msg = new Message ();
msg.send (url, "", msgEnv);

SOAPTransport st = msg.getSOAPTransport ();
BufferedReader br = st.receive ();
String line;
while ((line = br.readLine ()) != null) {
   System.out.println (line);
}
    }
  }
```

Before you run this application, you'll need to populate the service with temperature data for zip code 12345. (Redeploying the service with the new getTemperature( ) method destroys the data we saved earlier.) After putting some data into the service, run the client. It should spit out the following:

```
<WeatherDiaryResponse>
    <temperature>52.3</temperature>
    <recordTime>Wed Oct 31 14:58:48 EST 2001</recordTime>
</WeatherDiaryResponse>
```

We won't look at the SOAP envelope that was sent to the getTemperature( ) method, since you can figure out what it looks like by now. The only interesting part of the envelope is the response.

It would be nice to provide some more structure to the output; right now, we just dump a few XML elements. So let's build a document out of the response instead. The following code replaces everything after the msg.send( ) call. After we get the BufferedReader, we still need an instance of DocumentBuilder. But now, instead of building a document piece by piece, we'll use the content of the response instead. We create an instance of org.xml.sax.InputSource, passing the BufferedReader to the constructor. Now we call xdb.parse( ) with the InputSource as the parameter. This parses the XML in the response and builds a Document instance for us. After getting the root element, we print it so that we can be sure we're getting the element we're expecting. Then we get a list of all of the child elements of the root by calling getElementsByTagName("*"), passing it the wildcard (*). This method retrieves all of the child elements of the WeatherDiaryResponse root element. Finally, the list is traversed and each element is printed, with its associated data.

```
SOAPTransport st = msg.getSOAPTransport ();
BufferedReader br = st.receive ();

xdb = XMLParserUtils.getXMLDocBuilder();
InputSource is = new InputSource(br);
doc = xdb.parse(is);
elem = doc.getDocumentElement();
System.out.println("Root Element Is: " +
                              elem.getTagName());

NodeList children = elem.getElementsByTagName("*");
int cnt = children.getLength();
for (int i = 0; i < cnt; i++) {
   Node n = children.item(i);
   String name = n.getNodeName();
   String val = n.getFirstChild().getNodeValue();
   System.out.println(name + ": " + val);
}
```

Running the modified client produces the following output:

```
Root Element Is: WeatherDiaryResponse
temperature: 52.3
recordTime: Wed Oct 31 14:58:48 EST 2001
```

So with a little bit of XML manipulation we can return meaningful data from a message-style service, assuming the underlying transport supports the ability to provide a response.

Literal Encoding

We've seen how to use SOAP for RPC-type services, as well as how to pass around XML data in the less restrictive world of SOAP messaging services. But another possibility is to pass XML using RPC services. The problem is that RPC services rely on a type mapping mechanism to convert between XML elements and Java classes. It would be nice if you could use an RPC-style method invocation to pass parameters, with the result being standard XML. Well, you can. To do it, you need to use XML literal encoding, which tells the underlying SOAP framework that the data is XML and should remain that way.

Let's go back to the world of finance. We'll create a service that provides corporate information on companies in an XML format. The service is called urn: CorporateDataService, which has a method called getDataForSymbol. The service is an RPC service, and the method takes a stock symbol as the parameter. The data returned can include the company name, company address, year of incorporation, number of employees, and the high and low trading price for the past 52 weeks. This service will pull its data from another system that already keeps corporate data in XML format in a database. So it's not the responsibility of the service to format the data, only to pass it back to the caller. This scenario is perfect for using XML literal encoding. If the service were going to process the data in some way, it might just as well be designed to return a complex type that can be mapped to a Java class. Another reason for using literal encoding is that the client application may want to get the data in the XML format used on the back-end. It would be a waste of time to convert the XML on the server side, only to have the client put it back into XML. In this case, we're using SOAP to provide access to existing data, and then relying on existing software systems to do the processing.

To create a Java method with an appropriate signature, we need a class that encapsulates an XML document, since that's what we want to return to the caller. org.w3c. dom.Element does what we want, so we'll define our service method to return an instance of that class. The javasoap.book.ch8.CorporateDataService class in the following listing implements the service. The service opens a file whose name is the symbol passed to it with the extension *.xml*. The file is expected to be in the same directory as the class itself. (We're assuming that some other system has already generated the corporate data XML files that the service loads.) A java.io.FileReader is created, using the filename as the parameter to its constructor. Next we create an instance of DocumentBuilder, and call its parse() method to turn the contents of the file into an XML document object. The parameter passed to the parse() method is an instance of org.xml.sax.InputSource, which we create using the FileReader as the constructor's parameter. Now all we need to do is return the root element, which we can retrieve by calling doc.getDocumentElement(). You can deploy this service just like the other services in this book, listing getDataForSymbol as the sole service method. No special mappings are needed.

```
package javasoap.book.ch8;
import java.io.*;
import java.util.*;
import org.apache.soap.*;
import org.w3c.dom.*;
import org.apache.soap.util.xml.*;
import javax.xml.parsers.*;
import org.xml.sax.*;
public class CorporateDataService {
    public CorporateDataService() {
    }
    public Element getDataForSymbol(String symbol)
         throws Exception {
       FileReader fr = new FileReader(symbol + ".xml");
       DocumentBuilder xdb = XMLParserUtils.getXMLDocBuilder();
       Document doc = xdb.parse(new InputSource (fr));
       if (doc == null) {
          throw new SOAPException(Constants.FAULT_CODE_SERVER,
                         "Invalid Data");
       }
       return doc.getDocumentElement();
    }
}
```

Let's take a look at a corporate data file that contains a sample of the XML that our service will return to the caller:

```xml
<corporateData>
    <symbol>MINDSTRM</symbol>
    <name>MindStream Software, Inc.</name>
    <address>
        <address1>111 Smithtown Bypass</address1>
        <address2>Suite 208</address2>
        <city>Hauppauge</city>
        <state>NY</state>
        <zip>11788</zip>
    </address>
    <incorpYear>1998</incorpYear>
    <numEmployees>unknown</numEmployees>
    <tradeHistory>
        <yearlyHigh>75.5</yearlyHigh>
        <yearlyLow>60</yearlyLow>
    </tradeHistory>
</corporateData>
```

Now we can write a client application to invoke the getDataForSymbol method:

```java
package javasoap.book.ch8;
import java.io.*;
import java.util.*;
import java.net.*;
import org.w3c.dom.*;
import org.apache.soap.util.xml.*;
import org.apache.soap.*;
import org.apache.soap.encoding.*;
import org.apache.soap.encoding.soapenc.*;
import org.apache.soap.rpc.*;
public class GetDataClient {
    public static void main(String[] args)
            throws Exception {
        URL url = new URL(
            "http://georgetown:8080/soap/servlet/rpcrouter");
        Call call = new Call();
        call.setTargetObjectURI("urn:CorporateDataService");
        call.setMethodName("getDataForSymbol");
        call.setEncodingStyleURI(Constants.NS_URI_LITERAL_XML);
        String symbol = "MINDSTRM";
        Vector params = new Vector();
        params.addElement(new Parameter("symbol", String.class,
                    symbol, Constants.NS_URI_SOAP_ENC));
        call.setParams(params);
        Response resp;
        try {
            resp = call.invoke(url, "");
        }
        catch (SOAPException e) {
            System.out.println(e.getMessage());
            return;
```

```
        }
        if (!resp.generatedFault( )) {
            Parameter ret = resp.getReturnValue( );
            Element bookEl = (Element)ret.getValue( );
            System.out.println(DOM2Writer.nodeToString(bookEl));
        }
    }
}
```

We need to set the encoding style to XML literal encoding, both because we want the server to serialize its response as a literal XML document, and because we want the response to be interpreted that way. To do this, we call call. setEncodingStyleURI( ) with the argument Constants.NS_URI_LITERAL_XML. In Apache SOAP, this sets the encoding style for the Body element. That's the highest level at which the encodingStyle attribute will be set. However, we don't want the parameter that we're passing (the stock symbol) to be interpreted as XML; after all, it's just a string. We want to use the standard SOAP encoding for the parameter, so we want the encodingStyle attribute to appear on the symbol element as well, with the appropriate value for SOAP encoding. To specify the encoding style for this parameter, we set the fourth argument of the Parameter constructor to Constants.NS_URI_SOAP_ENC. In all of the previous examples, we've set this value to null, which means that the encodingStyle attribute need not appear at the parameter level; the encoding style for the parameter defaults to the encoding style set for the body. Setting the encoding style for the symbol element explicitly overrides the body's encoding style.

Now we invoke the method as usual, but we cast the return value to an instance of Element, since we're expecting the return value to be literal XML. I pass the resulting Element to the DOM2Writer.nodeToString( ) method so that I can print the XML to the console. Let's take a look at the SOAP envelope that was sent to the service:

```
<SOAP-ENV:Envelope
xmlns:SOAP-ENV="http://schemas.xmlsoap.org/soap/envelope/"
xmlns:xsi="http://www.w3.org/2001/XMLSchema-instance"
xmlns:xsd="http://www.w3.org/2001/XMLSchema">
<SOAP-ENV:Body>
<ns1:getDataForSymbol
xmlns:ns1="urn:CorporateDataService"
SOAP-ENV:encodingStyle="http://xml.apache.org/xml-soap/literalxml">
<symbol xsi:type="xsd:string"
SOAP-ENV:encodingStyle="http://schemas.xmlsoap.org/soap/encoding/">
MINDSTRM
</symbol>
</ns1:getDataForSymbol>
</SOAP-ENV:Body>
</SOAP-ENV:Envelope>
```

As you can see, the encodingStyle attribute is set to literal XML encoding for the SOAP Body element. The symbol element overrides this setting to use SOAP encoding. Now, here's the response envelope. You can see that the return value uses XML literal encoding, as the entire response is XML data.

```
<SOAP-ENV:Envelope
xmlns:SOAP-ENV=http://schemas.xmlsoap.org/soap/envelope/
xmlns:xsi=http://www.w3.org/2001/XMLSchema-instance
xmlns:xsd="http://www.w3.org/2001/XMLSchema">
<SOAP-ENV:Body>
<ns1:getDataForSymbolResponse
xmlns:ns1="urn:CorporateDataService"
SOAP-ENV:encodingStyle="http://xml.apache.org/xml-soap/literalxml">
<return>
<corporateData>
    <symbol>MINDSTRM</symbol>
    <name>MindStream Software, Inc.</name>
    <address>
        <address1>111 Smithtown Bypass</address1>
        <address2>Suite 208</address2>
        <city>Hauppauge</city>
        <state>NY</state>
        <zip>11788</zip>
    </address>
    <incorpYear>1998</incorpYear>
    <numEmployees>unknown</numEmployees>
    <tradeHistory>
        <yearlyHigh>75.5</yearlyHigh>
        <yearlyLow>60</yearlyLow>
    </tradeHistory>
</corporateData>
</return>
</ns1:getDataForSymbolResponse>
</SOAP-ENV:Body>
</SOAP-ENV:Envelope>
```

You can use the same technique if you want to send literal XML as a parameter to an RPC service method. Just specify the `Constants.NS_URI_LITERAL_XML` encoding style when you call the `Parameter` constructor. There's no requirement that you use the same encoding style for all the parameters; do whatever is appropriate to your application.

SOAP with Attachments

Many SOAP implementations allow you to send data along with the SOAP envelope as an attachment. Attachments are useful when the data would put a large and unnecessary burden on the SOAP processor. For example, consider how you would send an audio or video file as part of a SOAP message. These can be very large files, and they are not encoded in XML. You could certainly include them in your SOAP envelope using a binary encoding scheme like base64, but that would cause the data to be loaded and processed by your SOAP engine. It would certainly work, but it's a lot of overhead for no gain: why should your SOAP engine process a huge amount of binary data that it can't do anything with? Attaching the data allows you to send it along without incurring the overhead, but also without the structure of XML.

Let's create a buying and selling service for used cars. We'll have methods that list a car for sale and that retrieve information about available cars. We need a custom type to represent a listing; this type encapsulates the details of the car and the contact information for the car's seller. Here's the code for the javasoap.book.ch8. Listing class that we'll use to pass this information. It includes a toString( ) method so we can easily display its contents.

```java
package javasoap.book.ch8;
public class Listing {
    String _make;
    String _model;
    int    _year;
    int    _miles;
    String _ownerName;
    String _ownerEmail;
    public Listing( ) {
    }
    public Listing(String make, String model,
      int year, int miles, String ownerName, String ownerEmail) {
        setMake(make);
        setModel(model);
        setYear(year);
        setMiles(miles);
        setOwnerName(ownerName);
        setOwnerEmail(ownerEmail);
    }
    public void setMake(String make) {
        _make = make;
    }
    public String getMake( ) {
        return _make;
    }
    public void setModel(String model) {
        _model = model;
    }
    public String getModel( ) {
        return _model;
    }
    public void setYear(int year) {
        _year = year;
    }
    public int getyear( ) {
        return _year;
    }
    public void setMiles(int miles) {
        _miles = miles;
    }
    public int getMiles( ) {
        return _miles;
    }
    public void setOwnerName(String ownerName) {
        _ownerName = ownerName;
    }
```

```
    public String getOwnerName( ) {
       return _ownerName;
    }
    public void setOwnerEmail(String ownerEmail) {
       _ownerEmail = ownerEmail;
    }
    public String getOwnerEmail( ) {
       return _ownerEmail;
    }
    public String toString( ) {
       String result = String.valueOf(_year) + " " +
                    _make + " " + _model +
                    " with " + String.valueOf(_miles) +
                    " miles:" +
                    "\n    Owned by " + _ownerName + "(" +
                    _ownerEmail + ")";
       return result;
    }
}
```

The Listing class has string properties called Make and Model, which represent the manufacturer of the car and the model name, respectively. The Year is an integer property representing the year the car was built, and the Miles integer property is the mileage of the car. The OwnerName and OwnerEmail are string properties for the name and email address of the person who owns the car. The get and set methods for the properties conform to the JavaBeans patterns, so we won't need to write a custom serializer for the Listing class.

Now let's create a class to implement the urn:UsedCarListingService service. sending listings to the service. The addListing( ) method,* which sends listings to the service, takes an instance of Listing as its first parameter and returns an integer that represents the listing's ID. We'll allow the caller to attach an image file to an invocation of the addListing( ) web service method, so the second parameter is an instance of javax.activation.DataHandler that encapsulates the attachment. Apache SOAP already has a serializer for the DataHandler class, and takes advantage of the Java-Beans Activation Framework (JAF) for handling MIME attachments. This framework makes receiving attachments in an RPC service as simple as passing a parameter. The work of referencing and extracting the attachment is done for you, and you can work with the data through the JAF API. The search( ) method has String parameters for the make and model of the car, and returns an array of listing IDs. And finally, a getListing( ) method takes a listing ID as its parameter and returns an instance of Listing, and a getImage( ) method also takes the listing ID as its parameter and returns the associated image file as an attachment. Here is the javasoap.book.ch8.UsedCarListingService class:

```
    package javasoap.book.ch8;
    import java.util.*;
```

---

* Of course a removeListing would be a good idea too, but it's not important for the example.

```
import java.io.*;
import javax.activation.*;
import org.apache.soap.util.mime.*;
public class UsedCarListingService {
    Hashtable _listings = new Hashtable( );
    int _nextId = 100;
    public int addListing(Listing listing, DataHandler handler)
                throws Exception {
        _listings.put(new Integer(_nextId), listing);
        int listno = _nextId;
        _nextId++;
        if (handler != null) {
            String fname = String.valueOf(listno) + ".bin";
            DataSource ds = handler.getDataSource( );
            ByteArrayDataSource bsource =
                    new ByteArrayDataSource(ds.getInputStream( ),
                                            handler.getContentType( ));
            bsource.writeTo(new FileOutputStream(fname));
        }
        return listno;
    }
    public Integer[] search(String make, String model) {
        Vector v = findListingIds(make, model);
        int cnt = v.size( );
        if (cnt == 0)
            return null;
        Integer ids[] = new Integer[cnt];
        for (int i = 0; i < cnt; i++) {
            ids[i] = (Integer)v.elementAt(i);
        }
        return ids;
    }
    protected Vector findListingIds(String make, String model) {

        Vector result = new Vector( );
        for (Enumeration e = _listings.keys( ) ;
                            e.hasMoreElements( ) ;) {
            Integer i = (Integer)e.nextElement( );
            Listing listing = (Listing)_listings.get(i);
            if (make.equals(listing.getMake( )) &&
                model.equals(listing.getModel( ))) {
                result.add(i);
            }
        }

        return result;
    }
    public Listing getListing(int id) {
        Listing listing = (Listing)_listings.get(new Integer(id));
        return listing;
    }
    public DataHandler getImage(int id)
            throws Exception {
        String fname = String.valueOf(id) + ".bin";
```

```
        DataSource ds =
            new ByteArrayDataSource(new File(fname), null);
        DataHandler dh = new DataHandler(ds);
        return dh;
    }
}
```

The service operates at application scope, so all of the listings are available as long as the service is running. We don't bother to keep the listings in any kind of persistent storage, although you obviously would in the real world. The attached files, however, are stored in files on disk. We'll keep all of the listings in a hash table called _listings, where the keys are the unique listing IDs. New ID values are generated by incrementing the value of _nextId each time the addListing( ) method is invoked. The first part of addListing( ) stores the listing passed as a parameter in the hash table. The key to the hash table is an Integer based on the value of _nextId, which is subsequently incremented. The next step is to extract the attachment and store its contents in a local file. The filename is just the listing number with a *.bin* extension. We get a reference to a javax.activation.DataSource by calling the getDataSource( ) method of the handler parameter, and then create an org.apache.soap.util.mime. ByteArrayDataSource. The first parameter to its constructor is a java.io.InputStream for the data, which we get by calling ds.getInputStream( ). The other parameter is a String containing the MIME type of the data, which we get by calling handler. getContentType( ). Now we can save the contents of the attachment in a file by calling the writeTo( ) method of the ByteArrayDataSource, passing it an instance of java. io.FileOutputStream based on the filename we generated earlier. Now that the attachment data has been stored locally, we just return the listing number to the caller.

The search( ) method calls a local method called findListingIds( ), which returns a Vector containing Integer objects. Note that findListingIds( ) is not exposed as a service method. Each entry in the Vector represents the ID of a listing that matches the specified make and model. Then an Integer[] is allocated, populated with the values in the Vector, and returned to the caller. This array allows the caller to use the list of IDs to retrieve the actual listings as well as the associated images.

The getListing( ) method takes a single integer parameter, the listing ID. This ID is used to get the Listing object from the _listings hash table. The Listing is then returned to the caller. The getImage( ) method also takes the listing ID as an integer parameter, and uses it to generate the filename for the image associated with the listing. That name is used to instantiate a java.io.File, which is passed to the constructor of a ByteArrayDataSource. It's not necessary to specify the content type of the data, so null is used as the second parameter. A new DataHandler is created using the data source; this handler is returned to the caller. Now you can deploy the service, exposing the addListing, search, getListing, and getImage service methods. Remember to add a mapping entry for the custom listing type, as shown:

```
<isd:map encodingStyle="http://schemas.xmlsoap.org/soap/encoding/"
        xmlns:x="urn:UsedCarListingService" qname="x:Listing"
```

```
          javaType="javasoap.book.ch8.Listing"
java2XMLClassName="org.apache.soap.encoding.soapenc.BeanSerializer"
xml2JavaClassName="org.apache.soap.encoding.soapenc.BeanSerializer"/>
```

Now let's work on a client application that sends a listing to the service. We won't send a large binary file because we want to verify that the data is correct, so we'll use a small human-readable file named *data.bin*:

```
1:Rob
2:Englander
3:MindStream Software, Inc.
```

Here's the code for the client application:

```
package javasoap.book.ch8;
import java.io.*;
import java.util.*;
import java.net.*;
import org.apache.soap.util.mime.*;
import org.apache.soap.*;
import org.apache.soap.encoding.*;
import org.apache.soap.encoding.soapenc.*;
import org.apache.soap.rpc.*;
import javax.activation.*;
import javax.mail.internet.*;
import org.apache.soap.util.xml.*;
public class AddListingClient {
    public static void main(String[] args)
            throws Exception {
        URL url = new URL(
            "http://georgetown:8080/soap/servlet/rpcrouter");
        Call call = new Call();
        call.setTargetObjectURI("urn:UsedCarListingService");
        call.setMethodName("addListing");
        call.setEncodingStyleURI(Constants.NS_URI_SOAP_ENC);
        SOAPMappingRegistry smr = new SOAPMappingRegistry();
        BeanSerializer beanSer = new BeanSerializer();
        call.setSOAPMappingRegistry(smr);
        smr.mapTypes(Constants.NS_URI_SOAP_ENC,
            new QName("urn:UsedCarListingService", "Listing"),
                javasoap.book.ch8.Listing.class,
                beanSer, beanSer);
        Vector params = new Vector();
        Listing listing = new Listing("Pontiac", "Firebird", 1968,
            105000, "Rob Englander", "rob@mindstrm.com");
        params.addElement(new Parameter("listing",
                javasoap.book.ch8.Listing.class, listing, null));
        DataSource ds = new
                ByteArrayDataSource(new File("data.bin"), null);
        DataHandler dh = new DataHandler(ds);
        params.addElement(new Parameter("handler",
                javax.activation.DataHandler.class, dh, null));
        call.setParams(params);

        Response resp;
```

```
        try {
            resp = call.invoke(url, "");
        }
        catch (SOAPException e) {
            System.out.println(e.getMessage());
            return;
        }
        if (!resp.generatedFault()) {
            Parameter ret = resp.getReturnValue();
            System.out.println("The listing number is " +
                                    ret.getValue());
        }
        else {
            Fault fault = resp.getFault();
            System.out.println ("Fault Code = " +
                    fault.getFaultCode());
            System.out.println ("     String = " +
                    fault.getFaultString());
        }
    }
}
```

The client application starts by setting up the call to invoke the addListing service method. Since we're going to pass an instance of Listing, we map it to an instance of BeanSerializer. A listing is created for a 1968 Pontiac Firebird with 105,000 miles on it, owned by me. This is the first parameter for the method invocation. Next, an instance of ByteArrayDataSource is created. The first parameter is a java.io.File based on the *data.bin* filename. Once again, we don't specify the content type, so null is used for the second parameter. The data source is then used to construct a DataHandler object, which serves as the second parameter of the method invocation.

Run this example and you'll get the following output:

```
The listing number is 100
```

Since the service is application scoped, the listing number will increase by 1 each time you run the client.

The SOAP envelope sent to the server does not contain the contents of the image file. The transport is using a MIME multipart message in which the SOAP envelope is the first part and the attached file contents are the second part. So the XML element for the handler parameter is a reference to the second part, and looks like this:

```
<handler href ="cid:6889270.1004989967097.apache-soap.georgetown"/>
```

When you run the example, the value of the reference will be different because it's generated on the fly and includes the name of the source (here, the source is georgetown). But the important part is that the contents of the attached file do not appear within the SOAP envelope. In this example those contents are small, but imagine if we attached a 10 MB audio file, or a video clip of the car running in a stock car race. If you were to snoop at the HTTP stream sent to the server for this invocation, you'd see the following after the close of the SOAP envelope.

```
Content-Type: application/octet-stream
Content-Transfer-Encoding: 8bit
Content-ID: <6889270.1004989967097.apache-soap.georgetown>
Content-Length: 52

1: Rob
2: Englander
3: MindStream Software, Inc.
```

This is the encoded content of the attachment. In a real application, the attachment would probably be a large stream of encoded binary data, but in this program it's just a short message that allows us to verify that the attachment was handled correctly.

Now let's write a client that retrieves the listings and their associated image files. First we'll invoke the search method, passing "Pontiac" and "Firebird" as the parameters. Assuming we've run AddListingClient only once, we should get back an integer array with a single element of value 100. This is the ID for the first and only listing. We'll use the ID to retrieve the listing as well as the image file (as an attachment). Here is the code:

```
package javasoap.book.ch8;
import java.io.*;
import java.util.*;
import java.net.*;
import org.apache.soap.util.mime.*;
import org.apache.soap.*;
import org.apache.soap.encoding.*;
import org.apache.soap.encoding.soapenc.*;
import org.apache.soap.rpc.*;
import javax.activation.*;
import javax.mail.internet.*;
import org.apache.soap.util.xml.*;
public class SearchClient {
    public static void main(String[] args)
            throws Exception {
        URL url = new URL(
            "http://georgetown:8080/soap/servlet/rpcrouter");
        Call call = new Call();
        call.setTargetObjectURI("urn:UsedCarListingService");
        call.setMethodName("search");
        call.setEncodingStyleURI(Constants.NS_URI_SOAP_ENC);
        SOAPMappingRegistry smr = new SOAPMappingRegistry();
        BeanSerializer beanSer = new BeanSerializer();
        call.setSOAPMappingRegistry(smr);
        smr.mapTypes(Constants.NS_URI_SOAP_ENC,
            new QName("urn:UsedCarListingService", "Listing"),
            javasoap.book.ch8.Listing.class, beanSer, beanSer);
        Vector params = new Vector();
        String make = "Pontiac";
        String model = "Firebird";
        params.addElement(new Parameter("make",
                java.lang.String.class, make, null));
```

```
params.addElement(new Parameter("model",
        java.lang.String.class, model, null));
call.setParams(params);

Response resp;
try {
   resp = call.invoke(url, "");
}
catch (SOAPException e) {
   System.out.println(e.getMessage());
   return;
}
if (!resp.generatedFault()) {
   Parameter ret = resp.getReturnValue();
   int[] ids = (int[])ret.getValue();
   int cnt = ids.length;
   for (int i = 0; i < cnt; i++) {
      call.setMethodName("getListing");
      params = new Vector();
      params.addElement(new Parameter("id",
          java.lang.Integer.class, new Integer(ids[i]),
          null));
      call.setParams(params);
      try {
         resp = call.invoke(url, "");
      }
      catch (SOAPException e) {
         System.out.println(e.getMessage());
         return;
      }
      ret = resp.getReturnValue();
      Listing listing = (Listing)ret.getValue();
      System.out.println(listing);
      call.setMethodName("getImage");
      try {
         resp = call.invoke(url, "");
      }
      catch (SOAPException e) {
         System.out.println(e.getMessage());
         return;
      }
      ret = resp.getReturnValue();
      DataHandler handler = (DataHandler)ret.getValue();
      DataSource ds = handler.getDataSource();
      String fname = "EX17." +
              String.valueOf(ids[i]) + ".bin";
      ByteArrayDataSource bsource =
           new ByteArrayDataSource(ds.getInputStream(),
                             handler.getContentType());
      bsource.writeTo(new FileOutputStream(fname));
      System.out.println(
          "   Image File Stored In " + fname);
   }
}
```

```
    else {
        Fault fault = resp.getFault( );
        System.out.println ("Fault Code = " +
                fault.getFaultCode( ));
        System.out.println ("      String = " +
                fault.getFaultString( ));
    }
  }
}
```

The first part of the code should be really familiar by now. We set up the call for the search method, map the Listing type, and add two string parameters for searching for listings of Pontiac Firebirds. The return value of the call is cast to an int[ ]. (Even though the service class returns an Integer[ ], the Apache SOAP framework maps an array of primitive data elements to a corresponding array of primitive Java types, so we get back an int[ ].) Now we can loop over the array of listing IDs. For each one, we set the method name to getListing, and we use the listing ID from the ids array to create a Parameter for the call. Now we invoke the method, this time casting the result to an instance of Listing. Since Listing implements a toString( ) method, we can just pass the listing object to System.out.println( ) to display its contents. Next, we set the method name to getImage( ) and invoke again, this time casting the return value to a DataHandler and getting its DataSource. We write the contents of the attachment to a local file using the same technique we used in the UsedCarListingService class. The filename takes the form *EX17.xxx.bin*, where *xxx* is the listing ID.

The last step is to display the name of the file that contains the contents for the given listing. Here's what the output looks like:

```
1968 Pontiac Firebird with 105000 miles:
    Owned by Rob Englander(rob@mindstrm.com)
    Image File Stored In EX17.100.bin
```

If you look at the contents of the file *EX17.100.bin*, you'll find that it's identical to the contents of the original attachment:

```
1: Rob
2: Englander
3: MindStream Software, Inc.
```

If you want to work with attachments in Apache SOAP message-style services, you have to work at a lower level, without the nice abstractions provided at the RPC level of the API. GLUE also supports SOAP attachments using a straightforward API. Although we won't cover that here, I'm sure you'll find the GLUE abstractions easy to understand and use.

The alternative SOAP mechanisms we've discussed in this chapter, used along with all of the other techniques we've covered, allow you to use SOAP for just about any kind of data transfer model.

CHAPTER 9

SOAP Interoperability and WSDL

All of the examples to this point have used the same SOAP implementation for both client and server. Our Apache SOAP server examples were accessed using Apache SOAP client applications, and our GLUE server examples were accessed by GLUE client applications. In those rare occasions when you have control over the technology used at every node of a distributed system, it's easiest to use the same technology throughout. However, that opportunity doesn't present itself all that often, and it's fundamentally at odds with the web services vision of the computing world. So it's necessary to investigate how SOAP implementations interoperate with each other.

There are dozens of SOAP implementations available right now, and others will be showing up every day. Over time, you'll probably find lots of existing enterprise systems making themselves accessible via a SOAP mechanism over a variety of transports. Some systems will undoubtedly use SOAP under the covers, so you won't have to deal with it at all. And new distributed software frameworks based on SOAP will certainly sprout up. How well can we expect these systems to interoperate with one another? After all, software is still developed largely by companies and individuals that are competing in one way or another, which usually leads to problems with interoperability. Sometimes the problems arise because the specification has one or more sections that are open to interpretation, and developers working for different organizations interpret things differently. The fact that these problems occur doesn't necessarily indicate that the specification is flawed; it only indicates that software development is ultimately a human enterprise, and humans are prone to disagree.

One frequent cause of interoperability problems is the SOAPAction field, which SOAP uses to send information to a recipient outside the bounds of the SOAP envelope. This field is carried as part of the underlying transport's header information; for example, when the SOAP message is carried over an HTTP transport, this field is sent as an HTTP header. (It's not clear how SOAPAction should be handled for transports other than HTTP.) The content of the field is a URI intended to provide information to the recipient. This information might be the service namespace, service method name, or something else. Whatever it is, it's intended to give the recipient some clue about the contents of the envelope, without requiring the recipient to parse the XML. Some SOAP implementations don't require any data value to be sent in the SOAPAction field, while others do. Knowing what is required and making sure to include it in the message is critical to SOAP interoperability. We'll look at the SOAPAction requirements of some current SOAP implementations and the APIs for setting its value in the examples in this chapter. But first, we'll look at the Web Services Definition Language (WSDL), an important standard that promises to help solve interoperability problems.

Web Services Definition Language

One way to avoid interoperability problems with SOAP-based services is to use a structured language to describe the service, its location, the service methods, parameters, data types, and so on. The Web Services Definition Language (WSDL) does just that. WSDL is an XML grammar for describing web services. Systems can determine the programmatic interface of a web service by looking at the WSDL document associated with that service. The document describes the service methods along with their parameters and return types, and may also include the address, or endpoint, of the service. One of the greatest benefits of WSDL is that it is a single, accepted standard* for describing web services, which among other things motivates SOAP developers to avoid using their own mechanism for that task.

Does WSDL eliminate the problems associated with human (or machine) interpretation? Well, not completely. It does mean that service descriptions are far less ambiguous than they would be if there were no standard, but on the other hand, WSDL has a specification of its own, and that specification has the potential to be interpreted differently by multiple parties. WSDL isn't a perfect solution, but it certainly puts those of us working with these technologies in a better place than we'd be in otherwise.

Overview of WSDL

We're not going to cover WSDL in detail, as it's a large subject that warrants a book of its own. But it's a major contributor toward achieving SOAP interoperability, so it's important to spend some time looking at it. Some SOAP implementations, like GLUE, incorporate WSDL as an integral part of their operation. GLUE examples throughout this book have used the wsdl2java utility to generate the client-side Java code for accessing a GLUE-based service. wsdl2java reads a WSDL document that describes a service in order to create the Java interface and class files. We didn't have to actually write the WSDL document in those examples because GLUE generates

---

* You can find the WSDL specification at *http://www.w3.org/TR/wsdl*.

WSDL automatically. The GLUE client-side binding process also uses the WSDL for the service; that's how it creates the binding that is hidden behind the Java interface you use to interact with the service.

According to the WSDL specification:

> WSDL is an XML format for describing network services as a set of endpoints operating on messages containing either document-oriented or procedure-oriented information. The operations and messages are described abstractly, and then bound to a concrete network protocol and message format to define an endpoint. Related concrete endpoints are combined into abstract endpoints (services).

A WSDL document is a collection of one or more service definitions. The document contains a root XML element named definitions; this element contains the service definitions. The definitions element can also contain an optional targetNamespace attribute, which specifies the URI associated with the service definitions. WSDL uses namespaces and namespace IDs in the same way we've been using them in SOAP envelopes, so it's common to find a number of namespaces declared at the definitions level of the document.

WSDL defines services as collections of network endpoints. These endpoints, in WSDL terminology, are known as ports. WSDL separates the service ports and their associated messages from the network protocol that the service is bound to (binding). The combination of a binding and a network address results in a port, and a service is a collection of those ports.

The WSDL specification defines the main document sections as follows:

types
    A container for data type definitions using some type system (such as XSD)

message
    An abstract, typed definition of the data being communicated

operation
    An abstract description of an action supported by the service

portType
    An abstract set of operations supported by one or more endpoints

binding
    A concrete protocol and data format specification for a particular port type

port
    A single endpoint defined as a combination of a binding and a network address

service
    A collection of related endpoints

Let's take a look at a service that provides delayed stock quotes and news headlines based on a stock symbol. The service is called urn:CorpDataServices. It has a method called getHeadlines that takes a single String parameter for the stock symbol and returns a String[] that contains news headlines related to the company represented by the stock symbol. The service also contains a method named getQuote that takes the stock symbol as its parameter. The method returns an instance of a custom data type called Quote that contains the stock symbol, last trade price, change in price compared to its opening price, the number of shares of the stock traded so far today, and the timestamp of the information provided.

The following code implements the Quote custom type. I have placed this class in the services package. I'm separating the server-side classes from the client-side classes because I don't want to share the classes between client and server; there will be another package called clients for client-side classes. We'll use the techniques covered so far to map any custom types for use by client code.

```
package javasoap.book.ch9.services;
import java.io.*;
import java.util.*;
import java.net.*;
public class Quote {
    String _symbol;
    float  _lastPrice;
    float  _change;
    String _timeStamp;
    long   _volume;
    public String getSymbol() {
        return _symbol;
    }
    public void setSymbol(String symbol) {
        _symbol = symbol;
    }
    public float getLastPrice() {
        return _lastPrice;
    }
    public void setLastPrice(float lastPrice) {
        _lastPrice = lastPrice;
    }
    public float getChange() {
        return _change;
    }
    public void setChange(float change) {
        _change = change;
    }
    public String getTimeStamp() {
        return _timeStamp;
    }
    public void setTimeStamp(String timeStamp) {
        _timeStamp = timeStamp;
    }
    public long getVolume() {
        return _volume;
    }
    public void setVolume(long volume) {
        _volume = volume;
```

```
        }
    }
```

This is the only custom type we'll need for now; the rest of the data uses built-in types. Next we'll need a Java class that implements the service:

```
package javasoap.book.ch9.services;
import java.util.Vector;
public class CorpDataService {
    public Quote getQuote(String symbol)
            throws Exception {
        QuoteParser qp = new QuoteParser( );
        return qp.getQuote(symbol);
    }
    public String[] getHeadlines(String symbol)
            throws Exception {
        HeadlineParser hp = new HeadlineParser( );
        Vector v = hp.getHeadlines(symbol);
        int len = v.size( );
        String[] result = new String[len];
        for (int i = 0; i < len; i++) {
            result[i] = (String)v.elementAt(i);
        }
        return result;
    }
}
```

The getQuote( ) method of our CorpDataService class makes use of a class called QuoteParser. That class parses the data stream of a web-based quote service and packages the result in an instance of javasoap.book.ch9.services.Quote; however, I don't show the code for that class because it's specific to the quote system I'm using. I've made this service available at *http://www.mindstrm.com/soap.htm* so you won't need to run the service yourself. (I'll give you the information you need to access this service a little later.) Similarly, the getHeadlines( ) method uses a class called HeadlineParser that collects news headlines as Strings and returns them in an instance of java.util.Vector. getHeadlines( ) creates a String[] based on the contents of the vector and returns the array to the caller.

I've decided to implement this service using GLUE. The service is located at *http://mindstrm.com:8004/glue/urn:CorpDataServices.** Here's the javasoap.book.ch9.services.CorpDataServices class that I used to publish the service:

```
package javasoap.book.ch9.services;
import electric.util.Context;
import electric.server.http.HTTP;
import electric.registry.Registry;
public class CorpDataServices {

    public static void main( String[] args )
```

---

* Be sure to use *mindstrm.com*, not *www.mindstrm.com*. These URLs do not resolve to the same address.

```
                    throws Exception {
        String ns = "urn:CorpDataServices";
        HTTP.startup("http://mindstrm.com:8004/glue");
        Context context = new Context();
        context.addProperty("activation", "application");
        context.addProperty("namespace", ns);
        context.addProperty("description", "Corporate Services Demo");
        Registry.publish(ns,
            Javasoap.book.ch9.services.CorpDataService.class, context);
    }
}
```

After you run the CorpDataServices example, you can request the WSDL document associated with the published services. We've done this with virtually every GLUE example. The binding process requests the WSDL, which is generated automatically by the server. Of course, you're free to generate your WSDL by hand; I prefer to let the system do it for me. The easiest way to get a look at the WSDL for a GLUE service is through your web browser. The WSDL for the urn:CorpDataServices service is located at *http://mindstrm.com:8004/glue/urn:CorpDataServices.wsdl*. Some browsers, like Internet Explorer, display the WSDL in a way that allows you to expand the various nodes to see their underlying contents. Regardless of which browser you're using, the WSDL returned by our service application is the same:

```
<definitions name="CorpDataService"
  targetNamespace="http://www.themindelectric.com/wsdl/CorpDataService/"
  xmlns:tns="http://www.themindelectric.com/wsdl/CorpDataService/"
  xmlns:electric="http://www.themindelectric.com/"
  xmlns:soap="http://schemas.xmlsoap.org/wsdl/soap/"
  xmlns:http="http://schemas.xmlsoap.org/wsdl/http/"
  xmlns:mime="http://schemas.xmlsoap.org/wsdl/mime/"
  xmlns:xsd="http://www.w3.org/2001/XMLSchema"
  xmlns:soapenc="http://schemas.xmlsoap.org/soap/encoding/"
  xmlns:wsdl="http://schemas.xmlsoap.org/wsdl/"
  xmlns="http://schemas.xmlsoap.org/wsdl/">
<types>
  <schema xmlns="http://www.w3.org/2001/XMLSchema"
  xmlns:tns="http://www.themindelectric.com/package/java.lang/"
  targetNamespace="http://www.themindelectric.com/package/java.lang/">
    <complexType name="ArrayOfstring">
      <complexContent>
        <restriction base="soapenc:Array">
          <attribute ref="soapenc:arrayType" wsdl:arrayType="string[]" />
        </restriction>
      </complexContent>
    </complexType>
  </schema>
  <schema xmlns="http://www.w3.org/2001/XMLSchema"
    xmlns:tns=
      "http://www.themindelectric.com/package/javasoap.book.ch9.services/"
    targetNamespace=
      "http://www.themindelectric.com/package/javasoap.book.ch9.services/">
    <complexType name="Quote">
```

```xml
      <sequence>
        <element name="_symbol" nillable="true" type="string" />
        <element name="_lastPrice" type="float" />
        <element name="_change" type="float" />
        <element name="_timeStamp" nillable="true" type="string" />
        <element name="_volume" type="long" />
      </sequence>
    </complexType>
  </schema>
</types>
<message name="getQuote0SoapIn">
  <part name="arg0" type="xsd:string" />
</message>
<message name="getQuote0SoapOut">
  <part name="Result"
    xmlns:ns1=
      "http://www.themindelectric.com/package/javasoap.book.ch9.services/"
    type="ns1:Quote" />
</message>
<message name="getHeadlines1SoapIn">
  <part name="arg0" type="xsd:string" />
</message>
<message name="getHeadlines1SoapOut">
  <part name="Result"
    xmlns:ns1="http://www.themindelectric.com/package/java.lang/"
    type="ns1:ArrayOfstring" />
</message>
<portType name="CorpDataServiceSoap">
  <operation name="getQuote" parameterOrder="arg0">
    <input name="getQuote0SoapIn" message="tns:getQuote0SoapIn" />
    <output name="getQuote0SoapOut" message="tns:getQuote0SoapOut" />
  </operation>
  <operation name="getHeadlines" parameterOrder="arg0">
    <input name="getHeadlines1SoapIn"
           message="tns:getHeadlines1SoapIn" />
    <output name="getHeadlines1SoapOut"
           message="tns:getHeadlines1SoapOut" />
  </operation>
</portType>
<binding name="CorpDataServiceSoap" type="tns:CorpDataServiceSoap">
  <soap:binding style="rpc"
      transport="http://schemas.xmlsoap.org/soap/http" />
  <operation name="getQuote">
    <soap:operation soapAction="getQuote" style="rpc" />
    <input name="getQuote0SoapIn">
     <soap:body use="encoded" namespace="urn:CorpDataServices"
       encodingStyle="http://schemas.xmlsoap.org/soap/encoding/" />
    </input>
    <output name="getQuote0SoapOut">
     <soap:body use="encoded" namespace="urn:CorpDataServices"
       encodingStyle="http://schemas.xmlsoap.org/soap/encoding/" />
    </output>
  </operation>
  <operation name="getHeadlines">
```

```
    <soap:operation soapAction="getHeadlines" style="rpc" />
     <input name="getHeadlines1SoapIn">
      <soap:body use="encoded" namespace="urn:CorpDataServices"
        encodingStyle="http://schemas.xmlsoap.org/soap/encoding/" />
     </input>
     <output name="getHeadlines1SoapOut">
      <soap:body use="encoded" namespace="urn:CorpDataServices"
        encodingStyle="http://schemas.xmlsoap.org/soap/encoding/" />
     </output>
    </operation>
   </binding>
   <service name="CorpDataService">
     <documentation>Corporate Services Demo
     </documentation>
     <port name="CorpDataServiceSoap" binding="tns:CorpDataServiceSoap">
       <soap:address
         location="http://mindstrm.com:8004/glue/urn:CorpDataServices" />
     </port>
   </service>
   </definitions>
```

Let's walk through the WSDL generated for the urn:CorpDataServices service. There's quite a bit to look at, considering that we've got only two service methods and a single custom data type. (WSDL documents tend to be lengthy and hard to understand, even for extremely simple services. That's why you're best off letting a tool generate the WSDL for you.) Figure 9-1 illustrates the high-level structure of the WSDL document for our service. The "(n)" after some element names indicates that there is more than one element of a particular type.

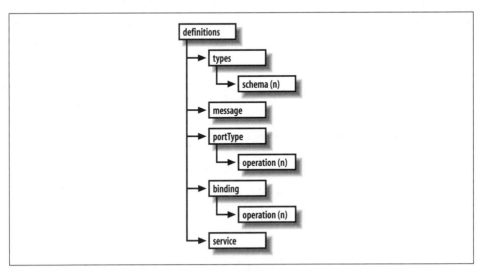

Figure 9-1. High-level structure of a WSDL document

The definitions element is the root of the document; everything else lies within it. The name attribute contains the name of the service definitions contained within, which in this case is CorpDataService. Note that this is not the name of the service, urn:CorpDataServices, but the name given to the definitions of the service. This name is derived from the name of the Java class that implements the service, javasoap.book.ch9.services.CorpDataService. The targetNamespace attribute declares the namespace associated with the service definition. Its default name is created automatically by appending the name of the definition to http://www.themindelectric.com/wsdl.* The definitions element includes a number of namespace identifier declarations, all of which are pretty self-explanatory. The last attribute sets the overall namespace to http://schemas.xmlsoap.org/wsdl, which reflects the namespace for WSDL itself.

Next is the types element. This element defines the custom types used by the service. Each custom type is defined using a schema element, where each schema is a direct child of types. The first schema is used to define the string array returned by the getHeadlines service method. This string array is a complexType; remember that even an array is considered a complex type because it has multiple values. The name attribute is assigned the value "ArrayOfstring". Inside complexType, we find an element named complexContent, which specifies that the type is restricted to an array of strings. The second schema element has a name attribute value of "Quote". This is the custom type used to return stock quote data from the service, also defined using the complexType element. In this case the complexType contains a sequence element that, in turn, contains the data fields for the custom quote data type. Each field is defined using an element tag, and contains a name attribute that specifies the name of the data field. GLUE uses the actual member names from the javasoap.book.ch9.services.Quote class. Each element has its type specified as well.

The message elements come next. These elements define the information passed between client and server. Each message contains a name attribute, formed by starting with the service method name and adding a number to make sure that the name is unique. Finally, GLUE appends SoapIn to the name if the message is an in parameter, or SoapOut if the message is an out parameter. From the standpoint of the message element, there is no such thing as an in/out parameter; all messages are sent either into a service, or out from it.

Each message contains 0 or more part elements. For input messages of an RPC-style service like ours, each part represents a method parameter. The service's out parameters won't appear in the description of an input message, since no associated value would be passed from the client to the server. In this example, the message named getQuote0SoapIn contains a single part named arg0 of type string. That message part corresponds to the first (and only) parameter of the getQuote service method: a

---

* GLUE uses www.themindelectric.com in quite a few of the namespace definitions it generates in the WSDL. You can override the targetNamespace by calling context.addProperty() with "targetNamespace" as the property name, and the value you want as the second parameter. However, that won't eliminate the use of www.themindelectric.com in other sections of the WSDL.

string containing the stock symbol. The getQuoteSoapOut message also contains a single part, this time named Result. That's the return value of the getQuote method. Notice that Result is defined as an instance of type Quote, and that it is namespace-qualified using http://www.themindelectric.com/package/javasoap.book.ch9. services/. This refers to the custom quote type defined earlier in the WSDL document. The getHeadlines messages follow the same pattern, so we won't discuss them. If there were any out or in/out parameters that returned values in any of these messages, they would be defined as part elements immediately following the Result part of the corresponding xxxSoapOut message. For instance, if the getQuote method used an in/out parameter for the stock symbol, the message element for the outbound response would look like this:

```
<message name="getQuote0SoapOut">
 <part name="Result"
 xmlns:ns1="http://www.themindelectric.com/package/javasoap.book.ch9.services/"
    type="ns1:Quote" />
 <part name="arg0" type="xsd:string" />     \
 </message>
```

The portType element is an abstraction that defines a set of operations and their associated messages. Our portType has a name attribute with a value "CorpDataServiceSoap". In this file, the name is derived by appending "Soap" to the name used earlier in the WSDL document. There are two operation elements inside portType, each corresponding to a service method. The first one contains a name attribute with a value of "getQuote", which is the service name. It also contains a parameterOrder attribute that specifies the order in which the method parameters should appear. The getQuote method has only one parameter, so that value is "arg0". For operations that contain more than one parameter, the value of the parameterOrder attribute lists each parameter, separated by spaces. Each operation contains a single input and a single output element, each of which contains a name and a message attribute. The name contains the name of the message, and the message contains the namespace-qualified name of the message element defined earlier in the WSDL.

The next major section of the WSDL document is binding. This section combines the abstract portType with a physical protocol. The name attribute of the binding is, once again, CorpDataServiceSoap. The type attribute refers to the port type being implemented by this binding; in this case it refers back to the portType element defined in the previous WSDL section. Under the binding element we find another binding tag, but this one is namespace-qualified by the soap namespace identifier defined at the root of the document. This element specifies the SOAP binding information. The style attribute has a value of "rpc", specifying that this is an RPC-style service binding. The transport attribute specifies the underlying transport; in this case, the transport is http://schemas.xmlsoap.org/soap/http, which represents the HTTP transport. Following the soap:binding element are operation elements for each of the service operations, or methods, present in the binding. Let's look at the first one, which has a `name` attribute with the value "getQuote". It contains an element called `soap:operation`, which has two attributes. The `style` attribute has the value "rpc", which means that this binding represents an RPC-style SOAP invocation. The `soapAction` attribute has the value "getQuote", which is the name of the method itself. This is a subtle but important part of SOAP interoperability. It's necessary to send the correct value for the `SOAPAction` header field when invoking services; this is an area where you could run into trouble with some SOAP implementations if you aren't paying attention. In this example, the attribute tells us that the service wants the name of the method being invoked to be supplied in the `SOAPAction` header field. If you don't supply the appropriate header, things aren't going to work. Each `operation` also has an `input` and an `ouput` element. These two elements share the same structure, so we'll only look at the `input`. The `input` element has a `name` attribute with the value "getQuote0SoapIn". Recognize that name? That's the message that the WSDL defined earlier; now we're associating the message with this binding operation. There's also a `soap:body` element that specifies the namespace of the binding and the type of encoding used. You can see that this example uses standard SOAP encoding, and that the namespace is the service name itself; `urn:CorpDataServices`. We set this namespace in the `CorpDataServices` class by calling the `context.setProperty( )` method.

The last stop in our WSDL example is the service element. This element combines a binding with a specific address. The `name` attribute contains the service name, which in this case is `CorpDataService`. This is followed by a `documentation` tag that contains a brief textual description of the service. The data contained under this element came from the `context.addProperty("description", "Corporate Services Demo")` method call we made in the `CorpDataServices` application that published this service. If you don't provide a service description, GLUE derives a description based on the name of the implementing Java class. The last element is named `port`, and it's the one that combines the binding with the physical address. The `name` attribute is set to "CorpDataServiceSoap". Although this is just a name and has no real implications, at this stage of the WSDL I like this style of naming because it tells me immediately that I'm talking about the `CorpDataService` using a SOAP binding. Anyway, the `binding` attribute is set to `tns:CorpDataServiceSoap`, which refers to the `binding` that we reviewed earlier. The `soap:address` element contains a `location` attribute that contains the actual location of the service. For our service, the location is *http://mindstrm.com:8004/glue/urn:CorpDataServices*, the URL where the service has been published.

Calling a GLUE Service from an Apache SOAP Client

Since we already have a GLUE service running, let's try to access it with a client written using Apache SOAP. It's nice of the service to publish WSDL, but Apache SOAP

---

clients can't do anything with that data. So we'll have to derive whatever information we need from the WSDL ourselves. Before we get into that, though, let's write a quick application that tries to call the getHeadlines method of the urn: CorpDataServices service.

First we need to determine the proper URL. When we were calling Apache SOAP services, the URL pointed to the rpcrouter servlet. In this case, a GLUE server application is hosting the service, so the URL we want is *http://mindstrm.com:8004/glue/ urn:CorpDataServices*.

With pure Apache SOAP examples, we always called call.setTargetObjectURI() and passed the service name as the parameter, but here we've already specified the service name in the URL. It turns out that this is the right choice, but we've got to call setTargetObjectURI() with some value or we'll get a client-side error. GLUE doesn't appear to care what value we use, since we've already arrived at the target endpoint, so we can just use any nonempty string when we call setTargetObjectURI(). I'm inclined to use the service name again, but it seems to work no matter what we do. Here's the code for the Apache2Glue application:

```
package javasoap.book.ch9;
import java.net.*;
import java.util.*;
import org.apache.soap.*;
import org.apache.soap.rpc.*;
import org.apache.soap.encoding.*;
import org.apache.soap.util.xml.*;
import org.w3c.dom.*;
public class Apache2Glue {
    public static void main(String[] args)
        throws Exception {

        URL url =
            new URL("http://mindstrm.com:8004/glue/urn:CorpDataServices");

        Call call = new Call();
        call.setTargetObjectURI("XYZ");

        call.setEncodingStyleURI(Constants.NS_URI_SOAP_ENC);
        String stock = args[0];
        Vector params = new Vector();
        params.addElement(new Parameter("stock", String.class,
                            stock, null));
        call.setParams(params);

        try {
            call.setMethodName("getHeadlines");
            Response resp = call.invoke(url, "");
            if (resp.generatedFault()) {
                Fault fault = resp.getFault();
                String code = fault.getFaultCode();
                String desc = fault.getFaultString();
```

```
            System.out.println(code + ": " + desc);
            Vector v = fault.getDetailEntries();
            int cnt = v.size();
            for (int i = 0; i < cnt; i++) {
                Element n = (Element)v.elementAt(i);
                Node nd = n.getFirstChild();
                System.out.println(n.getNodeName() + ": " +
                                        nd.getNodeValue());
            }
        }
        else {
            Parameter ret = resp.getReturnValue();
            String[] value = (String[])ret.getValue();
            int cnt = value.length;
            for (int i = 0; i < cnt; i++) {
                System.out.println(value[i]);
            }
        }
    }
    catch (SOAPException e) {
        System.err.println("Caught SOAPException (" +
                    e.getFaultCode() + "): " +
                    e.getMessage());
    }
  }
}
```

The rest of the code is the same as if we were accessing an Apache SOAP server. That wasn't very painful. It's just a matter of understanding the location of the service. If you look back at the WSDL for this service, you'll find that the answer is right in front of you: the location attribute of the soap:address element in the service section tells you the URL. The fact that GLUE doesn't really care about the target object URI is interesting, but it certainly won't get you into any trouble.

If you run the Apache2Glue application with a valid stock symbol as the command-line parameter, it spits back some headlines of news stories related to the stock symbol. For example, the following command asks for headlines related to General Motors:

```
java javasoap.book.ch9.clients.Apache2Glue GM
```

Here's the result:

```
GMAC files shelf for $8.1 billion in notes
Vivendi Pays $1.5B for EchoStar Slice
Product Is King--Again
GM plans to form venture with SAIC-Wuling in China
Vivendi Pays $1.5B for EchoStar Slice
Daewoo Mtr makes first loan payment in a year-report
'Twas the Night Before Q4
Valeo Says U.S. Unit Filed for Bankruptcy
Honda's tank in the SUV wars
Daewoo Says to Resume Operations Monday
```

Since my service takes these headlines from a live feed, you'll get different results when you run this program.

Now that we have a working client, let's modify it to call the getQuote() service method. In this case, we have to deal with a custom data type. So before we go any further, we must create a quote class that we can map to the value returned by the service method. The WSDL describes the custom quote type for us. Here's the relevant part of the document:

```
<complexType name="Quote">
  <sequence>
    <element name="_symbol" nillable="true" type="string" />
    <element name="_lastPrice" type="float" />
    <element name="_change" type="float" />
    <element name="_timeStamp" nillable="true" type="string" />
    <element name="_volume" type="long" />
  </sequence>
</complexType>
```

There's no need to write a custom serializer to handle this; we can write a Java bean with appropriate set and get methods. The property names and data types must correspond to the name and type attribute values of the elements of the Quote type. For example, the class must have a property named _symbol, so we'll need a get_symbol() method and a set_symbol() method. We'll also add a toString() method to make it easy to display the object's contents after we retrieve it from the service. Here's the code for the client-side Quote class:

```java
package javasoap.book.ch9.clients;
import java.io.*;
import java.util.*;
import java.net.*;
public class Quote {
    String _symbol;
    float  _lastPrice;
    float  _change;
    String _timeStamp;
    long   _volume;
    public String get_symbol() {
        return _symbol;
    }
    public void set_symbol(String symbol) {
        _symbol = symbol;
    }
    public float get_lastPrice() {
        return _lastPrice;
    }
    public void set_lastPrice(float lastPrice) {
        _lastPrice = lastPrice;
    }
    public float get_change() {
        return _change;
    }
```

```
    public void set_change(float change) {
        _change = change;
    }
    public String get_timeStamp() {
        return _timeStamp;
    }
    public void set_timeStamp(String timeStamp) {
        _timeStamp = timeStamp;
    }
    public long get_volume() {
        return _volume;
    }
    public void set_volume(long volume) {
        _volume = volume;
    }
    public String toString() {
        String result = "Symbol:      " + get_symbol() +
                        "\nLast Price: " + get_lastPrice() +
                        "\nChange:      " + get_change() +
                        "\nTime Stamp: " + get_timeStamp() +
                        "\nVolume:      " + get_volume();
        return result;
    }
}
```

Now we're ready to modify the client program. I'll call the new class Apache2Glue_v2. We need to map the data returned from getQuote to the Quote class. To make this mapping, we need to know the namespace that the data type comes from. Once again, the WSDL gives us this information:

```
<schema xmlns="http://www.w3.org/2001/XMLSchema"
    xmlns:tns=
      "http://www.themindelectric.com/package/javasoap.book.ch9.services/"
    targetNamespace=
      "http://www.themindelectric.com/package/javasoap.book.ch9.services/">
    <complexType name="Quote">
      <sequence>
        <element name="_symbol" nillable="true" type="string" />
        <element name="_lastPrice" type="float" />
        <element name="_change" type="float" />
        <element name="_timeStamp" nillable="true" type="string" />
        <element name="_volume" type="long" />
      </sequence>
    </complexType>
</schema>
```

The targetNamespace for the custom quote type is defined in the WSDL document as http://www.themindelectric.com/package/javasoap.book.ch9.services/. We use this namespace in the QName constructor when we map the data to our quote class, but that's getting somewhat ahead of the story. The client creates an instance of SOAPMappingRegistry and an instance of BeanSerializer, just as in Chapter 5. We then use the mapping registry's mapTypes() method to map the object returned by getQuote to our Quote object. Next, we set up the method call in the standard way, make the call, and pass the Quote object we get back to System.out.println( ). Here's the code for Apache2Glue_v2:

```
package javasoap.book.ch9.clients;
import java.net.*;
import java.util.*;
import org.apache.soap.*;
import org.apache.soap.rpc.*;
import org.apache.soap.encoding.*;
import org.apache.soap.encoding.soapenc.*;
import org.apache.soap.util.xml.*;
import org.w3c.dom.*;
public class Apache2Glue_v2 {
    public static void main(String[] args)
        throws Exception {

        URL url =
            new URL("http://mindstrm.com:8004/glue/urn:CorpDataServices");
        SOAPMappingRegistry smr = new SOAPMappingRegistry();
        BeanSerializer beanSer = new BeanSerializer();
        smr.mapTypes(Constants.NS_URI_SOAP_ENC,
          new QName(
            "http://www.themindelectric.com/package/javasoap.book.ch9.services/",
            "Quote"),
            Quote.class, beanSer, beanSer);

        Call call = new Call();
        call.setSOAPMappingRegistry(smr);
        call.setTargetObjectURI("XYZ");
        call.setEncodingStyleURI(Constants.NS_URI_SOAP_ENC);
        String stock = args[0];
        Vector params = new Vector();
        params.addElement(new Parameter("stock", String.class,
                                    stock, null));
        call.setParams(params);

        try {
            call.setMethodName("getQuote");
            Response resp = call.invoke(url, "");
            if (resp.generatedFault()) {
                Fault fault = resp.getFault();
                String code = fault.getFaultCode();
                String desc = fault.getFaultString();
                System.out.println(code + ": " + desc);
                Vector v = fault.getDetailEntries();
                int cnt = v.size();
                for (int i = 0; i < cnt; i++) {
                    Element n = (Element)v.elementAt(i);
                    Node nd = n.getFirstChild();
                    System.out.println(n.getNodeName() + ": "
                                            + nd.getNodeValue());
                }
```

```
        }
        else {
            Parameter ret = resp.getReturnValue();
            Quote value = (Quote)ret.getValue();
            System.out.println(value);
        }
    }
    catch (SOAPException e) {
        System.err.println("Caught SOAPException (" +
                    e.getFaultCode() + "): " +
                    e.getMessage());
    }
  }
}
```

Here's the result:

```
Symbol:     GM
Last Price: 47.28
Change:     -0.2
Time Stamp: 4:03PM
Volume:     3490100
```

A Proxy Service Using Apache SOAP

I'm going to use *http://mindstrm.com:8004/glue/urn:CorpDataServices* as the back-end for the services we develop through the rest of this chapter. In this example we'll create an Apache SOAP service called urn:QuoteProxyService that gets its data from the GLUE-based service we've been working with. In other words, this new Apache SOAP service acts as a proxy to the quote retrieval part of the GLUE-based service. This setup is depicted in Figure 9-2.

Figure 9-2. A proxy service

Instead of simply replicating the getQuote() service method from urn:CorpDataServices, let's do something more interesting. After all, we're free to design the proxy service any way we want; the fact that it gets its data from another service is really just an implementation detail. So let's add some value to urn:QuoteProxyService by giving it a method that can handle multiple stock symbols in a single call. This facility would be convenient for client applications that work with multiple stocks at one time. The method name is getQuotes(); it takes a single string array as its parameter. Each element of the array is a stock symbol, and the return value of the method is an array of quotes. The new service doesn't proxy the getHeadlines() method of the urn:CorpDataServices service. There's no real reason for this; I just chose to design my proxy that way.

Once again we're going to need a Java quote class for the proxy server to return. To be consistent with our package naming convention, this class belongs in javasoap. book.ch9.services. To avoid any confusion with earlier Java quote classes, let's name this one ProxyQuote. This class contains the same information as the other quote classes, but the property names and accessor methods are different. The only reason for this difference is to avoid confusion; the names really don't matter. Here's the code for the ProxyQuote class:

```java
package javasoap.book.ch9.services;
import java.io.*;
import java.util.*;
import java.net.*;
public class ProxyQuote {
    String _sym;
    float  _last;
    float  _diff;
    String _time;
    long   _vol;
    public String getStockSymbol( ) {
        return _sym;
    }
    public void setStockSymbol(String symbol) {
        _sym = symbol;
    }
    public float getLast( ) {
        return _last;
    }
    public void setLast(float last) {
        _last = last;
    }
    public float getDiff( ) {
        return _diff;
    }
    public void setDiff(float diff) {
        _diff = diff;
    }
    public String getTime( ) {
        return _time;
    }
    public void setTime(String time) {
        _time = time;
    }
    public long getVol( ) {
        return _vol;
    }
    public void setVol(long vol) {
        _vol = vol;
```

```
        }
    }
```

So now we have a Java class that represents the quote data from the urn:
QuoteProxyService. But let's not forget that this service is also a client to the urn:
CorpDataService. When we wrote an Apache SOAP client for that service, we needed
a Java class to map the return quote data. We can steal this from Quote: just change
the package name to javasoap.book.ch9.services, delete the toString( ) method,
and change its name to RemoteQuote. Here's the result:

```
package javasoap.book.ch9.services;
import java.io.*;
import java.util.*;
public class RemoteQuote {
    String _symbol;
    float  _lastPrice;
    float  _change;
    String _timeStamp;
    long   _volume;
    public String get_symbol( ) {
        return _symbol;
    }
    public void set_symbol(String symbol) {
        _symbol = symbol;
    }
    public float get_lastPrice( ) {
        return _lastPrice;
    }
    public void set_lastPrice(float lastPrice) {
        _lastPrice = lastPrice;
    }
    public float get_change( ) {
        return _change;
    }
    public void set_change(float change) {
        _change = change;
    }
    public String get_timeStamp( ) {
        return _timeStamp;
    }
    public void set_timeStamp(String timeStamp) {
        _timeStamp = timeStamp;
    }
    public long get_volume( ) {
        return _volume;
    }
    public void set_volume(long volume) {
        _volume = volume;
    }
}
```

Now we've got all the support classes we need, and can move ahead with the code
for the urn:QuoteProxyService. The Java class is named QuoteProxyService, and the

code is pretty simple. The service exposes one method, called getQuotes( ), which retrieves an arbitrary number of quotes based on the array of stock symbols. The method returns a ProxyQuote[], which is an array of ProxyQuote instances, one for each stock symbol. Each quote is obtained by calling the getStockQuote( ) method, which returns a single ProxyQuote based on the stock symbol passed as its parameter. Each quote is stored in a local Vector, the contents of which are used to populate an appropriately sized ProxyQuote[]. That array is then returned. The process used by the getStockQuote( ) method is essentially the same one used by the Apache2Glue_v2 client application. The only differences are that we don't bother with any returned fault elements, and we need to pull the data out of the resulting RemoteQuote instance in order to populate the ProxyQuote instance; remember that the quote data type returned by the back-end service is not the same as the quote data type that this new service returns to its clients. And that's how it should be. While it would be simplest for this example to return RemoteQuote instances, that's not how the service would work in the real world; a proxy service shouldn't expose the existence of the back-end service in any way. Here's the code for QuoteProxyService:

```java
package javasoap.book.ch9.services;
import java.net.*;
import java.util.*;
import org.apache.soap.*;
import org.apache.soap.rpc.*;
import org.apache.soap.encoding.*;
import org.apache.soap.encoding.soapenc.*;
import org.apache.soap.util.xml.*;
import org.w3c.dom.*;
public class QuoteProxyService {
    public QuoteProxyService( ) {
    }
    public ProxyQuote[] getQuotes(String[] symbols)
                        throws Exception {
        Vector v = new Vector( );
        int cnt = symbols.length;
        for (int i = 0; i < cnt; i++) {
            v.add(getStockQuote(symbols[i]));
        }
        cnt = v.size( );
        ProxyQuote[] quotes = new ProxyQuote[cnt];
        for (int i = 0; i < cnt; i++) {
            quotes[i] = (ProxyQuote)v.elementAt(i);
        }
        return quotes;
    }
    ProxyQuote getStockQuote(String symbol)
                        throws Exception {
        URL url = new URL("http://mindstrm.com:8004/glue/urn:CorpDataServices");
        SOAPMappingRegistry smr = new SOAPMappingRegistry( );
        BeanSerializer beanSer = new BeanSerializer( );
        smr.mapTypes(Constants.NS_URI_SOAP_ENC,
            new QName(
```

```
              "http://www.themindelectric.com/package/javasoap.book.ch9.services/",
              "Quote"),
              RemoteQuote.class, beanSer, beanSer);

        Call call = new Call( );
        call.setSOAPMappingRegistry(smr);
        call.setTargetObjectURI("XYZ");
        call.setEncodingStyleURI(Constants.NS_URI_SOAP_ENC);
        String stock = symbol;
        Vector params = new Vector( );
        params.addElement(new Parameter("stock", String.class,
                                stock, null));
        call.setParams(params);

        call.setMethodName("getQuote");
        Response resp = call.invoke(url, "");
        ProxyQuote quote = new ProxyQuote( );
        if (resp.generatedFault( )) {
            throw new Exception("Service Call Failed");
        }
        else {
            Parameter ret = resp.getReturnValue( );
            RemoteQuote value = (RemoteQuote)ret.getValue( );
            quote.setStockSymbol(value.get_symbol( ));
            quote.setLast(value.get_lastPrice( ));
            quote.setDiff(value.get_change( ));
            quote.setTime(value.get_timeStamp( ));
            quote.setVol(value.get_volume( ));
        }
        return quote;
    }
}
```

We can deploy this service the same way we've deployed all the Apache SOAP services we've created throughout the book. We'll need to include a mapping for the ProxyQuote class. The fully qualified name for the quote type is urn: QuoteProxyService:Quote. We used a JavaBeans-compliant property naming scheme, so the mapping uses the BeanSerializer class for the conversions. Here's what the deployment descriptor looks like:

```
<isd:service xmlns:isd="http://xml.apache.org/xml-soap/deployment"
            id="urn:QuoteProxyService">
  <isd:provider type="java"
              scope="Application"
              methods="getQuotes">
    <isd:java class="javasoap.book.ch9.services.QuoteProxyService"
    static="false"/>
  </isd:provider>
  <isd:faultListener>org.apache.soap.server.DOMFaultListener
  </isd:faultListener>
  <isd:mappings>
    <isd:map encodingStyle="http://schemas.xmlsoap.org/soap/encoding/"
      xmlns:x="urn:QuoteProxyService" qname="x:Quote"
```

```
        javaType="javasoap.book.ch9.services.ProxyQuote"
        java2XMLClassName="org.apache.soap.encoding.soapenc.BeanSerializer"
        xml2JavaClassName="org.apache.soap.encoding.soapenc.BeanSerializer"/>
    </isd:mappings>
  </isd:service>
```

Calling an Apache SOAP Service from a GLUE Client

This time, we'll write a GLUE client that accesses the urn:QuoteProxyService we just created. But how do we begin? GLUE creates service bindings dynamically based on a WSDL document. In our GLUE-to-GLUE examples, GLUE automatically generated the WSDL document describing the service, but Apache SOAP doesn't do that. We could certainly write an appropriate WSDL document by hand... but that's a lot of work, and the chances of ending up with a WSDL document that's correct are fairly small, unless you want to learn a lot more about WSDL than anyone should have to know. Instead, we'll use the java2wsdl tool that comes with GLUE to generate the WSDL.[*] This tool doesn't care that the Java code isn't for a GLUE-based service; it simply reads the Java code and generates the WSDL. java2wsdl doesn't give us a perfect WSDL document for the Apache-based service, but it's much less work to modify the document by hand than it is to write the whole thing. So let's generate the WSDL:

```
java2wsdl javasoap.book.ch9.services.QuoteProxyService -n
    urn:QuoteProxyService -t urn:QuoteProxyService -s
    -e http://georgetown:8080/soap/servlet/rpcrouter
```

The first parameter to java2wsdl is the Java class that implements the service. The -n option allows us to specify the namespace; we'll use the name of the service as the namespace. The -t option allows us to specify the value of the targetNamespace attribute. These two options are applied only to the definitions element of the generated WSDL. We'll need to modify the rest by hand, as you'll see shortly. The -s option tells the tool to generate a SOAP binding. We need this option because we are creating a service definition for a known endpoint (the location where the service was deployed), and therefore we know what transport we're using. (It's reasonably common to define the interface to the service and its binding separately, so that the same service can be deployed with different endpoints and using different protocols.) For this reason, we also include the -e option, which allows us to specify that endpoint. Since our RPC-style Apache SOAP services are all routed through the rpcrouter servlet, the endpoint is *http://georgetown:8080/soap/servlet/rpcrouter*.[†]

---

[*] Other tools for this purpose are available from other sources. For example, the IBM web services toolkit includes a similar utility.

[†] This location is part of my local network. You'll need to use your own appropriate network address for the location you used to deploy the service.

Now that we've generated a WSDL file, let's make the needed adjustments. The modified parts of the file are shown in bold.

```xml
<?xml version='1.0' encoding='UTF-8'?>
<definitions
name='urn:QuoteProxyService'
targetNamespace='urn:QuoteProxyService'
xmlns:tns='urn:QuoteProxyService'
xmlns:soap='http://schemas.xmlsoap.org/wsdl/soap/'
xmlns:http='http://schemas.xmlsoap.org/wsdl/http/'
xmlns:mime='http://schemas.xmlsoap.org/wsdl/mime/'
xmlns:xsd='http://www.w3.org/2001/XMLSchema'
xmlns:soapenc='http://schemas.xmlsoap.org/soap/encoding/'
xmlns:wsdl='http://schemas.xmlsoap.org/wsdl/'
xmlns='http://schemas.xmlsoap.org/wsdl/'>
  <types>
    <schema xmlns='http://www.w3.org/2001/XMLSchema'
        xmlns:tns='urn:QuoteProxyService'
        targetNamespace='urn:QuoteProxyService'>
      <complexType name='Quote'>
        <sequence>
          <element name='stockSymbol' nillable='true' type='string'/>
          <element name='last' type='float'/>
          <element name='diff' type='float'/>
          <element name='time' nillable='true' type='string'/>
          <element name='vol' type='long'/>
        </sequence>
      </complexType>
      <complexType name='ArrayOfQuote'>
        <complexContent>
          <restriction base='soapenc:Array'>
            <attribute ref='soapenc:arrayType'
                 wsdl:arrayType='tns:Quote[]'/>
          </restriction>
        </complexContent>
      </complexType>
    </schema>
    <schema xmlns='http://www.w3.org/2001/XMLSchema'
        xmlns:tns='urn:QuoteProxyService'
        targetNamespace='urn:QuoteProxyService'>
      <complexType name='ArrayOfstring'>
        <complexContent>
          <restriction base='soapenc:Array'>
            <attribute ref='soapenc:arrayType' wsdl:arrayType='string[]'/>
          </restriction>
        </complexContent>
      </complexType>
    </schema>
  </types>
  <message name='getQuotes0SoapIn'>
    <part name='arg0'
        xmlns:ns1='urn:QuoteProxyService' type='ns1:ArrayOfstring'/>
  </message>
```

```
<message name='getQuotes0SoapOut'>
  <part name='Result'
      xmlns:ns1='urn:QuoteProxyService' type='ns1:ArrayOfQuote'/>
</message>
<portType name='QuoteProxyServiceSoap'>
  <operation name='getQuotes' parameterOrder='arg0'>
    <input name='getQuotes0SoapIn' message='tns:getQuotes0SoapIn'/>
    <output name='getQuotes0SoapOut' message='tns:getQuotes0SoapOut'/>
  </operation>
</portType>
<binding name='QuoteProxyServiceSoap' type='tns:QuoteProxyServiceSoap'>
  <soap:binding style='rpc'
      transport='http://schemas.xmlsoap.org/soap/http'/>
  <operation name='getQuotes'>
    <soap:operation soapAction='getQuotes' style='rpc'/>
    <input name='getQuotes0SoapIn'>
      <soap:body use='encoded' namespace='urn:QuoteProxyService'
          encodingStyle='http://schemas.xmlsoap.org/soap/encoding/'/>
    </input>
    <output name='getQuotes0SoapOut'>
      <soap:body use='encoded' namespace='urn:QuoteProxyService'
          encodingStyle='http://schemas.xmlsoap.org/soap/encoding/'/>
    </output>
  </operation>
</binding>
<service name='QuoteProxyService'>
  <port name='QuoteProxyServiceSoap'
          binding='tns:QuoteProxyServiceSoap'>
    <soap:address
          location='http://georgetown:8080/soap/servlet/rpcrouter'/>
  </port>
</service>
</definitions>
```

We need to modify the namespace and target namespace values for all of the elements except definitions; this element was handled correctly because of the -n and -t command-line parameters we supplied to java2wsdl. That's why you see modified values for all of the namespace and targetNamespace attributes. The values generated contain names based on the Java classes used by the service implementation. They're just names, but I don't want that kind of information exposed. In other parts of the document, I stripped similar Java class package names that preceded otherwise acceptable names. For example, the value of the name attribute of the binding element was preceded by the name of the package where our service classes reside. The name modifications weren't necessary for interoperability, but I think they eliminate any confusion regarding the need to expose Java class and package names.

A few modifications are needed in the definition of the custom quote type. The generated name for the type was ProxyQuote, which comes from the Java class name that implements the custom type on the server side. However, that's not the name we chose for the type in the mapping section of the deployment descriptor. Let's take another look at the relevant part of the deployment descriptor:

```
<isd:map encodingStyle="http://schemas.xmlsoap.org/soap/encoding/"
xmlns:x="urn:QuoteProxyService" qname="x:Quote"
javaType="javasoap.book.ch9.services.ProxyQuote"
java2XMLClassName="org.apache.soap.encoding.soapenc.BeanSerializer"
xml2JavaClassName="org.apache.soap.encoding.soapenc.BeanSerializer"/>
```

The namespace is urn:QuoteProxyService. We already modified the corresponding part of the WSDL, so that part is good. But look at the qname attribute. We gave it a value of Quote,* not ProxyQuote. That means that when the response envelope is encoded, the quote data will be typed as a Quote, namespace-qualified by urn: QuoteProxyService. The java2wsdl generator has no way of knowing about that because the information resides outside of the Java code itself.

Finally, we need to change the names of the data elements that make up the custom quote type. The java2wsdl utility doesn't use JavaBeans property accessors by default; instead it looks directly at the member variables in the implementing class. So the names it used were sym, _last, etc. But the BeanSerializer class that encodes instances of the ProxyQuote class uses property names based on the JavaBeans naming standards. Well, almost. They actually aren't encoded as expected. If you were to look at the SOAP envelope returned by the service, you'd see that the elements of the custom quote data type all use lowercase for the first letter of the property name. According to the Java Beans specification, read and write accessors named setThing( ) and getThing( ) mean that the name of the property is Thing. But the BeanSerializer encodes them as thing. This problem hasn't affected us with Apache-to-Apache examples, but it does make a difference to GLUE clients. So we have some minor problems introduced by quirks of both SOAP implementations. To correct these problems, the element names are changed to be stockSymbol, last, diff, time, and vol.

There's also a definition for the array of quotes, which is what the getQuotes service method returns. The value of the name attribute is changed to ArrayOfQuote, and the value of wsdl:arrayType is changed to tns:Quote[]. Essentially we're removing "Proxy" from the definition of the quote and associated quote array. The second message definition refers to the quote array, so it needs to be modified as well to reflect the proper name of the quote array type.

Now we need to publish this WSDL document. My Apache SOAP engine is hosted by an Apache Tomcat server. This server is listening on port 8080 and running on a machine named georgetown on my local network. The *webapps/soap* directory under my Apache SOAP installation directory is a perfectly good place to put the WSDL

---

* The value is actually x:Quote, but for the sake of clarity I'm referring only to the local part of the name instead of the fully qualified name.

file. This means I can access it using the URL *http://georgetown:8080/soap/QuoteProxyService.wsdl.*

At this point, we're ready to write a GLUE client to access the urn:QuoteProxyService. All the classes for this application should be in the javasoap.book.ch9.clients package. We're not going to use the wsdl2java utility to create the classes and interfaces for binding to this service because we can't control the class names. We need the ability to control the class names because we're putting all of our client-side classes in the javasoap.book.ch9.clients package, and we already have a Quote class; we want the local Java class that gets mapped to the quote data type to be named ProxyQuote instead. You could run the wsdl2java from a directory other than the one corresponding to the javasoap.book.ch9.clients package; rename the generated Quote class and filename to ProxyQuote; change the references to it in the *QuoteProxyService.map* file; then move the files into the package directory. Here, though, we'll just write the classes by hand. It's not difficult, and it'll give us another chance to look inside the pieces needed for the GLUE client application.

So, let's create a client-side class named ProxyQuote to represent the quote data that's returned by the service. This class needs a public data field for each element of the quote, and we'll add a toString( ) method to make it easy to display. Here's the code for the ProxyQuote class:

```
package javasoap.book.ch9.clients;
public class ProxyQuote {
    public String stockSymbol;
    public float last;
    public float diff;
    public String time;
    public long vol;
    public String toString( ) {
        String result = "Symbol:      " + stockSymbol +
                        "\nLast Price: " + last +
                        "\nChange:     " + diff +
                        "\nTime Stamp: " + time +
                        "\nVolume:     " + vol;
        return result;
    }
}
```

We'll need a map file that describes the mapping from the data returned by the service to the ProxyQuote class. The file is named *QuoteProxyService.map*. I put it in the same directory as the javasoap.book.ch9.clients classes so that it will be loaded automatically. Here's the map file:

```
<?xml version='1.0' encoding='UTF-8'?>
<mappings xmlns='http://www.themindelectric.com/schema/'>
  <schema xmlns='http://www.w3.org/2001/XMLSchema'
      targetNamespace='urn:QuoteProxyService'
      xmlns:electric='http://www.themindelectric.com/schema/'>
```

```
<complexType
        name='Quote'
        electric:class='javasoap.book.ch9.clients.ProxyQuote'>
    <sequence>
      <element name='stockSymbol' nillable='true'
              electric:field='stockSymbol' type='string'/>
      <element name='vol'
              electric:field='vol' type='long'/>
      <element name='last'
              electric:field='last' type='float'/>
      <element name='diff'
              electric:field='diff' type='float'/>
      <element name='time' nillable='true'
              electric:field='time' type='string'/>
    </sequence>
  </complexType>
 </schema>
</mappings>
```

Note that we've given the name attribute of the complexType element a value of Quote. That matches what we used in the deployment descriptor for the Apache service, and it matches the modification we made to the WSDL file. The name attributes of all the element tags match the names of the elements of the quote data coming from the service, and the electric:field attribute values match the member variable names of the mapped ProxyQuote class. The targetNamespace attribute that governs this entire mapping document has a value of urn:QuoteProxyService. That's the value expected to be used by the service for namespace-qualifying the return Quote type; and that matches the WSDL as well.

Here's a Java interface that we'll use to bind to the service. It contains the one and only service method, getQuotes( ).

```
package javasoap.book.ch9.clients;
public interface IQuoteProxyService {
   ProxyQuote[] getQuotes(String[] symbols);
}
```

We now have everything we need to write a client application. We'll use the command-line arguments to specify the stock symbols for which we want quotes. We'll bind to the service using the address of the WSDL document we published, invoke the getQuotes( ) method using args as the parameter, and display the results by iterating over the returned array. Here's the code:

```
package javasoap.book.ch9.clients;
import electric.registry.Registry;
public class Glue2Apache {
   public static void main( String[] args )
           throws Exception {
      IQuoteProxyService service = (IQuoteProxyService)Registry.bind(
           "http://georgetown:8080/soap/QuoteProxyService.wsdl",
           IQuoteProxyService.class);
```

```
        ProxyQuote[] quotes = service.getQuotes(args);
        int cnt = quotes.length;
        for (int i = 0; i < cnt; i++) {
            System.out.println(quotes[i]);
            System.out.println("");
        }
    }
}
```

I ran the service with four stock symbols on the command line:

```
java javasoap.book.ch9.clients.Glue2Apache IBM MSFT GM MMM
```

Here are the results I got:

```
Symbol:     IBM
Last Price: 123.1
Change:     -0.79
Time Stamp: 1:59PM
Volume:     3916800
Symbol:     MSFT
Last Price: 67.701
Change:     -1.789
Time Stamp: 2:04PM
Volume:     21485800
Symbol:     GM
Last Price: 47.36
Change:     -0.74
Time Stamp: 1:59PM
Volume:     1719700
Symbol:     MMM
Last Price: 118.51
Change:     -1.29
Time Stamp: 2:00PM
Volume:     953400
```

Accessing .NET Services

Although it's not based on Java, there's no way to avoid a discussion of Microsoft's .NET technology. If you're interacting with web services, you'll certainly run into .NET more than once. To show how to achieve interoperability between .NET and web services written in Java, I've written a .NET web service using the C# language and published it on the Internet at *http://mindstrm.com:8199/CorpDataService/Proxy.asmx.*[*] For those of you working with .NET, it's necessary to specify that your service style is RPC, since that is not the .NET default service style. To do so, use the [SoapRpcService( )] declaration in your C# code. My .NET service acts as a proxy to the urn:CorpDataServices service running at *http://mindstrm.com:8004/glue/urn:CorpDataServices.* Figure 9-3 depicts the relationships involved.

---

[*] The code for the service is located at *http://www.mindstrm.com/soap.htm.*

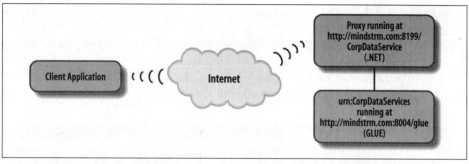

Figure 9-3. Interactions between a client, a proxy, and a service

The Proxy service has a getHeadlines method as well as a getQuote method, just like the urn:CorpDataServices service. Each method takes a single string parameter containing a stock symbol. getHeadlines returns an array of strings, and getQuote returns a custom quote data type. You can find information about .NET services simply by navigating to their URL. So enter the URL *http://mindstrm.com:8199/CorpDataService/Proxy.asmx* in your browser and you'll end up at the page shown in Figure 9-4.

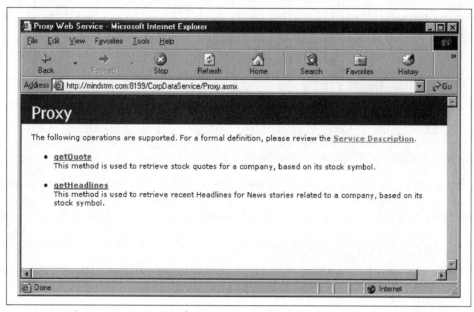

Figure 9-4. Information about a .NET service

If you click on the getQuote link or the getHeadlines link, you'll be taken to a page that allows you to see examples of the XML for sending requests to the service method, as well as the associated responses. There's also a basic user interface that allows you to use the service method without having to write any code. Clicking on Service Description gives you the WSDL for the entire Proxy service. We could look through the WSDL to find the required SOAPAction, namespaces, etc., so that we can set up our Apache SOAP client correctly. However, there's an easier way. Since clicking on the name of a method takes you to a page that shows the XML for messages passed between a client and the service method, we can use the browser to figure out what sorts of messages to send. Figure 9-5 shows the section of that page that shows what the request envelope should look like for invoking getQuote.

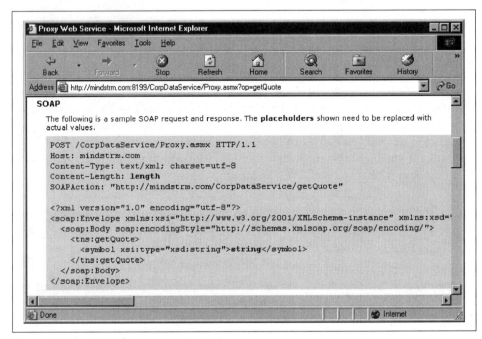

Figure 9-5. The SOAP document sent to getQuote

This gives us just about everything we need to access the service, except for its address. Although the Host field of the HTTP header shows that the server name is mindstrm.com, it doesn't show which port to use to access the service. To get the proper address, we need to peek at the WSDL. Here's the service section of the WSDL document for this service:

```
<service name="Proxy">
  <port name="ProxySoap" binding="s2:ProxySoap">
  <soap:address
    location="http://mindstrm.com:8199/CorpDataService/Proxy.asmx" />
  </port>
```

So now we see that the URL is *http://mindstrm.com:8199/CorpDataService/Proxy. asmx*. Next we need the value of the SOAPAction header field. Yes, in this case it matters! If you don't get this right, .NET will not invoke your service. So we need to specify the SOAPAction in our application, using the value http://mindstrm.com/ CorpDataService/getQuote. Remember, this is not an address to be used as the location of a service or service method, and therefore doesn't include details like a port number. It's a URI, a name that indicates to the .NET framework what the enclosed SOAP envelope is about.

Now we need to determine the namespace used to qualify the getQuote element. getQuote is qualified using the namespace identifier tns. (This doesn't show up in Figure 9-5, but you'll see it if you scroll to the right.) Here's the namespace declaration:

```
xmlns:tns=http://mindstrm.com/CorpDataService
```

This declaration tells us that the namespace we want is http://mindstrm.com/CorpDataService. The last thing to notice is the name of the parameter being passed to the getQuote method. Its name is symbol, and it matters to .NET.

Before we write any code, we should look at the response that the service will send back. This response tells us what we need to know about the custom quote data type we have to deal with. Figure 9-6 shows an example of the response envelope.

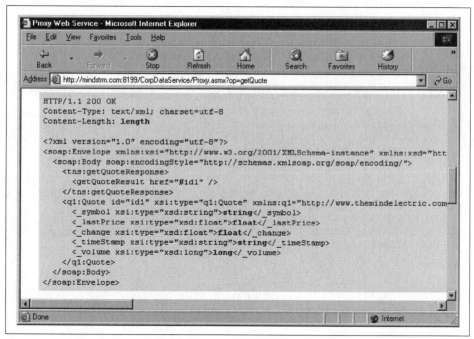

Figure 9-6. The response to a call to getQuote

getQuoteResponse is qualified by tns, which has the same value as it does in the request envelope: http://mindstrm.com/CorpDataService. (The namespace isn't on the visible part of the page.) Also note that the Quote element is namespace-qualified as well, using the identifier q1. Again, the namespace is cut off, so here's what it actually contains:

```
xmlns:q1="http://www.themindelectric.com/package/javasoap.book.ch9.services/"
```

What's www.themindelectric.com doing in this XML? When developing the .NET service, I used .NET Visual Studio to generate a C# class that accesses the urn: CorpDataServices service implemented in GLUE. It does so by requesting the WSDL, which is generated automatically by the GLUE-based server. That server uses www.themindelectric.com and the Java package name when it creates the namespace. Remember, it's just a name. Knowing the name will be convenient when we map this type to a Java class.

Here's the code for an Apache SOAP client application that accesses the .NET service:

```
package javasoap.book.ch9.clients;
import java.net.*;
import java.util.*;
import org.apache.soap.*;
import org.apache.soap.rpc.*;
import org.apache.soap.encoding.*;
import org.apache.soap.encoding.soapenc.*;
import org.apache.soap.util.xml.*;
import org.w3c.dom.*;
public class Apache2DotNet {
    public static void main(String[] args)
        throws Exception {

        URL url =
            new URL("http://mindstrm.com:8199/CorpDataService/Proxy.asmx");
        SOAPMappingRegistry smr = new SOAPMappingRegistry();
        BeanSerializer beanSer = new BeanSerializer();
        smr.mapTypes(Constants.NS_URI_SOAP_ENC, new QName(
          "http://www.themindelectric.com/package/javasoap.book.ch9.services/",
          "Quote"),
           Quote.class, beanSer, beanSer);

        Call call = new Call();
        call.setSOAPMappingRegistry(smr);
        call.setTargetObjectURI("http://mindstrm.com/CorpDataService");
        call.setEncodingStyleURI(Constants.NS_URI_SOAP_ENC);
        String stock = args[0];
        Vector params = new Vector();
        params.addElement(new Parameter("symbol",
                                  String.class, stock, null));
        call.setParams(params);

        try {
            call.setMethodName("getQuote");
            Response resp = call.invoke(url,
                  "http://mindstrm.com/CorpDataService/getQuote");
            if (resp.generatedFault()) {
                Fault fault = resp.getFault();
                String code = fault.getFaultCode();
                String desc = fault.getFaultString();
                System.out.println(code + ": " + desc);
                Vector v = fault.getDetailEntries();
                int cnt = v.size();
```

```
            for (int i = 0; i < cnt; i++) {
                Element n = (Element)v.elementAt(i);
                Node nd = n.getFirstChild( );
                System.out.println(n.getNodeName( ) + ": " +
                                                nd.getNodeValue( ));
            }
        }
        else {
            Parameter ret = resp.getReturnValue( );
            Quote value = (Quote)ret.getValue( );
            System.out.println(value);
        }
    }
    catch (SOAPException e) {
        System.err.println("Caught SOAPException (" +
                    e.getFaultCode( ) + "): " +
                    e.getMessage( ));
    }
  }
}
```

The `Apache2DotNet` Java class is similar to the `Apache2Glue_v2` class we developed earlier, so let's just review the changes instead of revisiting the entire class. The changes are shown in bold so you can pick them out easily.

The URL needed to access the service is *http://mindstrm.com:8199/CorpDataService/Proxy.asmx*. Since we're going to invoke getQuote, we'll get back an instance of a custom quote data type. You may have noticed in Figure 9-6 that the data fields of that quote type are exactly the same as the data fields of the `Quote` type returned by `urn:CorpDataServices`. So we can reuse some code here by mapping the `Quote` class we developed when we wrote the Apache SOAP client for accessing the GLUE service. It turns out that the namespace we need to qualify the quote type is also the same: `http://www.themindelectric.com/package/javasoap.book.ch9.services`.

The next modification is the parameter passed to the `call.setTargetObjectURI( )` method. In this case we pass `http://mindstrm.com/CorpDataService`, which is the namespace used to qualify the getQuote element in the WSDL. We also need to change the name of the parameter specified in the `Parameter( )` constructor to symbol, since that's the name we found earlier when we looked at the request envelope.

The last change is that we need to specify the value of the SOAPAction associated with this method invocation. To set this value, we use the second parameter of the `call.invoke( )` method. In our other Apache SOAP clients, we passed an empty string as the second parameter because we had no need to specify a SOAPAction. However, when invoking .NET service methods, we must include the correct SOAPAction. Earlier, we found that SOAPAction needed to have the value `http://mindstrm.com/CorpDataService/getQuote`, so that's what we pass to `call.invoke( )`.

The rest of the code is unchanged. If you run the `Apache2DotNet` application, it invokes the getQuote method on our .NET service, which in turn invokes the getQuote method on the urn:CorpDataServices service. Here's what the output looked like when I ran the application, passing GM as the stock symbol:

```
Symbol:     GM
Last Price: 48.05
Change:     0.35
Time Stamp: 11:06AM
Volume:     1078700
```

Writing an Apache Axis Client

The Apache group is currently working on a completely new SOAP implementation known as Axis.* It's really too early in the evolution of that project to spend much time on it. It's likely to change quite a bit before it stabilizes, and right now it's not ready for production use. The plan is for Axis to conform to JAX-RPC, an emerging API standard for SOAP RPC. Nevertheless, Axis is out there now and can be used to experiment a bit. So let's take a brief look at Axis and get a feel for how it's likely to work. Later, in Chapter 11, we'll take a look at JAX-RPC.

The heart of the client is Axis2DotNet. It invokes the getHeadlines method on the .NET service that we used before.

```
package javasoap.book.ch9.clients;
import org.apache.axis.AxisFault;
import org.apache.axis.client.Call;
import org.apache.axis.client.Service;
import org.apache.axis.client.Transport;
import org.apache.axis.encoding.XMLType;
import org.apache.axis.transport.http.HTTPConstants;
import org.apache.axis.utils.Options;
import java.net.URL;
import java.util.*;
public class Axis2DotNet {
    public static void main(String args[]) {
        try {
            URL url =
             new URL("http://mindstrm.com:8199/CorpDataService/Proxy.asmx");
            Service  service = new Service();
            Call call = (Call) service.createCall();
            call.setTargetEndpointAddress( url );
            call.setOperationName("getHeadlines");
            call.setProperty(Call.NAMESPACE,
                    "http://mindstrm.com/CorpDataService");
            call.setProperty(HTTPConstants.MC_HTTP_SOAPACTION,
                 "http://mindstrm.com/CorpDataService/getHeadlines");
            call.addParameter("symbol", XMLType.XSD_STRING, Call.PARAM_MODE_IN);
```

---

* The actual name is currently being debated, but as of this writing it is still called Axis. The examples in this book are based on the Axis release dated December 5, 2001. Obviously, you can expect changes to the APIs as things develop.

```
            call.setReturnType(XMLType.SOAP_ARRAY);
            ArrayList ret = (ArrayList)call.invoke(new Object[] {args[0]});
            Object[] res = ret.toArray();
            int cnt = res.length;
            for (int i = 0; i < cnt; i++) {
                System.out.println((String)res[i]);
            }
        }
        catch (Exception e) {
            System.out.println(e);
        }
    }
}
```

Axis appears to be headed toward a more structured API, which is a welcome change from the Apache SOAP implementation. That's not a knock on the work in Apache SOAP; it's a nice achievement, and it certainly works. The smarter object-oriented API emerging in Axis couldn't have been done without the lessons learned from building Apache SOAP.

So let's take a quick look at the code. We start by creating an instance of java.net. URL, just like we do in Apache SOAP examples. The next step is to create an instance of org.apache.axis.client.Service, which acts as a factory for creating org.apache. axis.client.Call objects, an instance of which is created by calling service. createCall( ). From this point on, everything is done via the Call object. We pass the URL to call.setTargetEndpointAddress( ) and set the method name using call. setOperationName( ). The next step is to set the namespace. We determined in a previous example that the namespace we want to use is http://mindstrm.com/ CorpDataService. The namespace is set as a property of the Call object by using the call.setProperty( ) method. The namespace property is specified in the first parameter by passing Call.NAMESPACE, and the appropriate namespace is passed as a string in the second parameter. We also need to set the SOAPAction property in the same way, this time using the Call.MC_HTTP_SOAPACTION constant as the property name, and http: //mindstrm.com/CorpDataService/getHeadlines as the value. Remember, .NET services require you to specify a SOAPAction value that corresponds to the service method.

The next step is to set up the parameters of the Call, using call.addParameter( ). The first parameter of this method is the name of the parameter to be passed to the service. This name is used as the element name in the SOAP envelope. The second parameter specifies the data type; in this case the constant XMLType.XSD_STRING is used to indicate that the parameter is an instance of the built-in string type. The last parameter, Call.PARAM_MODE_IN, indicates that the parameter is an in parameter. (Axis supports out and in/out parameters too.) It's interesting that the values of the parameters aren't specified in the call.addParameter( ) method. Instead, an Object[] is passed to the subsequent call.invoke( ) method, where each entry in the object array corresponds to the value of the parameter already set up using call. addParameter( ). We have only one parameter: the string found in args[0], which contains the stock symbol. So we use args[0] to create an instance of Object[] with just one entry.

The return value of the call.invoke( ) method is an instance of java.util.ArrayList that contains the headlines returned for the stock symbol passed to the service method. Calling the toArray( ) method of the returned ArrayList returns an Object[] in which each entry is a java.lang.String containing a headline. We iterate over that array and write the headline to the console. I ran Axis2DotNet and passed GM on the command line. Here is the result I got:

```
Autos: Year of Big Sales, Little Profits
Autos: Year of Zero Financing and Profits
Report: EchoStar May Invest in Spaceway
EchoStar may invest $1 billion in Spaceway-WSJ
GM-Daewoo Motor deal due by Jan 20 - creditor bank
In Detroit, a New Definition of 'Quality'
GM's bright idea; Ford's e-commerce plans take root
GM invests in Lutz's Cunningham Motors
December U.S. Auto Sales Seen Up Over '00
RESEARCH ALERT-UBS Warburg ups GM EPS view
```

It seems pretty easy to write Axis clients of .NET services. Axis can also use a services WSDL on the fly, but we won't cover that here.

Let's modify the code to access the GLUE-based service named urn: CorpDataServices running at *http://mindstrm.com:8004/glue*. The new class name is Axis2Glue. We need to make only one modification to the Axis2DotNet class to make it work with our GLUE service: the URL needs to be changed to *http://tokyo:8004/ glue/urn:CorpDataServices*. Everything else can remain the same. Now that's promising! Apparently the Axis team has worked toward normalizing the API, and Axis may be a very interesting implementation when it matures.

CHAPTER 10

SOAP Headers

The SOAP envelope may contain a Header element that encompasses data outside the boundaries of an RPC (or other) style invocation. The header is an extension mechanism that can carry any kind of information that lies outside the semantics of the message in the body, but is nevertheless useful or even necessary for processing the message properly. Routing information might contain transaction identifiers, authentication keys, or other information related to the message's processing or routing.

Putting routing information in the SOAP header is useful when a message is sent to an intermediary, which in turn sends the message on to its final destination. In Chapter 9 we developed some proxy services that used another service to perform their tasks. In those cases, the client application was not aware that the service it was calling was actually a proxy. However, it's possible for proxy services to forward messages to specified endpoints or make use of other endpoints in the performance of their tasks. We'll develop an example of this kind of proxy, or intermediary, service.

Although SOAP does not currently specify any security mechanism, the Header element is a good place to encode authentication data such as usernames and passwords. Using the Header to store authentication data allows you to develop your service methods using only the parameters necessary and relevant to the method's task, and still gives you a mechanism to pass other related data to the recipient. The semantics of using the SOAP header for authentication are implementation dependent, but it's a reasonable mechanism in the absence of some other standard.

GLUE has considerable support for SOAP headers,* but Apache SOAP really lacks in that area. I'll walk you through a technique for working with headers in Apache SOAP client and services.

---

* The GLUE documentation is more than enough to get you going with headers in GLUE.

Apache SOAP Providers and Routers

The Apache SOAP engine does not provide direct support for working with SOAP headers. However, it provides just enough Java class support and functional hooks to let you add headers without too much pain. Most of the work involved will be on the service side. Basically, we want a way to gain access to the SOAP header from within the service methods we implement. But before we delve into any code, let's look at the way Apache SOAP handles and routes SOAP messages. Figure 10-1 shows the path taken by an RPC message sent to an Apache SOAP service. The objects shown in gray are part of the Apache SOAP framework, while those in white are the Java classes we've been writing throughout the book.

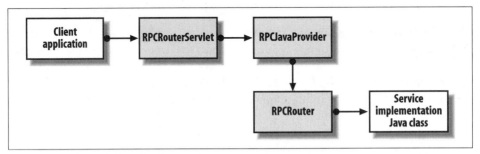

Figure 10-1. The path from the client to the service implementation

Apache SOAP is based on Java servlets. When you send an RPC-style SOAP message, you're actually sending the message to the `org.apache.soap.server.http. RPCRouterServlet` class. It's up to the servlet to determine the appropriate provider class for the specific invocation. All of our Apache SOAP services so far have used the default Java provider. Here is the relevant part of the deployment descriptor:

```
<isd:provider type="java"
```

In every case, we've assigned the `type` attribute the value `"java"`. This is nothing more than an alias for telling the framework that we want it to use the default Java provider, which is `org.apache.soap.providers.RPCJavaProvider`. The servlet uses that provider class, and all provider classes, to locate and invoke the service method. The default provider uses `org.apache.soap.server.RPCRouter` to route the message to the appropriate service implementation class. The router loads the service class and invokes the specified method using Java reflection. To specify some other provider implementation, assign the provider's full Java class name as the value of the `type` attribute.

Replacing the Provider and Router Classes

In order to make the SOAP header available to our service methods, we'll need to replace the router class with one of our own design. We could modify the org.

apache.soap.server.RPCRouter class and rebuild the Apache SOAP source tree, but that's a bit messy; we'd have to go through the process again for every new release of the Apache SOAP engine. Luckily, Apache SOAP makes use of a concept called *pluggable providers*. This means that you can plug in your own provider to be used with a given service deployment. To use your own provider, you must implement your own provider class. This is just the hook we're looking for. Creating our own provider lets us use our own router, which can pass the SOAP header to our service methods. For instance, if we implement a provider class called BetterRPCJavaProvider, we can associate it with a service deployment by modifying the isd:provider element in the relevant deployment descriptor:

```
<isd:provider type="javasoap.book.ch10.services.BetterRPCJavaProvider"
```

This element tells the RPC router servlet to use our new provider class instead of the default provider. That's exactly what we want. So let's write our own provider.

All providers must implement the org.apache.soap.util.Provider interface, which contains locate( ) and invoke( ) methods. The locate( ) method locates the service deployment information in preparation for the method invocation. The invoke( ) method invokes the service method, assuming that a preceding call to locate( ) was successful.

We don't need to reinvent the entire wheel here. The org.apache.soap.providers. RPCJavaProvider class does a perfectly good job of locating the service, so let's just extend it so that we can modify the invoke( ) method for our purpose. Here's the code for our new provider, BetterRPCJavaProvider:

```
package javasoap.book.ch10.services;

import java.io.*;
import javax.servlet.*;
import javax.servlet.http.*;
import org.apache.soap.*;
import org.apache.soap.rpc.*;
import org.apache.soap.server.*;
import org.apache.soap.server.http.*;
import org.apache.soap.util.*;

public class BetterRPCJavaProvider
        extends org.apache.soap.providers.RPCJavaProvider {

   public void invoke(SOAPContext reqContext, SOAPContext resContext)
              throws SOAPException {
      try {
         Response resp = BetterRPCRouter.invoke(envelope.getHeader( ), dd,
              call, targetObject, reqContext, resContext);
         Envelope env = resp.buildEnvelope( );
         StringWriter sw = new StringWriter( );
         env.marshall(sw, call.getSOAPMappingRegistry( ), resContext);
         resContext.setRootPart(sw.toString( ),
                    Constants.HEADERVAL_CONTENT_TYPE_UTF8);
```

```
      }
      catch(Exception e) {
          if (e instanceof SOAPException)
              throw (SOAPException )e;

          throw new SOAPException(Constants.FAULT_CODE_SERVER, e.toString( ));
      }
   }
}
```

I lifted the code for the invoke( ) method from the org.apache.soap.providers.
RPCJavaProvider source code. The only changes I made appear in bold. The first
change is to call the static invoke( ) method of BetterRPCRouter, which takes an
instance of org.apache.soap.Header as its first parameter. We haven't implemented
that class yet, but we will shortly; we need it because the default router, org.apache.
soap.server.RPCRouter, doesn't allow us to pass the header to its invoke( ) method.
The remaining parameters are the same as in org.apache.soap.server.RPCRouter.
One benefit of extending the default provider is that it does the work of obtaining
the SOAP envelope inside its implementation of the locate( ) method, which it
stores in the envelope class variable (an instance of org.apache.soap.Envelope). So all
we need to do is pass envelope.getHeader( ) as the first parameter of the invoke( )
method of our new router class.

Now we can move on to implementing our own router. Once again, we don't need
to write the whole class; instead we'll extend org.apache.soap.server.RPCRouter. We
only need to implement the invoke( ) method, as the rest of the base class is fine.
Our invoke( ) method will take an org.apache.soap.Header as its first parameter. The
trick will be finding a way to pass the header to our service class methods.

One of the nice things about having access to source code is that you can sometimes
find gems that aren't otherwise noticeable. It turns out that the org.apache.soap.
server.RPCRouter implementation actually anticipates that your service methods may
be taking an instance of org.apache.soap.rpc.SOAPContext as their first parameter.
Under those circumstances, the default router simply uses the rest of the parameters
starting from position 1. You can try this if you like. Go back to any of the Apache
SOAP service classes from previous chapters and stick an instance of org.apache.
soap.rpc.SOAPContext into the method signature as its first parameter, effectively
pushing the rest of the parameters to the right. If you rebuild and deploy the service
after making this change, everything will work just as before; the router deals with the
possibility that you included this special first parameter, but it doesn't require you to
do it. This feature comes close to fulfilling our need to access the SOAP header. The
problem is that obtaining the header from the org.apache.soap.rpc.SOAPContext is a
lot of work. Still, the mechanism is perfect for our needs. The result is a router that
allows us to implement service methods that can take an instance of org.apache.soap.
Header as the first parameter. Here's the code for the BetterRPCRouter class. Again,
most of the code comes from the base class, with the modifications shown in bold.

```
package javasoap.book.ch10.services;

import org.apache.soap.server.*;
import java.io.*;
import java.util.*;
import java.lang.reflect.*;
import org.w3c.dom.*;
import org.apache.soap.util.Bean;
import org.apache.soap.util.MethodUtils;
import org.apache.soap.util.IOUtils;
import org.apache.soap.*;
import org.apache.soap.rpc.*;
import org.apache.soap.util.StringUtils;

public class BetterRPCRouter extends org.apache.soap.server.RPCRouter {

    public static Response invoke(Header hdr, DeploymentDescriptor dd,
                      Call call, Object targetObject, SOAPContext reqCtx,
                      SOAPContext resCtx)
         throws SOAPException {
      byte providerType = dd.getProviderType();
      Vector params = call.getParams();
      String respEncStyle = call.getEncodingStyleURI();
      Object[] args = null;
      Class[] argTypes = null;
      if (params != null) {
         int paramsCount = params.size();
         args = new Object[paramsCount];
         argTypes = new Class[paramsCount];
         for (int i = 0; i < paramsCount; i++) {
            Parameter param = (Parameter)params.elementAt(i);
            args[i] = param.getValue();
            argTypes[i] = param.getType();
            if (respEncStyle == null) {
               respEncStyle = param.getEncodingStyleURI();
            }
         }
      }

      if (respEncStyle == null) {
         respEncStyle = Constants.NS_URI_SOAP_ENC;
      }

      Bean result = null;
      try {
         if (providerType == DeploymentDescriptor.PROVIDER_JAVA ||
             providerType == DeploymentDescriptor.PROVIDER_USER_DEFINED) {
            Method m = null ;
            try {
               m = MethodUtils.getMethod (targetObject,
                       call.getMethodName(), argTypes);
            } catch(NoSuchMethodException e) {
               try {
                  int paramsCount = 0 ;
```

```
                        if (params != null) paramsCount = params.size();
                        Class[] tmpArgTypes = new Class[paramsCount+1];
                        Object[] tmpArgs = new Object[paramsCount+1];
                        for (int i = 0 ; i < paramsCount ; i++)
                            tmpArgTypes[i+1] = argTypes[i] ;

                        argTypes = tmpArgTypes;
                        argTypes[0] = Header.class;
                        m = MethodUtils.getMethod(targetObject,
                                    call.getMethodName(),argTypes);
                        for (int i = 0 ; i < paramsCount ; i++)
                            tmpArgs[i+1] = args[i];

                        tmpArgs[0] = hdr;
                        args = tmpArgs;
                    }
                    catch (NoSuchMethodException e2) {
                        throw e;
                    }
                catch (Exception e2) {
                    throw e2;
                }
            }            catch (Exception e) {
                throw e;
            }

            result = new Bean(m.getReturnType(),
                            m.invoke(targetObject, args));
        }
        else {
            Class bc = Class.forName("org.apache.soap.server.InvokeBSF");
            Class[] sig = {DeploymentDescriptor.class,
                            Object.class,
                            String.class,
                            Object[].class};
            Method m = MethodUtils.getMethod(bc, "service", sig, true);
            result = (Bean) m.invoke (null,
                        new Object[] {dd, targetObject,
                                        call.getMethodName (), args});
        }
    }
    catch (InvocationTargetException e) {
        Throwable t = e.getTargetException();
        if (t instanceof SOAPException) {
            throw (SOAPException)t;
        }
        else {
            throw new SOAPException(Constants.FAULT_CODE_SERVER,
                "Exception from service object: " + t.getMessage(), t);
        }
    }
    catch (ClassNotFoundException e) {
        throw new SOAPException (Constants.FAULT_CODE_SERVER,
                "Unable to load BSF: script services " +
```

```
                      "unsupported without BSF", e);
       }
       catch (Throwable t) {
          throw new SOAPException (Constants.FAULT_CODE_SERVER,
            "Exception while handling service request: " + t.getMessage( ), t);
       }

       Parameter ret = null;
       if (result.type != void.class) {
          ret = new Parameter (RPCConstants.ELEM_RETURN, result.type,
                              result.value, null);
       }

       return new Response(call.getTargetObjectURI(), call.getMethodName ( ),
                          ret, null, null, respEncStyle, resCtx);
       }
   }
```

The first parameter of the invoke( ) method is an instance of org.apache.soap.Header that contains the SOAP header from the request envelope. Using Java reflection, an attempt is made to obtain the service class method, assuming that the method's parameters and their associated types are a direct match to those found in the SOAP body. If that fails, the code tries again, this time looking for a method that has all of the SOAP body parameters as well as a first parameter of type org.apache.soap. Header. To set this up, we assign argTypes[0] the value Header.class, and assign tmpArgs[0] the value hdr (the first parameter to our invoke( ) method). These arrays are used by the Java reflection mechanism when finding and subsequently invoking Java methods dynamically. As you can see, the vast majority of the code is unchanged. Much of it deals with finding an appropriate service class method, dealing with the possibility that a BSF script implements the service,[*] and handling faults.

An Apache SOAP Service That Handles SOAP Headers

We now have a provider and router that can pass the SOAP header to our service methods, so let's go ahead and implement a service that uses the SOAP header. The urn:ProxyQuoteService from Chapter 9 is a good place to start. Its implementation hardcoded the physical address of the back-end service as *http://mindstrm.com:8004/glue/urn:CorpDataServices*; we'll ask the client application to provide that information as part of the SOAP header. Our proxy service defaults to a bogus address of *http://mindstrm.com:8899/glue/urn:CorpDataServices* if no routing data appears in

---

[*] Apache SOAP allows you to implement services using BSF scripting. Refer to the Apache SOAP documentation if you're interested in that subject.

the header. You might use a similar technique if the service accesses a default back-end service but can also be directed to a client-specified service via the SOAP header.

Let's design our SOAP header so that it contains a single child element named targetAddress. This element contains the back-end service address that the proxy should use. The elements within the header may use the SOAP-ENV:mustUnderstand attribute with a value of "1" to indicate that the recipient of the envelope must understand the header element and properly use the data provided. The SOAP header sent by a client that demands the understanding of the targetAddress should look like this:

```
<SOAP-ENV:Header>
<targetAddress SOAP-ENV:mustUnderstand="1">
http://mindstrm.com:8004/glue/urn:CorpDataServices
</targetAddress>
</SOAP-ENV:Header>
```

So let's design our service to understand the targetAddress header element, but not any other header elements. If any other header elements appear with a mustUnderstand attribute value of "1", the service returns a SOAP fault. The new service will be called urn:DirectedQuoteProxyService, implemented by the DirectedQuoteProxyService class:

```
package javasoap.book.ch10.services;

import java.net.*;
import java.util.*;
import org.apache.soap.*;
import org.apache.soap.rpc.*;
import org.apache.soap.encoding.*;
import org.apache.soap.encoding.soapenc.*;
import org.apache.soap.util.xml.*;
import org.w3c.dom.*;

import javasoap.book.ch9.services.RemoteQuote;
import javasoap.book.ch9.services.ProxyQuote;

public class DirectedQuoteProxyService {

    static final String TARGETADDRESS = "targetAddress";
    static final String DEFAULTTARGET =
            "http://mindstrm.com:8899/glue/urn:CorpDataServices";

    public DirectedQuoteProxyService() {
    }

    String getTargetAddress(Header header)
            throws SOAPException  {

        String target = DEFAULTTARGET;

        Vector entries = header.getHeaderEntries();
```

```java
        for (int i = 0; i < entries.size(); i++) {
            Element el = (Element)entries.elementAt(i);
            String name = el.getLocalName();
            String val = el.getAttributeNS(Constants.NS_URI_SOAP_ENV,
                Constants.ATTR_MUST_UNDERSTAND);

            if (name.equals(TARGETADDRESS)) {
                target = el.getFirstChild().getNodeValue();
            }
            else if (val != null && val.equals("1")) {
                if (!name.equals(TARGETADDRESS))
                throw new SOAPException("MustUnderstand",
                    "Service Doesn't Understand Header Element: " + name);
            }
        }
    }

    return target;
}

public ProxyQuote getQuote(Header hdr, String symbol)
                throws SOAPException, Exception {

    String target = getTargetAddress(hdr);

    URL url = new URL(target);

    SOAPMappingRegistry smr = new SOAPMappingRegistry();

    BeanSerializer beanSer = new BeanSerializer();

    smr.mapTypes(Constants.NS_URI_SOAP_ENC,
        new QName(
        "http://www.themindelectric.com/package/javasoap.book.ch9.services/",
        "Quote"),
        RemoteQuote.class, beanSer, beanSer);

    Call call = new Call();
    call.setSOAPMappingRegistry(smr);
    call.setTargetObjectURI("XYZ");
    call.setEncodingStyleURI(Constants.NS_URI_SOAP_ENC);

    String stock = symbol;

    Vector params = new Vector();
    params.addElement(new Parameter("stock", String.class, stock, null));
    call.setParams(params);

    call.setMethodName("getQuote");
    Response resp = call.invoke(url, "");
    ProxyQuote quote = new ProxyQuote();
    if (resp.generatedFault()) {
        throw new Exception("Service Call Failed");
    }
    else {
```

```
        Parameter ret = resp.getReturnValue( );
        RemoteQuote value = (RemoteQuote)ret.getValue( );
        quote.setStockSymbol(value.get_symbol( ));
        quote.setLast(value.get_lastPrice( ));
        quote.setDiff(value.get_change( ));
        quote.setTime(value.get_timeStamp( ));
        quote.setVol(value.get_volume( ));
    }

    return quote;
  }
}
```

The code is mostly the same as the QuoteProxyClass we developed in Chapter 9. The getQuote( ) method now takes an org.apache.soap.Header as its first parameter, and a String containing the stock symbol as its second parameter. Before constructing the URL, a call is made to the getTargetAddress( ) method, with the header passed as its parameter. The getTargetAddress( ) method returns either the bogus default address if no targetAddress element appears in the header, or the value of the targetAddress element if it does exist. We iterate over all of the header elements, looking for the targetAddress element. While we're at it, we look to see if any of the other header elements contain a SOAP-ENV:mustUnderstand attribute with a value of "1", and throw an appropriate SOAPException if we find any other header elements that we're required to understand. Throwing the exception results in a corresponding SOAP fault being returned to the caller. The returned value of getTargetAddress( ) is used to construct the URL. The remainder of the code is the same as it was for javasoap.book.ch9.services.QuoteProxyService.

Let's deploy the service, remembering to use our BetterRPCJavaProvider class as the value of the type attribute of the provider element. Here's what the deployment descriptor should look like:

```
<isd:service xmlns:isd="http://xml.apache.org/xml-soap/deployment"
             id="urn:DirectedQuoteProxyService">
  <isd:provider type="javasoap.book.ch10.services.BetterRPCJavaProvider"
                scope="Application"
                methods="getQuote">
  <isd:java class="javasoap.book.ch10.services.DirectedQuoteProxyService"
        static="false"/>
  </isd:provider>

  <isd:faultListener>org.apache.soap.server.DOMFaultListener
  </isd:faultListener>

  <isd:mappings>
    <isd:map encodingStyle="http://schemas.xmlsoap.org/soap/encoding/"
        xmlns:x="urn:QuoteProxyService" qname="x:Quote"
        javaType="javasoap.book.ch9.services.ProxyQuote"
        java2XMLClassName="org.apache.soap.encoding.soapenc.BeanSerializer"
        xml2JavaClassName="org.apache.soap.encoding.soapenc.BeanSerializer"/>
  </isd:mappings>
</isd:service>
```

Now let's write an Apache SOAP client application that can access the urn: DirectedQuoteProxyService. Most of the code should look familiar by now, so I'll just describe the new parts related to setting up the SOAP header. The class is called HeaderClient:

```
package javasoap.book.ch10.clients;

import java.net.*;
import java.util.*;
import org.apache.soap.*;
import org.apache.soap.rpc.*;
import org.apache.soap.encoding.*;
import org.apache.soap.encoding.soapenc.*;
import org.apache.soap.util.xml.*;
import org.w3c.dom.*;
import javax.xml.parsers.DocumentBuilder;

import javasoap.book.ch9.services.ProxyQuote;

public class HeaderClient {
    public static void main(String[] args)
        throws Exception {

        URL url = new URL("http://georgetown:8080/soap/servlet/rpcrouter");

        SOAPMappingRegistry smr = new SOAPMappingRegistry();

        BeanSerializer beanSer = new BeanSerializer();

        smr.mapTypes(Constants.NS_URI_SOAP_ENC,
          new QName("urn:QuoteProxyService", "Quote"),
                ProxyQuote.class, beanSer, beanSer);

        Call call = new Call();
        call.setSOAPMappingRegistry(smr);
        call.setTargetObjectURI("urn:DirectedQuoteProxyService");
        call.setEncodingStyleURI(Constants.NS_URI_SOAP_ENC);

        String stocks = args[0];

        Header header = new Header();
        String must = Constants.NS_PRE_SOAP_ENV + ":" +
                                Constants.ATTR_MUST_UNDERSTAND;

        Vector entries = new Vector();
        DocumentBuilder builder = XMLParserUtils.getXMLDocBuilder();
        Document doc = builder.newDocument();
        Element elem = doc.createElement("targetAddress");
        elem.setAttribute(must, "1");
        Text txt = doc.createTextNode("");
        txt.setData("http://mindstrm.com:8004/glue/urn:CorpDataServices");
        elem.appendChild(txt);
        entries.addElement(elem);
```

```
                header.setHeaderEntries(entries);
                call.setHeader(header);

                Vector params = new Vector();
                params.addElement(new Parameter("stocks", String.class, stocks, null));
                call.setParams(params);

                try {
                    call.setMethodName("getQuote");
                    Response resp = call.invoke(url, "");

                    if (resp.generatedFault()) {
                        Fault fault = resp.getFault();
                        String code = fault.getFaultCode();
                        String desc = fault.getFaultString();
                        System.out.println(code + ": " + desc);

                        Vector v = fault.getDetailEntries();
                        int cnt = v.size();
                        for (int i = 0; i < cnt; i++) {
                            Element n = (Element)v.elementAt(i);
                            Node nd = n.getFirstChild();
                            //System.out.println(n.getNodeName()
                                    + ": " + nd.getNodeValue());
                        }
                    }
                    else {
                        Parameter ret = resp.getReturnValue();
                        ProxyQuote value = (ProxyQuote)ret.getValue();
                        System.out.println("Symbol:      " + value.getStockSymbol() +
                                "\nLast Price: " + value.getLast() +
                                "\nChange:       " + value.getDiff() +
                                "\nTime Stamp: " + value.getTime() +
                                "\nVolume:       " + value.getVol());
                    }
                }
                catch (SOAPException e) {
                    System.err.println("Caught SOAPException (" +
                                e.getFaultCode() + "): " +
                                e.getMessage());
                }
            }
        }
    }
```

We create an instance of org.apache.soap.Header called header that we'll use to build up the header elements. The String variable must holds the qualified name of the mustUnderstand attribute. We build the name using the constant values Constants. NS_PRE_SOAP_ENV and Constants.ATTR_MUST_UNDERSTAND, with a ":" between them. This results in the value SOAP-ENV:mustUnderstand. Now we'll have to work at the XML level, like we did when we developed custom fault detail entries in Chapter 7. We take the same approach here, except that we don't need to build the SOAP-ENV: Header element; that's taken care of by the org.apache.soap.Header class. We only need to build the child entries inside the header, so we create targetAddress as the first element of the document. Next we set the mustUnderstand attribute by calling elem.setAttribute( ), passing it the must string variable as well as a value of "1". Now we create a text node and set its data to http://mindstrm.com:8004/glue/urn: CorpDataServices, which is the endpoint we're directing the proxy service to use. The vector of header entries is added to the header by calling header.setHeaderEntries( ), and then the header is added to the call object using call.setHeader( ). Now the header we set up will be included when the SOAP envelope is created. I ran this client application with AMX on the command line, resulting in the following SOAP envelope being sent to the service:

```
<SOAP-ENV:Envelope
xmlns:SOAP-ENV="http://schemas.xmlsoap.org/soap/envelope/"
xmlns:xsi="http://www.w3.org/2001/XMLSchema-instance"
xmlns:xsd="http://www.w3.org/2001/XMLSchema">
<SOAP-ENV:Header>
<targetAddress SOAPENV:mustUnderstand="1">
http://tokyo:8004/glue/urn:CorpDataServices
</targetAddress>
</SOAP-ENV:Header>
<SOAP-ENV:Body>
<ns1:getQuote
xmlns:ns1="urn:DirectedQuoteProxyService"
SOAP-ENV:encodingStyle="http://schemas.xmlsoap.org/soap/encoding/">
<stocks xsi:type="xsd:string">AMX</stocks>
</ns1:getQuote>
</SOAP-ENV:Body>
</SOAP-ENV:Envelope>
```

CHAPTER 11

JAX-RPC and JAXM

With most software technologies, standardization occurs when the technology has gained a certain amount of momentum. Well, SOAP and web services have gained the requisite momentum, and standards (and their resulting acronyms) are sprouting up. There are a slew of API standards evolving for manipulating XML in Java, all of which fall under the umbrella of the Java APIs for XML (JAX). JAX is not a product—it's an API definition, and as such, it's no different from many of the countless API specifications associated with Java. However, since XML is such a wide-ranging area, JAX is made up of many components. Two of these are of particular interest to us: JAX-RPC and JAXM. JAX-RPC is the Java API for XML-based RPC. This is the API that, over time, I'd expect most significant SOAP RPC implementations to follow. JAXM is the Java API for XML Messaging, and, like JAX-RPC, it will likely become widely accepted.

These two APIs are new, and are not yet ready for the production world. The specifications for JAXM and JAX-RPC are in public review, and therefore are expected to change before they're complete; however, at this stage, the changes should be relatively minor. Nonetheless, Sun has produced a reference implementation that allows you to start working with these technologies. This reference implementation is included in the Java Web Services Developer Pack (Java WSDP) available at *http:// java.sun.com/webservices/webservicespack.html*. You can treat this release as an early beta; as long as you don't use it for a production server and don't expect it to have all the bugs worked out or the features you like, it will help you get up to speed so that you can build a production server as soon as possible when the standards are finalized. The Web Services Developer Pack uses a Tomcat 4 server, so if you've been using Apache SOAP with Tomcat up to this point, you should be pretty comfortable working with JAX. Even if you haven't been using Tomcat, the installation instructions for the pack are straightforward, and you shouldn't have much trouble with it.

To explore JAX-RPC, we'll build a few examples using the reference implementation of JAX. These examples will be new versions of the examples we developed earlier in this book. We'll move quickly, with the assumption that you've read every chapter up to this point. We won't attempt to cover JAX-RPC and JAXM completely; instead, we'll use this opportunity to take a quick look at how these APIs are structured, and how they compare to the Apache SOAP 2.X and GLUE APIs that we explored in earlier chapters. In other words, we'll be rebuilding a few of the service and client examples from previous chapters using JAX.

JAX-RPC

Let's start with JAX-RPC, since we've spent most of our time in the RPC world. Like GLUE, JAX-RPC hides the details of the underlying protocol (SOAP) from the programmer. To hide the underlying protocol, JAX-RPC makes use of objects known as stubs and ties. A *stub* is used by a client application to access a remote service. The stub looks like the service interface, but it runs as part of the local client process. The stub in turn uses the underlying framework to generate an appropriate SOAP message and send it over HTTP. So from the perspective of a client application programmer, if you have the stub you don't need to deal with any of the details of the SOAP message. Figure 11-1 shows the relationship between client code, stubs, and the runtime component of the JAX-RPC client framework.

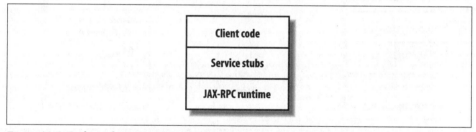

Figure 11-1. Stubs in the JAX-RPC architecture

A *tie* is conceptually similar to a stub, but exists on the server side. A tie acts as a bridge between the JAX-RPC runtime and the service implementation, and decouples your service code from the JAX-RPC framework. Inbound service messages are handled by the JAX-RPC runtime and passed to the service via a tie object. Service responses move back through the tie to the JAX-RPC runtime, where they are converted to SOAP response or SOAP fault messages and returned over HTTP. Figure 11-2 shows the relationship between service code, service ties, and the JAX-RPC runtime.

Think for a moment about the RPC mechanisms in Apache SOAP 2.X and GLUE. Apache exposes a great deal of the SOAP machinery to the Java programmer, and asks the programmer to deal with SOAP at a concrete level. Architecturally, JAX-RPC looks quite a bit more like GLUE in that it hides many of the low-level details. This is a positive trend in the evolution of SOAP APIs, whether or not they are proprietary.

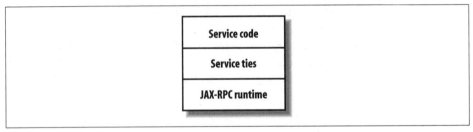

Figure 11-2. Ties in the JAX-RPC architecture

Regardless of the complexity of your API or the kind of distributed mechanism you choose, it's good practice to abstract and isolate the part of your software that deals with the distributed computing mechanism. This allows you to swap mechanisms with minimal impact on the rest of your work. The examples in this chapter use this approach, even though the examples are so simple that it may seem like overkill. Figure 11-3 shows the overall architecture of the RPC examples we'll develop using JAX-RPC.

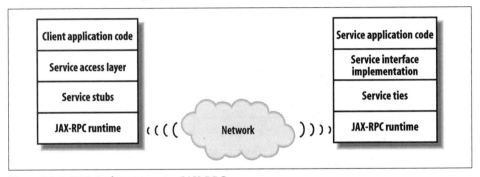

Figure 11-3. RPC Architecture using JAX-RPC

Working Without Ant

The Java Web Services Developer Pack tutorial relies heavily on a package called Ant. All Java source file compilation, directory creation, JAR file creation, etc., are managed by Ant configuration files. Although Ant is quite popular, and using it to build the kind of code in this chapter is a good idea, we're not going to cover its use here. (For more information about Ant, see *Ant: The Definitive Guide* by Jesse Tilly and Eric Burke.) Instead, I'm going to take you through the manual steps for the examples. If you know how to use Ant, you'll be able to gloss over some of the details in this chapter.

The most critical thing to set up is the classpath. The Early Access Release makes use of 10 JAR files that need to be on your classpath. These files are located in the *common\lib* directory underneath the root of your Developer Pack installation, and

---

it's up to you to make sure they are on your classpath using whatever technique you prefer. Here are the files:

> *jaxrpc-ri.jar*
> *jaxrpc-api.jar*
> *activation.jar*
> *dom4j.jar*
> *jaxm-api.jar*
> *jaxm-client.jar*
> *log4j.jar*
> *mail.jar*
> *xalan.jar*
> *xerces.jar*

Creating a JAX-RPC Service

Back in Chapter 9 we talked about building proxy services, which sit between client applications and other services. In that chapter, the back-end service with which the proxies communicated was located at *http://mindstrm.com:8004/glue/urn: CorpDataServices*. Let's do the same thing again, only this time we'll build our proxy service using the JAX-RPC reference implementation.* This example allows us to see how JAX-RPC interoperates with GLUE, and gives us a chance to build both a service and a client using JAX-RPC.

The first step in building the service is to write a Java interface for it, which I'll call javasoap.book.ch11.services.IStockServiceProxy. This interface must implement the java.rmi.Remote interface because JAX-RPC makes use of the Java RMI package. This strategy is fairly common because Java RMI provides a good distributed computing abstraction. The methods in the interface should be defined to throw RemoteException, which also comes from the java.rmi package. We'll define one method, getStockQuote( ), which takes a string parameter for the stock symbol and returns an instance of javasoap.book.ch9.services.ProxyQuote. There's no need to create a new class for returning a quote; we've already done it in Chapter 9. Here's what the code looks like for the IStockServiceProxy interface:

```
package javasoap.book.ch11.services;

import java.rmi.Remote;
import java.rmi.RemoteException;
import javasoap.book.ch9.services.ProxyQuote;

public interface IStockServiceProxy extends Remote {
```

---

* I'm assuming you've downloaded and installed the Java Web Services Developer Pack already, and verified that it is working properly.

```
    public ProxyQuote getStockQuote(String symbol) throws RemoteException;
}
```

Next, we need to write a Java class that implements the IStockServiceProxy interface, which I'll call javasoap.book.ch11.services.StockServiceProxyImpl. I don't
normally use the Impl suffix in my class names, but it's a common practice, and it
suits my purposes here. (Ordinarily, I'd just drop the "I" from the interface name
and call the implementation class StockServiceProxy, but I want to use that name for
something else. I want to decouple the class that really performs the work of the service from the classes that work with JAX-RPC or any other API.) So the
StockServiceProxyImpl class is part of the Service Interface Implementation layer
from Figure 11-3. We'll use another class, called javasoap.book.ch11.services.
StockServiceProxy, to do the actual work. Unlike StockServiceProxyImpl, this class
doesn't know anything about the JAX-RPC mechanism, nor does it know anything
about the IStockServiceProxy interface used by the tie object. This allows us to use
the class, without modification, regardless of the distributed computing mechanism
we're using. In other words, StockServiceProxy is part of the Service Application
Code layer shown in Figure 11-3. We'll use an instance of StockServiceProxy inside
the getStockQuote( ) method of the StockServiceProxyImpl class, as shown below:

```
package javasoap.book.ch11.services;

import javasoap.book.ch9.services.ProxyQuote;

public class StockServiceProxyImpl implements IStockServiceProxy {

    public ProxyQuote getStockQuote(String symbol) {
        StockServiceProxy sp = new StockServiceProxy( );
        return sp.getStockQuote(symbol);
    }
}
```

Now we'll implement the StockServiceProxy class, whose job it is to invoke the
GetQuote( ) method on the urn:CorpDataServices service. However, I want to hold off
on communicating with this GLUE-based service, as that involves the use of its
WSDL file. We'll get to that later. But for now, the getStockQuote( ) method of
StockServiceProxy will just return an instance of ProxyQuote with dummy data.
Here's the code:

```
package javasoap.book.ch11.services;

import javasoap.book.ch9.services.ProxyQuote;

public class StockServiceProxy {

        public ProxyQuote getStockQuote(String symbol) {

        ProxyQuote pq = new ProxyQuote( );
        pq.setStockSymbol(symbol);
```

```
                    // set dummy data for now
                    pq.setLast((float)0.0);
                    pq.setDiff((float)0.0);
                    pq.setTime("NA");
                    pq.setVol(0);

                    return pq;
            }
        }
```

These are all the Java classes and interfaces we'll need to implement the service. Go ahead and compile them. Now it's time to generate the stubs and ties for the service. A command-line tool called xrpcc generates these classes. xrpcc takes a configuration file as input. This file is an XML file that contains information about the classes, namespaces, service name, etc. I've named this file *CorpDataServices.xml*. Let's take a look at its contents:

```
<?xml version="1.0" encoding="UTF-8"?>
<configuration
  xmlns="http://java.sun.com/jax-rpc-ri/xrpcc-config">
  <rmi name="CorpDataServicesProxy"
    targetNamespace="http://mindstrm.com/wsdl"
    typeNamespace="http://mindstrm.com/types">
      <service name="CorpDataServices"
          packageName="javasoap.book.ch11.client">
        <interface name="javasoap.book.ch11.services.IStockServiceProxy"
          servantName="javasoap.book.ch11.services.StockServiceProxyImpl"/>
      </service>
  </rmi>
</configuration>
```

Everything lies underneath the configuration tag, which uses the xmlns attribute to define the global namespace as http://java.sun.com/jax-rpc-ri/xrpcc-config. Since we're using an interface based on RMI, the first child of configuration is named rmi.[*] The name attribute is used to specify the *model* name, which is essentially the name that will be used as a base for the files generated by this process. You can think of it as the name of the service definition. (It is used for just that purpose in the WSDL file that gets generated.) The targetNamespace and typeNamespace attributes are used to declare the namespaces that will be associated with the target service and the custom types, respectively. Under the rmi tag comes the service tag, which provides xrpcc information about the Java classes and interface used to implement the service. The name attribute contains the service name itself, and the packageName attribute contains the name of the Java package to use for the generated client-side code. Under service comes the interface tag, which tells the tool about the classes that implement the service interface. The name attribute contains the fully qualified

---

[*] xrpcc also allows the use of a WSDL document instead of RMI. We'll use that approach later in the chapter.

name of the Java interface for the service, and the `servantName` contains the fully qualified name of the Java class that implements that interface.

So let's go ahead and run xrpcc for our service. The root of my working classpath is `e:\projects\soap`, so I'll pass that on the command line as follows:

```
xrpcc -both -keep -classpath e:\projects\soap -d gen CorpDataServices.xml
```

The `-both` option tells `xrpcc` that we want it to generate the files for both the client and server side. If for some reason you prefer to generate client-side and server-side files separately, you'd use either `-client` or `-server` instead. If you specify `-keep`, as I did, the Java source files for the generated code will not be deleted. (By default, `xrpcc` compiles the generated code and then deletes the source files, since you don't really need them for anything. I used `-keep` so I could take a peek at the code. It's useful to see what classes and methods `xrpcc` is generating, particularly when you're getting started.) The `-classpath` option specifies the classpath for finding the input class files; the `-d` option specifies the directory to use as the root for the generated files. Finally, the last argument on the command line is the name of the configuration file.

Here's a listing of the files generated by `xrpcc`, organized by the subdirectories within xrpcc's working directory. Items in bold are directory names. For the sake of clarity, I didn't list the Java source files that were retained because of the `-keep` option. (In fact, I deleted them manually to ensure that they weren't packaged for deployment.)

gen

    CorpDataServices.wsdl

    CorpDataServicesProxy_Config.properties

javasoap\book\ch11\client

    CorpDataServicesProxy.class

    CorpDataServicesProxy_SerializerRegistry.class

    CorpDataServicesProxyImpl.class

javasoap\book\ch11\services

    GetStockQuote_RequestStruct.class

    GetStockQuote_RequestStruct_SOAPSerializer.class

    GetStockQuote_ResponseStruct.class

    GetStockQuote_ResponseStruct_SOAPBuilder.class

    GetStockQuote_ResponseStruct_SOAPSerializer.class

    IStockServiceProxy_Stub.class

    IStockServiceProxy_Tie.class

javasoap\book\ch9\services

    ProxyQuote_SOAPSerializer.class

I placed the files into a separate *gen* directory because they are going to be packaged in a JAR file a little later, and I don't want to package my entire javasoap.book package path. The first time I ran xrpcc, I noticed that the stub and tie classes were generated in the same package. I don't like to work that way. As you've seen throughout, I've kept my client-side and server-side classes in separate packages, but xrpcc doesn't give me that option. In addition, the serializer class (ProxyQuote_SOAPSerializer) for the javasoap.book.ch9.services.ProxyQuote class was put into the javasoap.book.ch9.services package. I suppose this makes sense, though it's not where I would want the serializer; but again, I don't have control over this. One could certainly mess around with the package names in the source code that xrpcc generates, and recompile by hand, but I won't bother. This is still an early-access release, and things will change. Just keep in mind that you may not be happy with the package structuring that xrpcc creates.

Next, we need to create a deployment descriptor. The information contained in the deployment descriptor is used to configure the service application on the web server. Here's the deployment descriptor for our service, which needs to be called *web.xml*; I put it into the *gen* directory. The text in bold represents code specific to this example.

```xml
<?xml version="1.0" encoding="UTF-8"?>

<!DOCTYPE web-app PUBLIC
    "-//Sun Microsystems, Inc.//DTD Web Application 2.3//EN"
    "http://java.sun.com/j2ee/dtds/web-app_2_3.dtd">

<web-app>
    <display-name>CorpDataServices</display-name>
    <description>Corporate Data Services</description>
    <servlet>
        <servlet-name>JAXRPCEndpoint</servlet-name>
        <display-name>JAXRPCEndpoint</display-name>
        <description>
            Endpoint for Corporate Data Services Application
        </description>
        <servlet-class>
            com.sun.xml.rpc.server.http.JAXRPCServlet
        </servlet-class>
        <init-param>
            <param-name>configuration.file</param-name>
            <param-value>
            /WEB-INF/CorpDataServicesProxy_Config.properties
            </param-value>
        </init-param>
        <load-on-startup>0</load-on-startup>
    </servlet>
    <servlet-mapping>
        <servlet-name>JAXRPCEndpoint</servlet-name>
        <url-pattern>/jaxrpc/*</url-pattern>
    </servlet-mapping>
```

```
<session-config>
    <session-timeout>60</session-timeout>
</session-config>
</web-app>
```

We aren't done yet. Now that we've implemented the Java classes and interfaces for our service, generated ties and stubs, and created a deployment descriptor, the next step is to package the service in a WAR file. A WAR file is a *web application archive*, i.e., a JAR file that contains the files needed to deploy and run a web application according to the Java servlet specification. We'll copy the class files for IStockServiceProxy, StockServiceProxyImpl, and StockServiceProxy into the appropriate directory underneath the *gen* directory, and do the same thing for the javasoap.book.ch9.services.ProxyQuote class. We need to organize our files and directories to be a proper WAR file. Everything should start from a root directory that must be called *WEB-INF* (all uppercase letters). Move the *web.xml*, *CorpDataServicesProxy_Config.properties*, and *CorpDataServices.wsdl* files into the *WEB-INF* directory. Now we need to put the Java classes into the proper directories. Create a directory called *classes* underneath the *WEB-INF* directory, and make it the root of the *javasoap* directory. In other words, move the *javasoap* directory and all of its contents into *WEB-INF\classes*. Ant would make managing the process a lot easier: you just set up some configuration files and it does the rest. But now you know what Ant would be doing behind the scenes.

Let's create our WAR file. From the *gen* directory, issue the command:

```
jar cvf corpdata.war WEB-INF
```

This packages everything we need into the WAR file named *corpdata.war*. Figure 11-4 shows the contents of the WAR file using the WinZip program.

Now are we finished? Not quite. The last step is to deploy the service, which is as simple as copying the WAR file to the *webapps* directory for Tomcat 4 (remember that Tomcat 4 is included with the Java Web Services Developer Pack). So go ahead and do this now. My Web Services Developer Pack is installed on *e:\jwsdp-1_0-ea1*, so I copied *corpdata.war* to *e:\jwsdp-1_0-ea1\webapps*. If you've got Tomcat 4 running, shut it down and restart it; that will get it to read the *corpdata.war* file and deploy the service. You can check to be sure the service is properly deployed by going to *http://localhost:8080/corpdata/jaxrpc* in your browser. If the service is deployed correctly, you'll see the following:

```
A Web Service is installed at this URL.
It supports the following ports: "IStockServiceProxy" (http://localhost:8080/
corpdata/jaxrpc/IStockServiceProxy)
```

Well, that was easy! Actually, it wasn't as bad as it seems. A lot of the work was in the packaging and deployment. If you use the Ant tool instead of doing it by hand, things go a lot quicker. Remember that this is an early-access release of a reference implementation, so you can be pretty sure that the production systems will have better deployment tools.

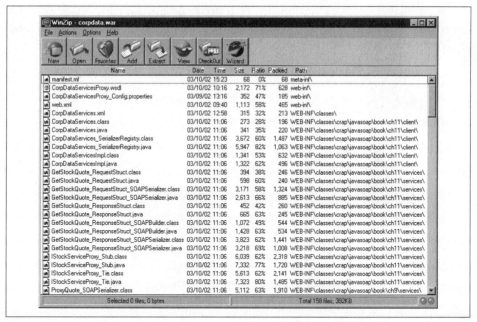

Figure 11-4. The contents of corpdata.war

Now that we've got a service deployed, let's take a moment to reflect. Is the development process better than the one we used in Apache SOAP? It seems to be. We didn't have to write any code other than that which implemented the service, while in Apache SOAP we had to write quite a bit of code related to the transport, type mapping, etc. In particular, notice that we didn't have to deal with our custom ProxyQuote class directly. The stubs and ties handled the entire mapping and serialization process.

How does this compare to GLUE in terms of service development? It's similar, although there are some subtle yet striking differences. As a developer, I know I'd certainly prefer not to deal with any generated code. Why should I have to manage those class files? Why should I have to even know they exist? With GLUE, some of this is handled dynamically, which makes it a bit easier to manage. You still need some client-side stubs, but service development hides everything. In my opinion, that's an advantage.

Creating a JAX-RPC Client

Before we start writing a client application, let make sure to copy all the class files generated earlier into their proper locations on the local filesystem. Remember that we have them in a WAR file, and we also have them under the *gen\WEB-INF\classes* directory. But neither of these locations is on my local classpath, so now is a good time to put them where they belong so the client application can access them.

Writing a client application for this service is pretty simple. All you need to do is get an instance of the stub that was generated earlier and call the desired service method on that object. Here's the code for a sample application class called `javasoap.book.ch11.client.StockQuoteApp`:

```
package javasoap.book.ch11.client;

import javasoap.book.ch11.services.*;
import javasoap.book.ch9.services.*;

public class StockQuoteApp {
    public static void main(String[] args) {
        try {
            CorpDataServicesProxyImpl proxy =
                new CorpDataServicesProxyImpl();
            IStockServiceProxy_Stub stub =
                (IStockServiceProxy_Stub)proxy.getIStockServiceProxy();
            stub._setTargetEndpoint(args[0]);
            ProxyQuote quote = stub.getStockQuote("IBM");
            System.out.println("Price is " + quote.getLast());
            System.out.println("Volume is " + quote.getVol());
            System.out.println("Timestamp is " + quote.getTime());
            System.out.println("Diff is " + quote.getDiff());
        } catch (Exception ex) {
            ex.printStackTrace();
        }
    }
}
```

We create an instance of `CorpDataServicesProxyImpl`, and then we call its `getIStockServiceProxy()` method. This gives us a reference to the stub, an instance of `IStockServiceProxy_Stub`. We need to pass the endpoint URL to the stub via its `_setTargetEndpoint()` method. The URL is *http://localhost:8080/corpdata/jaxrpc/IStockServiceProxy*, which is the location of the service endpoint we deployed earlier. Now we can simply call the `getStockQuote()` method, which results in an invocation of the service method of the same name. Notice that the return value is an instance of `javasoap.book.ch9.services.ProxyQuote`. Serialization of this custom type is handled automatically on both the client and service side. Running this application results in the following output:

```
Price is 0.0
Volume is 0
Timestamp is NA
Diff is 0.0
```

This is how you might use JAX-RPC to develop both the client and service code for a service. But that won't always be your situation. I mentioned earlier that xrpcc can make use of a WSDL file. That might be a nice way to generate stubs for accessing, say, a GLUE service. (And it will probably be the best way to generate stubs for accessing an arbitrary service somewhere on the network.) We'll try that next.

Generating Stubs from WSDL

Generating client code from WSDL is pretty simple. First we'll modify the *Corp-DataServices.xml* file that we used earlier as input to xrpcc. We have to remove the entire rmi section and replace it with a wsdl section. Here's what the modified file should look like:

```
<?xml version="1.0" encoding="UTF-8"?>
<configuration
  xmlns="http://java.sun.com/jax-rpc-ri/xrpcc-config">
  <wsdl name="CorpDataServicesProxy"
        location="http://mindstrm.com:8004/glue/urn:CorpDataServices.wsdl"
        packageName="javasoap.book.ch11.glueclient">
  </wsdl>
</configuration>
```

The name attribute specifies the model name, just like it did in the RMI example earlier. The location attribute contains the address of the WSDL resource for the service. We're going to use the GLUE service from Chapter 9; the WSDL for it is *http://mindstrm.com:8004/glue/urn:CorpDataServices.wsdl*. The packageName attribute, like before, specifies the package name of the generated code. This time we'll use javasoap.book.ch11.glueclient, since this code is meant to access our GLUE-based service. Generate the client-side code by issuing the command:

```
xrpcc -client -keep -classpath e:\projects\soap -d gen  CorpDataServices.xml
```

This is essentially the same command we used earlier, except that the -client option indicates that we're only interested in generating client code. When the process completes, the Java class files should be moved into the proper javasoap.book.ch11.glueclient directory so that they appear on the classpath. Take note of the javasoap.book.ch11.glueclient.Quote class. This is a custom type that represents the data returned from the GLUE service; it is already defined as a type in the WSDL document. Great! We don't have to do anything special to handle that type.

Let's write a client application called javasoap.book.ch11.glueclient.StockQuoteApp. It will look similar to our other StockQuoteApp, but it will talk to our existing GLUE-based service. Here's the code:

```
package javasoap.book.ch11.glueclient;

public class StockQuoteApp {
    public static void main(String[] args) {
        try {
            CorpDataServiceImpl proxy =
                new CorpDataServiceImpl();
            CorpDataServiceSoap_Stub stub =
                (CorpDataServiceSoap_Stub)proxy.getCorpDataServiceSoap();
            stub._setTargetEndpoint(args[0]);
            Quote quote = stub.getQuote("IBM");
            System.out.println("Price is " + quote.get_lastPrice());
            System.out.println("Volume is " + quote.get_volume());
```

```
        System.out.println("Timestamp is " + quote.get_timeStamp( ));
        System.out.println("Change is " + quote.get_change( ));
    } catch (Exception ex) {
      ex.printStackTrace( );
    }
  }
}
```

Running this application requires that the URL for the service endpoint be passed on the command line. In this case the proper URL is *http://mindstrm.com:8004/glue/urn: CorpDataServices*. When I ran this I got the following output:

```
Price is 105.09
Volume is 10726400
Timestamp is Mar  8
Change is 1.38
```

We could use the code from this example to make our earlier service talk to the GLUE service to get its data, instead of returning dummy data the way it does now. At this point you should be pretty clear on how to go about making that change, so I'll just run through it quickly. We'll need to modify the getStockQuote( ) method of the StockServiceProxy class. Here's what the modified code looks like:

```
package javasoap.book.ch11.services;

import javasoap.book.ch9.services.ProxyQuote;
import javasoap.book.ch11.glueclient.*;

public class StockServiceProxy {

    public ProxyQuote getStockQuote(String symbol) {

        ProxyQuote pq = new ProxyQuote( );
        try {
          CorpDataServiceImpl proxy =
              new CorpDataServiceImpl( );
          CorpDataServiceSoap_Stub stub =
              (CorpDataServiceSoap_Stub)proxy.getCorpDataServiceSoap( );
          stub._setTargetEndpoint(
              "http://mindstrm.com:8004/glue/urn:CorpDataServices");
          Quote quote = stub.getQuote(symbol);

          pq.setLast(quote.get_lastPrice( ));
          pq.setVol(quote.get_volume( ));
          pq.setTime(quote.get_timeStamp( ));
          pq.setDiff(quote.get_change( ));
        }
        catch (Exception ex) {
          ex.printStackTrace( );
        }

        return pq;
    }
}
```

The `javasoap.book.ch11.glueclient` package is imported; that package contains the stub code for talking to the `urn:CorpDataServices` service. This time we hardcode the URL passed to `_setTargetEndpoint( )`. After getting an instance of `Quote` back from the call to `getQuote( )`, we use it to populate an instance of `ProxyQuote`. Remember, the two services don't return the same data type. Then we simply return the `ProxyQuote` instance. This is pretty painless, thanks to WSDL. Of course, we had to compile the modified `StockServiceProxy` class, and create and deploy an updated WAR file to include the modified code along with the entire `javasoap.book.ch11.glueclient` package.

Dynamic Invocation Interface

At times, you want more control over the way your application interfaces with a service. One reason for wanting more control is that your application does not know the service methods and parameters in advance, making it impossible to generate stubs. It's also reasonably likely that the service you want to invoke does not provide a WSDL document describing it. The Dynamic Invocation Interface (DII) is an API that allows you to invoke services at a level much closer to the JAX-RPC runtime. We're not going to spend any time with DII, but you should be aware of it. We saw a glimpse of its structure in Chapter 9 when we developed a simple Axis example. It may not be identical, and these APIs are still evolving, but the approach is the same.

I see DII as a last-resort approach to writing code to communicate with SOAP web services. Letting a tool generate the low-level code based on a WSDL description is really the best choice, since WSDL is language and implementation independent, and is an accepted standard. If your SOAP tools can work with a WSDL file, that's your best bet.

JAXM, in Less Than a Nutshell

The APIs that JAXM provides for writing messaging clients and services are at a low level, similar to what we saw in Chapter 8. They require you to make a connection to the server (or an intermediary) and build up the XML that constitutes the message. Although this is a powerful technique, it gives you a lot of rope with which to hang yourself. I like the flexible nature of working directly with XML, but I still want the structure of RPC-style interaction. If you need to design your services to accept XML documents as parameters, you might find that literal encoding is sufficient within the context of RPC. If that's not enough, then you'll have to walk the messaging (or proprietary) path.

I suggest you take a look at the examples that come with the Java Web Services Developer Pack tutorial. Even though we don't develop a JAXM example here, you're armed with enough knowledge to understand what's happening. And something tells me that a future edition of this book will delve deep into JAXM, JAX-RPC, and the rest of the JAX Pack.

What Next?

You're now more than ready to start developing web services in Java. Don't be put off by the pace of change. Keep track of the latest technologies, including new releases of existing implementations. New versions of GLUE, Axis (Apache SOAP), .NET, and many others will make the development of services in Java easier, better, and more powerful. Finally, keep an eye on standardized APIs, security, service registries, and IDE integration; the list is growing as fast as the bandwidth requirements! Jump in.

Index

We'd like to hear your suggestions for improving our indexes. Send email to *index@oreilly.com*.

B

base64 character set, 34, 35
BasicTradingService class (example), 85
  Apache SOAP client, 86
  deploying in Apache SOAP, 86
  executeStockTrade() service method, 100
  getHighLow() service method, 110
  getMostActive() service method, 94
  heterogeneous array as method
    parameter, 88
  returning arrays from method
    calls, 94–97
      GLUE, deploying in, 96
BasicTradingServiceHelper class
  (example), 107
Bean class, 121
BeanSerializer class, 103, 112, 191
BetterRPCJavaProvider class (example), 215
BetterRPCRouter class (example), 216–219
BetterSOAPMappingRegistry class
  (example), 131
binary data
  encoding, 34–36
  sending as SOAP attachments, 153
bind() (Registry), 68
bindings
  GLUE services, 198
  SOAP, 198
  WSDL, 179, 186
    combining with physical address in
      port element, 187
    operation elements for service, 186
Body elements, 13, 21
  fault subelements, 22–24
  literal XML encoding style, setting, 166
body (SOAP messages), retrieving elements
  in, 155
browsers, displaying WSDL documents, 182
built-in data types, XML Schema Part 2, 32
  in SOAP, 26
byte arrays, 34
ByteArrayDataSource class, 171

C

C/C++ languages
  default values for method parameters in
    C++, 42
  structs, 37
Call class, 64, 211
  encoding style URI, setting, 77

  mapping custom types to Java
    classes, 103
  method parameters, setting, 77
  setHeader(), 225
  setTargetObjectURI(), 188
CallCounterApp class (example), 57
CallCounterService (example), 51
  deployment descriptor, 52
case, converting for stock symbol, 82
child elements, getting for root element, 162
classes
  Apache SOAP router and provider,
    replacing, 214–219
  helper, generating with GLUE console, 68
  holder, 82
  Java
    associating with Java objects, 121
    Call class, 64
    client-side, for GLUE service
      access, 60
    custom serialization, 118
    data structure, mapping to custom
      types, 107
    deserializing encoded data into class
      instance, 120
    designing custom, 97–99
    loading dynamically in Java SOAP, 52
    sharing in client/server
      programming, 105
    structs vs., 37
    Vector class, 77
client applications
  Apache Axis, for .NET service, 210–212
  Apache SOAP
    BasicTrading Service, accessing, 86
    calling from GLUE service, 187–193
    custom serialization, 132
    DataFeedService, accessing, 122
    fault with detail section, 147
    for .NET proxy service, 206
    .NET service, accessing, 208
    passing heterogeneous array as service
      method parameter, 89
    returning arrays from method calls, 94
    returning custom types, 111
    for service passing custom types as
      method parameters, 102
    SOAP headers, 223
    temperature data, requesting, 161
    WeatherDiary message
      service, 156–159
    XML document, passing, 165

---

literal encoding, 163–176
    attachments, 167–176
loading classes dynamically, Java SOAP
        implementations, 52
locate() (Provider), 215
location attribute (soap:address
        element), 189

M

main(), CallCounterApp (example class), 57
mapping
    array of primitive data elements to array of
        primitive Java types, 176
    custom data types, handling with stubs
        and ties, 235
    custom type data fields to Java data
        structure class, 106
    custom types to Java classes, 101, 107
    custom types to serializers in GLUE, 136
    service method return values to custom
        data type, 110, 191, 197
        QuoteProxyService.map
        (example), 202
mapping registry, 130
Mappings class, 136
mappings elements, 54
mapTypes() (SOAPMappingRegistry), 103,
        191
markup languages, 4
marshall(), 118
    namespace scope pushing and, 120
    serializing sparse arrays, 127
    xjmr class, 128
Message class, creating instance and calling
        send(), 158
message elements, WSDL document, 185
message passing systems, xi, 2
    SOAP-based (JAXM API), 7
message-oriented middleware (MOM), 4
messages, SOAP, 9–24
    actor attribute, 18
    Body element, 21
    encodingStyle attribute, 20
    Envelope element, 16
    envelope versions, 21
    envelopes, 13–16
    faults, 22–24
    Header element, 17
    HTTP binding, 9

HTTP request, 10
HTTP response, 11
mustUnderstand attribute, 19
transmitted by GLUE applications, 80
message-style services, 152–163
    stock quotes (example), designing
        message format, 3
    writing, 154–163
messaging, JAXM (Java API for XML
        Messaging), xii, 7, 226, 239
method calls, 2
method calls, SOAP RPC, 45–51
    Apache SOAP, 64
    Call class, 64
    fault responses, 49
    mapping to Java code, 47
    method response, 48
method parameters
    java2wsdl tool, 198
    parameterOrder attribute, 186
    passing arrays as, 85–93
        using GLUE, 91–93
    passing custom types as, 97–108
        mapping custom types to Java
            classes, 101
    passing to services, 75–84
        with GLUE APIs, 78–81
        in, out, and in/out, 81–84
    representing in WSDL document with
        part elements, 185
    SOAP RPC calls, in method invocation
        structs, 47
method signatures, 47
MethodCounter class (example), 52
methods
    C++, defining default parameter
        values, 42
    service, exposing in GLUE, 59
methods attribute (provider element), 53
Microsoft
    COM (Component Object Model), 2
        variant type, polymorphism in, 36
    .NET, 7, 204–210
MIME types
    attachments, handling with JAF, 169
    base64 encoding algorithm for byte
        arrays, 34
    multipart messages, 154
Mind Electric, The, 7
MOM (message-oriented middleware), 4
multi-dimensional arrays, 39

About the Author

Robert Englander is Principal Engineer and President of MindStream Software, Inc. (*www.mindstrm.com*). He provides consulting services in software architecture, design, and development, as well as developing frameworks for use on client projects. His focus is in the areas of component architectures and distributed systems.

Rob has built software in Java and C++ for clients ranging from small shops to large organizations. He has spoken at industry conferences, written articles for magazines and journals, and is the author of the O'Reilly book *Developing Java Beans*.

Colophon

Our look is the result of reader comments, our own experimentation, and feedback from distribution channels. Distinctive covers complement our distinctive approach to technical topics, breathing personality and life into potentially dry subjects.

The animal on the cover of *Java and SOAP* is a red firefish, *Pterois volitans*. These fish are found throughout the warm, tropical waters of the Indian and Pacific Oceans at depths up to 100 feet. They tend to sit nearly motionless on the ocean floor, often under ledges, waiting for potential prey—mainly small fish and crustaceans—to wander into range.

Red firefish are members of the family Scorpaenidae—scorpionfishes—named for the poisonous spines on their dorsal fins. Confident in their ability to defend themselves, firefish often do not back off even when a human approaches; instead, they point their venomous spines towards aggressors. Their confidence is well-placed: the sting of their spines, though not usually fatal to humans, is extremely painful.

In addition to their native ocean habitat, red firefish can also be found living in many home tropical aquariums. They can grow up to 16 inches in length and so require a fairly large tank. But despite their fearsome spines and predatory nature, they're actually very peaceful and sociable, and they get along well with other fish—except the ones small enough to be eaten.

Emily Quill was the production editor and copyeditor for *Java and SOAP*. Sarah Sherman and Matt Hutchinson provided quality control. Philip Dangler, David Chu, and Julie Flanagan provided production assistance. Ellen Troutman-Zaig wrote the index.

Emma Colby designed the cover of this book, based on a series design by Edie Freedman. The cover image is a 19th-century engraving from the Dover Pictorial Archive. Emma Colby produced the cover layout with QuarkXPress 4.1 using Adobe's ITC Garamond font.

Melanie Wang designed the interior layout, based on a series design by David Futato. Neil Walls converted the files from Microsoft Word to FrameMaker 5.5.6 using tools created by Mike Sierra. The text font is Linotype Birka; the heading font is Adobe Myriad Condensed; and the code font is LucasFont's TheSans Mono Condensed. The illustrations that appear in the book were produced by Robert Romano and Jessamyn Read using Macromedia FreeHand 9 and Adobe Photoshop 6. The tip and warning icons were drawn by Christopher Bing. This colophon was written by Leanne Soylemez.

 **More Titles from O'Reilly**

Java

Java Network Programming, 2nd Edition

By Elliotte Rusty Harold
2nd Edition August 2000
760 pages, ISBN 1-56592-870-9

Java Network Programming, 2nd Edition, is a complete introduction to developing network programs (both applets and applications) using Java, covering everything from networking fundamentals to remote method invocation (RMI). It includes chapters on TCP and UDP sockets, multicasting protocol and content handlers, and servlets. This second edition also includes coverage of Java 1.1, 1.2 and 1.3. New chapters cover multithreaded network programming, I/O, HTML parsing and display, the Java Mail API, the Java Secure Sockets Extension, and more.

Java Swing

By Robert Eckstein, Marc Loy & David Wood
1st Edition September 1998
1255 pages, ISBN 1-56592-455-X

The Swing classes eliminate Java's biggest weakness: its relatively primitive user interface toolkit. *Java Swing* helps you to take full advantage of the Swing classes, providing detailed descriptions of every class and interface in the key Swing packages. It shows you how to use all of the new components, allowing you to build state-of-the-art user interfaces and giving you the context you need to understand what you're doing. It's more than documentation; Java Swing helps you develop code quickly and effectively.

Java Pragramming with Oracle JDBC

By Donald K. Bales
1st Edition December 2001
496 pages, ISBN 0-596-00088-X

Here is the professional's guide to leveraging Java's JDBC in an Oracle environment. Readers learn the all-important mysteries of establishing database corrections; issuing SQL queries and getting results back; and advanced topics such as streaming large objects, calling PL/SQL procedures, and working with Oracle9*i*'s object-oriented features. Also covered: transactions, concurrency management and performance. This is an essential tool for all Java Oracle developers who need to work with both technologies.

Learning Wireless Java

By Qusay Mahmoud
1st Edition December 2001
264 pages, ISBN 0-596-00243-2

Learning Wireless Java is a solid introduction to working with the Mobile Information Device Profile (MIDP), which contains the APIs designed specifically for writing applications that need to run on wireless and embedded devices. It includes reference material on the core and javax.microedition classes, as well as on the classes specific to the various wireless platforms the J2ME supports.

Java Security, 2nd Edition

By Scott Oaks
2nd Edition May 2001
618 pages, ISBN 0-596-00157-6

The second edition focuses on the platform features of Java that provide security—the class loader, bytecode verifier, and security manager—and recent additions to Java that enhance this security model: digital signatures, security providers, and the access controller. The book covers in depth the security model of Java 2, version 1.3, including the two new security APIs: JAAS and JSSE.

Database Programming with JDBC and Java, 2nd Edition

By George Reese
2nd Edition August 2000
352 pages, ISBN 1-56592-616-1

This book describes the standard Java interfaces that make portable object-oriented access to relational databases possible, and offers a robust model for writing applications that are easy to maintain. The second edition has been completely updated for JDBC 2.0, and includes reference listings for JDBC and the most important RMI classes. The book begins with a quick overview of SQL for developers who may be asked to handle a database for the first time, and goes on to explain how to issue database queries and updates through SQL and JDBC.

O'REILLY®

TO ORDER: **800-998-9938** • *order@oreilly.com* • *www.oreilly.com*
ONLINE EDITIONS OF MOST O'REILLY TITLES ARE AVAILABLE BY SUBSCRIPTION AT **safari.oreilly.com**
ALSO AVAILABLE AT MOST RETAIL AND ONLINE BOOKSTORES

Java

Java Cookbook

By Ian Darwin
1st Edition June 2001
882 pages, ISBN 0-59600-170-3

This book offers Java developers short, focused pieces of code that are easy to incorporate into other programs. The idea is to focus on things that are useful, tricky, or both. The book's code segments cover all of the dominant APIs and many specialized APIs and should serve as a great "jumping-off place" for Java developers who want to get started in areas outside their specialization.

Java Performance Tuning

By Jack Shirazi
1st Edition September 2000
440 pages, ISBN 0-596-00015-4

Java Performance Tuning contains step-by-step instructions on all aspects of the performance tuning process, right from such early considerations as setting goals, measuring performance, and choosing a compiler. Extensive examples for tuning many parts of an application are described in detail, and any pitfalls are identified. The book also provides performance tuning checklists that enable developers to make their tuning as comprehensive as possible.

Java RMI

By William Grosso
1st Edition November 2001
576 pages, ISBN 1-56592-452-5

Enterprise Java developers, especially those working with Enterprise JavaBeans, and Jini, need to understand RMI technology in order to write today's complex, distributed applications. O'Reilly's *Java RMI* thoroughly explores and explains this powerful but often overlooked technology. Included is a wealth of real-world examples that developers can implement and customize.

Learning Java

By Pat Niemeyer & Jonathan Knudsen
1st Edition, May 2000
726 pages, Includes CD-ROM
ISBN 1-56592-718-4

For programmers either just migrating to Java or already working steadily in the forefront of Java development, *Learning Java* gives a clear, systematic overview of the Java 2 Standard Edition. It covers the essentials of hot topics like Swing and JFC; describes new tools for signing applets; and shows how to write networked clients and servers, servlets, JavaBeans, and state-of-the-art user interfaces. Includes a CD-ROM containing the Java 2 SDK, version 1.3.

Java Internationalization

By Andy Deitsch & David Czarnecki
1st Edition March 2001
451 pages, ISBN 0-596-00019-7

Java Internationalization shows how to write software that is truly multilingual, using Java's very sophisticated Unicode internationalization facilities. Java Internationalization brings Java developers up to speed for the new generation of software development: writing software that is no longer limited by language boundaries.

Java Message Service

By Richard Monson-Haefel & David Chappell
1st Edition December 2000
238 pages, ISBN 0-596-00068-5

This book is a thorough introduction to Java Message Service (JMS) from Sun Microsystems. It shows how to build applications using the point-to-point and publish-and-subscribe models; use features like transactions and durable subscriptions to make applications reliable; and use messaging within Enterprise JavaBeans. It also introduces a new EJB type, the MessageDrivenBean, that is part of EJB 2.0, and discusses integration of messaging into J2EE.

Java

Java Servlet Programming, 2nd Edition

By Jason Hunter with William Crawford
2nd Edition April 2001
780 pages, ISBN 0-596-00040-5

The second edition of this popular book has been completely updated to add the new features of the Java Servlet API Version 2.2, and new chapters on servlet security and advanced communication. In addition to complete coverage of the 2.2 specification, we have included bonus material on the new 2.3 version of the specification.

Java & XML, 2nd Edition

By Brett McLaughlin
2nd Edition September 2001
528 pages, ISBN 0-596-000197-5

New chapters on Advanced SAX, Advanced DOM, SOAP, and data binding, as well as new examples throughout, bring the second edition of *Java & XML* thoroughly up to date. Except for a concise introduction to XML basics, the book focuses entirely on using XML from Java applications. It's a worthy companion for Java developers working with XML or involved in messaging, web services, or the new peer-to-peer movement.

JavaServer Pages

By Hans Bergsten
1st Edition December 2000
572 pages, ISBN 1-56592-746-X

JavaServer Pages shows how to develop Java-based web applications without having to be a hardcore programmer. The author provides an overview of JSP concepts and illuminates how JSP fits into the larger picture of web applications. There are chapters for web authors on generating dynamic content, handling session information, and accessing databases, as well as material for Java programmers on creating Java components and custom JSP tags for web authors to use in JSP pages.

Java and XSLT

By Eric M. Burke
1st Edition September 2001
528 pages, ISBN 0-596-00143-6

Learn how to use XSL transformations in Java programs ranging from stand-alone applications to servlets. *Java and XSLT* introduces XSLT and then shows you how to apply transformations in real-world situations, such as developing a discussion forum, transforming documents from one form to another, and generating content for wireless devices.

Enterprise JavaBeans, 3rd Edition

By Richard Monson-Haefel
3rd Edition September 2001
592 pages, ISBN 0-596-00226-2

Enterprise JavaBeans has been thoroughly updated for the new EJB Specification. Important changes in Version 2.0 include a completely new CMP (container-managed persistence) model that allows for much more complex business function modeling; local interfaces that will significantly improve performance of EJB applications; and the "message driven bean," an entirely new kind of Java bean based on asynchronous messaging and the Java Message Service.

Java In a Nutshell Quick References

Java Enterprise in a Nutshell, 2nd Edition

By David Flanagan, Jim Farley &
William Crawford
2nd Edition April 2002
992 pages, ISBN 0-596-00152-5

Completely revised and updated to cover the
new 2.0 version of Sun Microsystems Java
Enterprise Edition software, *Java Enterprise
in a Nutshell* 2nd edition covers the RMI,
Java IDL, JDBC, JNDI, Java Servlet, and Enterprise JavaBeans APIs, with a fast-paced tutorial and compact reference material on each technology.

Java Foundation Classes in a Nutshell

By David Flanagan
1st Edition September 1999
748 pages, ISBN 1-56592-488-6

Java Foundation Classes in a Nutshell
provides an in-depth overview of the important
pieces of the (JFC), such as the Swing components and Java 2D. It also includes compact
reference material on all the GUI- and graphics-
related classes in the numerous javax.swing
and java.awt packages. Covers Java 2.

J2ME in a Nutshell

By Kim Topley
1st Edition, March 2002
462 pages, ISBN 0-596-00253-X

O'Reilly's *J2ME in a Nutshell* is as definitive a
reference to the heart of the J2ME platform
as the classic *Java in a Nutshell* is for the
Standard Java platform. Its solid introduction
to J2ME covers the essential APIs for different
types of devices and deployments; the profiles
(specifications of the minimum sets of APIs
useful for a set-top box, wireless phone, PDA, or other device);
and the Java virtual machine functions that support those APIs.
The meat of the book is its classic O'Reilly-style quick reference
to all the core Micro Edition classes.

Java in a Nutshell, 4th Edition

By David Flanagan
4th Edition March 2002
992 pages, ISBN 0-596-00283-1

This bestselling quick reference contains an
accelerated introduction to the Java programming language and its key APIs, so seasoned
programmers can start writing Java code right
away. The fourth edition of *Java in a Nutshell*
covers the new Java 1.4 beta edition, which contains significant changes from the 1.3 version.

Java Examples in a Nutshell, 2nd Edition

By David Flanagan
2nd Edition September 2000
584 pages, ISBN 0-596-00039-1

In *Java Examples in a Nutshell*, the author
of Java in a Nutshell has created an entire
book of example programs that not only
serve as great learning tools, but can also be
modified for individual use. The second edition of this best-selling book covers Java 1.3,
and includes new chapters on JSP and
servlets, XML, Swing, and Java 2D. This is the book for those who
learn best "by example."

O'REILLY®

TO ORDER: **800-998-9938** • *order@oreilly.com* • *www.oreilly.com*
ONLINE EDITIONS OF MOST O'REILLY TITLES ARE AVAILABLE BY SUBSCRIPTION AT **safari.oreilly.com**
ALSO AVAILABLE AT MOST RETAIL AND ONLINE BOOKSTORES

How to stay in touch with O'Reilly

1. Visit our award-winning web site

http://www.oreilly.com/

★ "Top 100 Sites on the Web"—PC Magazine
★ CIO Magazine's Web Business 50 Awards

Our web site contains a library of comprehensive product information (including book excerpts and tables of contents), downloadable software, background articles, interviews with technology leaders, links to relevant sites, book cover art, and more. File us in your bookmarks or favorites!

2. Join our email mailing lists

Sign up to get email announcements of new books and conferences, special offers, and O'Reilly Network technology newsletters at:

http://www.elists.oreilly.com

It's easy to customize your free elists subscription so you'll get exactly the O'Reilly news you want.

3. Get examples from our books

To find example files for a book, go to:

http://www.oreilly.com/catalog

select the book, and follow the "Examples" link.

4. Work with us

Check out our web site for current employment opportunites:

http://jobs.oreilly.com/

5. Register your book

Register your book at:

http://register.oreilly.com

6. Contact us

O'Reilly & Associates, Inc.
1005 Gravenstein Hwy North
Sebastopol, CA 95472 USA
TEL: 707-827-7000 or 800-998-9938
(6am to 5pm PST)
FAX: 707-829-0104

order@oreilly.com
For answers to problems regarding your order or our products. To place a book order online visit:

http://www.oreilly.com/order_new/

catalog@oreilly.com
To request a copy of our latest catalog.

booktech@oreilly.com
For book content technical questions or corrections.

proposals@oreilly.com
To submit new book proposals to our editors and product managers.

international@oreilly.com
For information about our international distributors or translation queries. For a list of our distributors outside of North America check out:

http://international.oreilly.com/distributors.html